The Metaphorical Society

The Metaphorical Society
An Invitation to Social Theory

Daniel Rigney

ROWMAN & LITTLEFIELD PUBLISHERS, INC.
Lanham • Boulder • New York • Toronto • Plymouth, UK

ROWMAN & LITTLEFIELD PUBLISHERS, INC.

Published in the United States of America
by Rowman & Littlefield Publishers, Inc.
A wholly owned subsidiary of The Rowman & Littlefield Publishing Group, Inc.
4501 Forbes Boulevard, Suite 200, Lanham, Maryland 20706
www.rowmanlittlefield.com

10 Thornbury Road
Plymouth PL6 7PP
United Kingdom

British Library Cataloguing in Publication Information Available

Library of Congress Cataloging-in-Publication Data

Rigney, Daniel, 1949–
     The metaphorical society : an invitation to social theory / Daniel Rigney.
         p.   cm.
     ISBN 0-7425-0937-0 — ISBN 0-7425-0938-9 (pbk.)
     1. Social sciences—Philosophy. I. Title.
     H61.15.R54 2001
     300'.1—dc21   00-045920

Printed in the United States of America

♾️™ The paper used in this publication meets the minimum requirements of
American National Standard for Information Sciences—Permanence of Paper for
Printed Library Materials, ANSI/NISO Z39.48—1992.

Contents

~

Preface

~

This book invites you to engage in stimulating acts of imagination. It invites you to view human societies through the poetic lens of metaphor and to ask questions of the following sort. How is a society like (and unlike) a living creature? How is it like (and unlike) a machine, or a battlefield, or a legal code, or a marketplace, or a game, or a theatrical production, or a great discourse extending across generations?

These are metaphors that have shaped the course of Western social theory in recent centuries. The eight major metaphors that we will consider in this book are certainly not the only poetic images that have ever guided human understandings of society. Other images of social life have been influential in other places, times, and cultures. A panoramic survey of societal metaphors across diverse cultures and historical epochs would no doubt make a fascinating (if encyclopedic) project in its own right. Such a project is, however, well beyond the scope of this book, which has the more modest aim of offering the inquisitive general reader a brief and distinctive introduction to social theory as a literary genre.

In a broad sense we are all social theorists already, struggling to comprehend our day-to-day experiences within the context of the larger structures and systems we inhabit. In a narrower sense, social theory is the *systematic* attempt to explain and interpret social phenomena. This book invites you to become both more systematic and more imaginative in your own thinking about social relations as you immerse yourself in the major metaphorical traditions of sociology and its neighboring disciplines.

This book is written especially for those who are open to seeing the world from more than one angle of vision. As you view the social world through each of the metaphorical lenses offered here, my hope is that you may come to see your own life and the world around you in fresh and unexpected ways. I hope, too, that these alternative perspectives will expand your sense of social connectedness and your active engagement in the work of making a more humane world. Social theory, far from being an impractical activity, can often throw new light on our daily practices, changing the way we see our lives and perhaps even the way we live them.

Throughout this book we will consider both the uses and abuses of metaphor in social theory. Metaphorical thinking has its powers, but also its hidden snares and pitfalls. Every metaphorical model of society is inevitably partial and selective, revealing only some aspects of the social whole while obscuring others. Every metaphor is at once both a way of seeing and a way of not seeing. Thus, while each metaphor may yield important insights, no single metaphor can tell the whole story.

To complicate matters further, the social reality that metaphors attempt to capture is elusive, many-faceted, and continually changing. A metaphor that seems to work in one cultural or historical context may be entirely inappropriate to another. Hence the quest to discover a universal or final model of human society comes to seem increasingly futile.

Given these and other limitations of metaphor, should we then abandon the metaphorical imagination entirely in favor of more prosaic strategies of discovery and argument? The view advanced here is that we should not and, indeed, cannot. Metaphors are both dangerous *and* inescapable. They are dangerous when we mistake them for final truths. But they are also impossible to expunge from thought. There is growing evidence that our capacity to forge figurative connections among seemingly unconnected experiences is fundamental to human cognition and creativity. Metaphorical thinking is constantly at work across the full spectrum of human endeavors, from the arts and sciences to religion, law, and the affairs of everyday life. It is doubtful that we could do without our metaphors even if we wanted to, because they are embedded in the very languages we speak, without which we could not survive. This book argues, then, not for the abolition of social metaphors but rather for their more conscious, critical, and creative use.

Social metaphors do not merely describe social reality. In some instances it is more apt to say that they play a part in its *creation* or *construction*. When our metaphorical images of reality serve as guides to action, they indirectly shape the very social world they purport to describe. By orienting our lives and choices around one or another metaphor, whether consciously or not, we act to produce one or another kind of world. Thus we make one kind of world, for instance, when we choose to view social life as a perpetual war, and a very different kind of world when we choose instead to regard our relationships as constructive and ongoing conversations.

Entire civilizations are organized, at least in part, around their dominant metaphors. Just as Spartan society was formed around its self-conception as a military organization, and ancient Hebrew society around the image of a sacred covenant, contemporary North American society is organized around its own set of dominant metaphors, particularly the imagery of the marketplace and the game. In important ways, the metaphors we embrace define who we are, not just as persons but as civilizations. It is crucial, then, that we become more aware of the metaphors we live by, for if we do not take conscious control of our metaphors, they are likely to take unconscious control of us.

What began more than twenty years ago as a promising idea is now finally a material artifact capable of stimulating further ideas. I thank all of my friends and colleagues who have shown an interest in this project along the way, with special thanks to a few in particular. My mentor Gideon Sjoberg, in his teaching and writing, first made me aware of the power of metaphors and analogies in sociological theory. My colleague Bernard Lee, S.M., would later rekindle my interest in social metaphors with his odd talk of "deep stories" and "dialogical communities." Both of these philosopher-citizens remain, for me, exemplars of creative scholarship and moral engagement. Wildlife sociologist Richard Machalek helped to sustain the project with his good-natured devil's advocacy. Dean Birkenkamp of Rowman & Littlefield deserves special thanks for his unfailing encouragement and support. I also thank Serina Beauparlant, John Bartkowski, Mary Lynne Hill, Donna Barnes, and several anonymous reviewers for their insightful comments on various portions and versions of this manuscript. I appreciate St. Mary's University for granting me a sabbatical leave to work on the project, and a generation of sociological theory students for participating actively and constructively in its development. Finally, I dedicate this book with gratitude to my parents, Margaret and Carl; my brothers; *mi esposa* the historian Alida Metcalf; and our sons Matthew and Benjamin for being my family, both literally and metaphorically, through the years. Where would we be without each other?

CHAPTER ONE

~

The Metaphorical
Imagination

The ancient Indian fable of the blind men and the elephant, popularized in English verse by the nineteenth-century American poet John Godfrey Saxe (1900), has amused schoolchildren for generations. You may recall the poem's opening lines:

It was six men of Indostan
  To learning much inclined,
Who went to see the Elephant
  (Though all of them were blind),
That each by observation
  Might satisfy his mind.
The *First* approached the Elephant,
  And happening to fall
Against his broad and sturdy side,
  At once began to bawl:
"God bless me! but the Elephant
  Is very like a wall!"

As the poem progresses, each scholar steps forward in turn to investigate the beast. One feels its tusk and decides that the elephant is like a spear. Another seizes the trunk and likens the elephant to a snake, and so on—each foolishly mistaking his limited perception of the part for the fuller reality of the whole. The poet concludes:

And so these men of Indostan
  Disputed loud and long,
Each in his own opinion
  Exceeding stiff and strong,
Though each was partly in the right
  And all were in the wrong!

1

Saxe's poem, originally composed as a satire on the certitudes of theologians, may be read more broadly as a story about fallible human attempts in every age to comprehend elusive realities of every kind. Although the poem may not rise to the level of a literary masterpiece, the fable on which it is based remains a powerful parable, as timely now as when it was first conceived. There is something strangely postmodern about this ancient tale in its frank recognition of the multiplicity and partiality of human perspectives, and of the limitations of vision and insight that we all share in common as human knowers.

Social theorists are in some ways like the seekers in Saxe's verse, and human societies are the elusive realities they seek to grasp. Like the fabled elephant, societies can be baffling in their scope and complexity. And social theorists, with their limited powers of observation and analysis, must somehow make sense of these complex wholes on the basis of partial and even seemingly contradictory evidence.

Who, after all, has ever seen a whole society? Even the simplest of human communities escapes total observation. If in our travels we should encounter a band of hunter–gatherers, we may witness hunters hunting, gatherers gathering, shamans dancing, and storytellers recounting the heroic deeds of the ancestors. But have we really observed the society in all of its parts and dimensions? Have we "seen" its linguistic rules, its kinship structures, the evolution of its technologies, or the worldview encoded in its myths? As finite observers, we cannot hope to grasp this many-sided and largely invisible totality all at once. At best, we experience fleeting fragments of some larger social entity whose nature we can only approach, gropingly, through conjecture.

If relatively small, simple, and stable societies are perplexing, how much more perplexing is the emerging world society. This global network of political, economic, and cultural organizations, linked together by high-speed postindustrial technologies, is so overwhelmingly complex and mutates so rapidly as to defy human comprehension. Just as we think we have understood it, it has changed again. To make matters even more complex, we are a part of the very creature we seek to understand. We are not detached observers of some fixed object, but rather active participant–observers in the process of creating, sustaining and interpreting social life (cf. Brown 1977: 97). This is a very strange elephant indeed.

Metaphor, Simile, and Analogy

Like the sages of Indostan, we often resort to *metaphors*, *similes*, and *analogies* in our attempts to reduce complex and unfamiliar phenomena to simpler and more familiar terms. (Indeed, the fable of the elephant may be read as a metaphor about our penchant for metaphors.) Metaphor is a mode of thought wherein we interpret one domain of experience through the language of another. A metaphor, or implied comparison, figuratively identifies one object of thought (A) with another (B), creating a fusion of images and associations between the two and inviting us to view one *as if* it were the other, as in William Shakespeare's dictum that "all the world's a stage." Of course, a metaphor is literal nonsense when it asserts an identity between nonidentical objects. All the world is not actually a stage. As Erving Goffman (1974: 1) wryly observes, even theater itself is not theatrical in every regard.

Simile is more literal than metaphor, asserting not that A *is* B, but only that A is *like* B in certain implied respects. In metaphor, politics is theater. In simile, politics is merely *like* theater. (The sages of Indostan are, strictly speaking, constructing similes when they liken the elephant to one or another familiar object.) Analogy goes one step beyond simile, specifying ways in which A and B are alike. We develop an analogy when we begin to explicate the points of resemblance that metaphor and simile only hint at. Thus, a political campaign is like a theatrical production in a variety of ways: (1) both are staged to win the approval of an audience; (2) both require elaborate behind-the-scenes preparation, and so forth. A special type of analogy, coming down to us from Aristotle and the ancient Greeks, is the ratio or proportion, written in the form $A_1:A_2::B_1:B_2$. Thus, the cynic may remark that "big donors are to political candidates as puppeteers are to puppets." Or to express the same idea as a simple metaphor, "big donors are the puppeteers of politics."

Every metaphor or analogy has its limits. To say that A and B are alike in some respects is to imply that they are not alike in others. The attributes that A and B share are called the *positive analogy,* whereas their unshared attributes are called the *negative analogy* or *disanalogy* (Hesse 1966: 8). When we analyze a metaphor or analogy, we must consider both its positive and negative aspects, identifying not only the metaphor's merits, but also the ways in which it may be partial, misleading, or mistaken. Finally, we will want to consider the *neutral analogy*—i.e., those respects in which the sameness or difference of two things is still unknown. Herein lies the heuristic value of an analogy: its capacity to raise new questions and lead us to new discoveries as we systematically explore its ambiguities (Hesse 1966: 8).

We frequently call upon metaphors and analogies when we are trying to make sense of mysteries. Thus, social analysts in the closing years of the twentieth century struggled to make sense of a strange new social phenomenon called the Internet by likening it to a variety of more familiar things—a superhighway, a spiderweb, a library, an organism, a cable or telephone system, a shopping mall, a town square, or a newly independent nation. Each metaphor captured one or another aspect of the electronic elephant, but none yielded a complete picture. Mark Stefik (1996) contends that such metaphors do more than merely describe the Internet. By shaping our conceptions, our imaginations and our choices, they may actually alter the course of the Internet's development.

So it is with social metaphors in general. George Lakoff and Mark Johnson (1980) argue convincingly that in every sphere of life our metaphors shape our perceptions of reality, our conceptual imaginations, and ultimately our actions. This implies that the metaphors we live by have the capacity not merely to describe or interpret social reality, but to transform it. To paraphrase one of sociology's favorite theorems (Thomas and Thomas 1928: 572), we may say that metaphors defined as real are real in their consequences. If this is so, then we had better choose our metaphors carefully, for the shape of our futures may depend on the metaphors we now choose to guide us.

In the natural and social sciences it was once supposed that metaphors are mere literary decorations, introduced by clever writers to amuse readers and to aid in their understanding, but otherwise of little value. Today, however, philosophers and historians of science generally acknowledge the crucial role that metaphors and analogies play in scientific creativity and discovery (Black 1962; Koestler 1964; Hesse 1966; Schön 1967; Boden 1992; Weisberg 1993; Holyoak and Thagard 1995). Some metaphors in the social sciences do indeed serve as clever stylistic devices, as when Vilfredo Pareto, following Niccolò Machiavelli, memorably refers to alternative types of political leaders as "lions" and "foxes." But in many other instances metaphors function not as mere ornaments, but as central organizing principles structuring entire bodies of thought. These are the guiding metaphors that will interest us throughout this book.

Social theorists are increasingly aware of the aesthetic, literary, and rhetorical dimensions of theory (e.g., Nisbet 1976; Agger 1989, 2000). Richard Harvey Brown (1977), in his plea for a "poetic for sociology," is perhaps foremost among sociologists in recognizing the power of metaphors to shape social analysis. Among anthropologists, Clifford Geertz (1973, 1983, 1988) has pioneered the literary analysis of ethnographic theory and research, while among economists Deirdre McCloskey (1985, 1990, 1994) has explored the many ways in which metaphorical imagery shapes economic theory and policy. Gareth Morgan (1997; Grant and Oswick 1996) and Paul Rosenblatt (1994) have skillfully excavated the metaphors that underlie organizational theory and family theory, respectively. Meanwhile, a growing number of linguists (e.g., Lakoff and Johnson 1980; Lakoff 1996; Tannen 1998; St. Clair 1994) have turned their attention to the analysis of social metaphors in public discourse and popular culture. These are clear signs that interest in the metaphorical imagination is alive and well in the social sciences and cultural studies.

Metaphors can be powerful sources of creative insight, but they also have their hidden dangers. Demagogues often abuse metaphors and analogies in public discourse, using them manipulatively in political and commercial messages to present one-sided or misleading simplifications of complex issues. Even well-meaning metaphorists may be oblivious to the hidden implications of their favorite images. Metaphors are notoriously seductive, and even those who warn against them seem unable to resist their charms. Aristotle exemplifies this attitude of ambivalence in the *Poetics* ([ca. 330 B.C.E.] 1935: 315–17). In one breath, he cautions against the excesses of metaphor and analogy; in the next, he asserts that to be master of the metaphor is "the greatest thing by far." It is a "mark of genius, for to be good at metaphor is to be intuitively aware of hidden resemblances." Thomas Hobbes ([1651] 1964: 29–30) observes that reasoning by metaphor and other such "senseless and ambiguous words . . . is wandering amongst innumerable absurdities." He then proceeds to develop the metaphor of the political state as a Leviathan or powerful giant. Alan Wolfe (1993: 164–69) remarks that we "will never understand society properly unless we are prepared to understand it on its own terms," moving beyond metaphors borrowed from nature and culture. Yet elsewhere he concedes that it is "impossible to capture the complexity and interconnectedness of human society without metaphors."

The view advanced here is that metaphorical thinking is both dangerous *and* unavoidable. Metaphors are powerful tools of thought. The hazards of metaphor in social theory are real enough, but they reside less in the nature of the tools themselves than in the carelessness with which they are often applied to social analysis. We must learn to use these tools of thought more consciously and critically, for they continue to shape the course of social theory, and even of societies themselves. The question is whether we will be the masters of our metaphors or they of us.

In this book we will review some of the major metaphorical traditions that have inspired and animated social theory through history, with special emphasis on metaphorical imagery in nineteenth- and twentieth-century Western social thought. We will examine both the constructive uses and the dangerous abuses of metaphorical thought, and we will suggest some ways in which social metaphors and analogies might be developed more systematically and more imaginatively. In short, we will be reading metaphorical models of society from three perspectives: first, with an appreciative eye toward their insights; second, with a critical eye toward their hidden ambiguities, contradictions and dangers; and finally with a creative "third eye" toward their unrealized possibilities.

In the tradition of the sociology of knowledge, we will want to remain continually aware of the wider social, political, and historical contexts within which metaphorical images of society are created, employed, criticized, and abandoned.

Metaphors do not, after all, come from nowhere. They come from particular people and groups in particular places and times, and they are inevitably shaped by the interests and historical circumstances of their makers (Mannheim 1936: 274–75). Consider, for example, some of the metaphors that Western leaders deployed following World War II as strategic rhetorical weapons, invoking a "cold war" against those "behind the iron curtain" who threatened to turn developing nations into "falling dominoes" if the United States and its allies did not defeat the Soviet Union in an ever-accelerating "arms race." These mental images locked millions of minds, including the minds of leaders themselves, into a particular view of U.S.–Soviet relations. With the easing of U.S.–Soviet hostilities, we now have the creative opportunity to rethink such militaristic and mechanistic images of international relations, and to propose fresh and constructive new metaphors to describe (and even, in subtle ways, to shape) world relations in the twenty-first century. In this and every other sphere of life we may draw upon the powers of the metaphorical imagination to help us think critically and creatively about the images that guide our thoughts and actions. Metaphorical images of society are not the exclusive province of social theory, but infuse the popular culture as well. For in the end, there is no sharp line separating social theory from other regions of public discourse, or our theoretical metaphors from the metaphors we live by in our daily lives.

Eight Metaphorical Images of Society

Social theorists, in their attempts to explain and interpret social life, have borrowed concepts and vocabularies freely from a wide variety of cultural domains, including the sciences, the arts, commerce, and daily life. Sociology, as a crossroads discipline lying near the center of the social sciences (Rigney and Barnes 1979), has been particularly receptive to metaphorical influences converging from many different directions. Thus we find sociological theorists, as well as their neighbors in anthropology and political science, variously comparing human societies to (1) biological systems, (2) machines, (3) wars, (4) legal codes, (5) economic markets, (6) games, (7) theatrical productions, and (8) linguistic discourses, among numerous other phenomena in human experience. In some instances a given metaphor links society to a natural phenomenon (e.g., society as organism). More often, however, the metaphor draws a figurative connection between society as a whole and one of its institutional domains (e.g., technology, the military, law, economy, or the arts), urging us to interpret all of society through that domain's own specialized vocabulary and discourse. Thus, a theorist may map the vocabulary of engineering, or neoclassical economics, or theater, or literary theory onto the social world, reducing that larger and more complex world to the size and shape of a single cultural province. Every social metaphor is in this sense provincial. Some social metaphors are imperial as well, particularly when their defenders insist that they capture definitively the *real* essence of society, and therefore must eventually absorb or vanquish all rival understandings of the social world.

Powerful "root metaphors" (Pepper 1942) such as those named above have been the source of many important theoretical models in the social sciences, generating simplified and selective representations of social reality that attempt to capture the essential features of social phenomena. And social theorists, like the sages of Indostan, have often argued vigorously among themselves about which of these partial representations is more nearly true (Rigney 1979). To guard against provincial and imperial claims to final truth about human societies in all of their variety and mercurial complexity, it is essential that we sharpen our powers of *metaphorical analysis*, learning to recognize both the strengths and the limitations of metaphorical models in the social sciences and cultural studies. We must be aware that each model smuggles hidden or unconscious assumptions into social theory from its domain of origin (Gouldner 1970: 31ff), and we must be alert to the hidden cargo of dubious implications that it may carry. But we must also remain open to the fresh insights and treasures that each metaphor may bring us, and to its heuristic potential for further development. Let us now briefly introduce each of the eight metaphorical images of society that we have named, returning in later chapters to explore each in further detail.

Society as Living System

Perhaps the oldest living metaphors in social theory are those that interpret social phenomena through the vocabulary of biology and medicine. We borrow imagery from reproductive biology each time we use kinship terminology to describe nonkin relations, as when we describe a school or religious organization as a family, or a labor union as a brotherhood, or a nation-state as a motherland. We call upon biological imagery again when we speak of society as an organism (as Auguste Comte, Emile Durkheim, and other early functionalists did), or of social evolution, or of the cultural ecology.

In general, biological metaphors call our attention to the relational and organically interconnected nature of social life, in contrast to more recent atomistic images, which tend to portray society as a loose collection of autonomous individuals. While biological metaphors imply that societies are *like* living systems, some biologists have seriously suggested the intriguing possibility that social and cultural phenomena are quite *literally* alive, a claim we will consider at the close of chapter 2.

Society as Machine

Chapter 3 takes up mechanical images of society, which emerged to prominence with the rise of modern science and the industrial revolution. In the nineteenth century, scientifically inclined philosophers known as "positivists" began to imagine the possibility of a rigorous science of society worthy of the name "social physics." With this positivist dream of a social physics came the corollary vision of a "social engineering." While the metaphor of social physics portrayed societies as natural mechanisms governed by immutable scientific laws, the social engineering metaphor offered a rather different view of societies as artificial machines capable of being designed and redesigned to solve human problems more efficiently. We call forth mechanistic imagery each time we speak of society as a system of social "forces" (pressures, stresses, strains, and the like) or describe social organizations in technological terms, as when we refer to a bureaucracy as a machine (as Max Weber did), or to the Constitution of the United States as a system of checks and balances (as did the American Founders). Historically, mechanical metaphors are linked to the technologies of their times. Thus, earlier images of society as a clockwork or an industrial assembly line are now giving way to the postindustrial image of society as a cybernetic or computer system—a metaphor that would have been inconceivable less than a century ago.

Society as War

Warmer than the image of society as machine is the fierce image of society as a battleground whereon adversaries wage a relentless struggle for scarce and valued resources. Metaphors of social warfare have been developed in widely varying ways by Machiavelli, Hobbes, Karl Marx, and many others in the diverse tradition of conflict theory. We marshal the metaphors of war when we refer to nonmilitary conflicts in military terms, as when we allude to the "battle of the sexes" or the "culture wars." War metaphors aptly describe many of the harsher aspects of human history and social life; yet as calls to action, they may exacerbate rather than ameliorate destructive conflicts. In chapter 4 we defend many aspects of the conflict perspective while arguing for the need to go beyond the rhetoric of warfare in search of more life-giving and less potentially destructive images of social life.

Society as Legal Order

Chapter 5 presents a tamer image of society as an intricate system of rules, regulations, or codes of conduct. Order and social control are central themes in this legalistic model of social life, which suggests that we are by nature the makers, followers, breakers, adjudicators, and enforcers of social norms, both formal and informal. Accordingly, we all, at one time or another, play the metaphorical roles of legislator, executive, police agent, criminal, advocate, judge, jury, and jailer. Critics may rightly challenge the fairness or effectiveness of particular rules or rule-making systems, but few will deny that *some* system of normative regulation is necessary if a society is to escape the social disorientation of *anomie*, or worse, the anarchic war of all against all.

Society as Marketplace

The metaphor of the social marketplace, examined in chapter 6, depicts society as an elaborate network of exchange relationships among individuals and groups. Inspired by Adam Smith's classical economics and developed by social exchange and rational choice theorists, this metaphor reflects the assumptions of the prevailing culture of capitalism, urging us to view social relations as transactions based on self-interested calculations of reward and cost. Critics of the market metaphor contend that it presents an overly individualistic view of society, representing human relations in cold, instrumental, and amoral terms as transactions among consumers who simultaneously use and are used by each other. We weigh the costs and benefits of this metaphor as we continue to make our way through the proverbial marketplace of ideas.

Society as Game

The popular image of society as game, like the image of society as marketplace, portrays social life as a spirited and intensely competitive quest for prizes and payoffs. Like the war metaphor (although usually less grim), the game metaphor highlights the importance of strategy and tactics, deception, and team loyalty in social relations. Like the legal metaphor, it also underscores the need for shared and agreed-upon rules in the regulation of competition. In chapter 7 we will consider both quantitative and qualitative versions of the game metaphor, from the mathematical theory of games to Goffman's cynical image of society as a con game. What can we learn about our own civilization from the fact that the game metaphor is among the most popular and influential in contemporary postmodern culture?

Society as Theater

"All the world's a stage," wrote Shakespeare, "and all the men and women merely players. They have their exits and their entrances, and one man in his time plays many parts." We call upon the language of theater when we describe people as social actors playing their prescribed roles in accordance with received cultural scripts or, alternatively, as improvisational actors making up their performances as they go along. The theatrical or dramaturgical model of society, as developed by Goffman, Victor Turner, and others, raises a host of intriguing questions. Is there anything more to us than the masks we wear and the roles we play? Is society just a made-up story? And if so, are there limits on our power to rewrite the cultural scripts we have been handed? These are among the questions we will meet in chapter 8.

Society as Discourse

If any one metaphor has come to dominate cultural analysis in recent decades, it is the image of human societies as linguistic creations—artificial realities constructed socially through the medium of symbols. The image of society as language or discourse, presented in chapter 9, has its roots in European philosophy and linguistics. It has inspired a wide range of intellectual movements in twentieth-century social thought, including symbolic interactionism, social phenomenology, ethnomethodology, hermeneutics, structuralism and semiotics, deconstruction, postmodernism, and postmodern forms of feminism.

Relying on linguistic images of society as discourse, some postmodern theorists have proposed to treat society as a kind of "text" that may be authored, edited, read, and interpreted in a variety of alternative ways. Other theorists prefer to speak of society as an ongoing "conversation" among a multitude of distinctive voices through time, viewing our identities as symbolic constructs that we create, sustain, and transform in dialogue with others. The image of society as an ongoing conversation is at once both contemporary and ancient. It was already vividly present in the dialogues between Socrates and the Sophists of ancient Athens. Today, more than two millennia later, we are still in conversation with the ghost of Socrates, and with each other, regarding the dialogical character of social life.

〜

Beneath the diversity and apparent fragmentation of social theory lies a powerful and (paradoxically) unifying process that we have called the metaphorical imagination. We do not make the imperial claim here that *all* theorizing is metaphorical, nor that metaphor is the only source of inspiration and insight available to social theorists. Metaphors, similes, and analogies involve associative and abductive modes of thought that complement, but certainly do not replace, conventional inductive and deductive modes of reasoning (as we discuss more fully in the postscript). Yet the history of social theory is so thoroughly woven and laced with metaphorical images that we can scarcely conceive its existence without them.

The eight images of society that we have chosen for special analysis are neither exhaustive of all social metaphors nor even mutually exclusive, for many theorists have relied upon multiple images of social life. Yet these eight guiding metaphors are arguably the most influential and enduring images of society to be found in Western social theory in recent centuries. Significant metaphors from other times, places, and cultures are unfortunately beyond the limited scope of this book. We must give short shrift, for instance, to the medieval image of the universe as a cosmic hierarchy—a "great chain of being" (Lovejoy 1964)—proceeding downward from God to the lowliest creature, with the society of Man (and his subordinate, woman) occupying some middle place between the angels and the apes. This hierarchical metaphor has been largely superseded by the more modern and egalitarian image of social life as a "web" or "network" of intricately interconnected elements (Wolfe 1993: 164), an image that underlies much of modern systems theory and network analysis (Turner 1998: 520–30; Willer 1999) and that more nearly reflects the spirit of the age of the Internet and the World Wide Web.

We can give only passing notice to other familiar metaphors that picture a society as a "melting pot," or as an interwoven "fabric" or textured "tapestry," or as a "mosaic" made of many diverse fragments bonded together to form a pattern (Wolfe 1993: 165), or to metaphors transposed from music to social discourse, including metaphors of harmony and dissonance, rhythm, resonance and orchestration. If we pass lightly over these and other popular images of social relations, it is only because they are not clearly associated with any of the major metaphorical traditions that have dominated social thought.

Which of the metaphors considered here are most insightful and which are most misleading or dangerous? Before we can attempt to answer this question, we must first confront the prior question: "How does one go about deciding whether one metaphor or analogy is better or worse than another?" Some possible answers to the latter question are offered in the postscript, "A Guide to

Metaphorical Analysis," which provides a more complete discussion of metaphor as a cognitive and cultural tool. Those who seek a more advanced introduction to social metaphors are urged to go directly to the postscript before proceeding to chapter 2. This guide will be of special interest to those who wish to pursue their own metaphorical analyses.

Cultivating a keen sense of the uses and abuses of metaphor leads us, as Robert Bellah (1970: 246) has said in another context, to "the rejection of all univocal understandings of reality, of all identifications of one conception of reality with reality itself." Like the blind sages of Indostan, we need reminding that no social perspective is total and that no metaphor or analogy can adequately capture the social whole in all of its layers and dimensions. Metaphors and analogies are both dangerous *and* unavoidable. We cannot escape them, for they are essential elements of human thought and imagination. We can, however, learn to use them more consciously, more critically, more creatively, and more wisely. This book is written toward that end.

CHAPTER TWO

~

Society as
Living System

Perhaps the oldest and most enduring of all social metaphors are those that invite us to visualize a society as a kind of living thing. We find biological images of social life in the oral and written traditions of societies of all kinds, from the simplest to the most complex and from the most ancient to the most modern. In general, biological metaphors draw our attention to the profound interconnectedness of social life and to its rootedness in the deeper organic processes of nature. Just as the organs of the body or the species in an ecosystem are intricately connected to each other and depend upon each other for their mutual survival, so too are the members of social systems mutually linked, from the micro-level of the family to the macro-level of the international economy.

Biological metaphors often establish symbolic connections between the members of a society and the natural world that surrounds them. Consider, for example, the practice of totemism in tribal societies. A totem is an object, usually an animal or plant species, that a clan adopts as a metaphorical symbol of its identity. (The seahawk, for instance, is a prominent totem among Native Americans of the Pacific Northwest, and more recently among football players and fans in the same region.) Organic metaphors of this sort are found in tribal societies around the world (Sapir and Crocker 1977; Fernandez 1991). If prehistoric societies were anything like the few remaining hunting and gathering societies of today, we may surmise that human beings were creating organic images of social life long before the beginning of recorded time.

We frequently encounter biological metaphors in early recorded history as well. Organic metaphors came naturally to agrarian and pastoral peoples, living as they did in close relationship with plants, animals, and the cycles of nature. The literature of the ancient Hebrew people, for example, abounds with organic metaphors reflecting their agrarian and pastoral lifeways, including references to the harvest (e.g., the separation of wheat and chaff) and herding (e.g., the separation of sheep and goats). Each of these images served to link the society metaphorically to its habitat, symbolizing its organic connectedness to other forms of life.

Society as Family

Among the most ancient of biological metaphors are those that depict social phenomena in the language of kinship and reproduction. Indeed, the earliest known written records, the ancient cuneiform texts of the Sumerians of Mesopotamia dating from the third millenium B.C.E., contain hymns and mythic tales that picture the social process of harvesting and storing grain as a metaphorical "marriage" of the god of fertility to the goddess of the storehouse (Lerner, Meacham, and Burns 1988: 37).

Kinship metaphors typically picture human communities as extended families, connected vertically by parent–child relations and horizontally by conjugal or sibling relations. (We should note here that families are the products not only of biological reproduction, but also of cultural construction, and hence that genetic kinship and reproduction, insofar as they are organized, regulated, and understood differently in different cultures, are not *merely* biological phenomena.) While other biological metaphors feature our connectedness to nature, family metaphors point toward our natural connectedness to each other—a counterpoint to the more atomistic and impersonal metaphors of the modern age that we will consider in later chapters.

Although we speak of kinship as metaphor, some have argued that we are all *literally* members of a single extended family with common ancestral roots. The nineteenth-century social theorist Auguste Comte, who regarded the family as the most fundamental unit of society, observed that "families become tribes, and tribes become nations: so that the whole human race might be conceived of as the gradual development of a single family" (in Turner and Beeghley 1981: 46). Biologists, however, do not normally employ the term *family* in such an expansive way. While we all ultimately share a common ancestral lineage, we are separated from most of our fellow human beings by vast genealogical distances. Thus, when we invoke metaphors such as "the human family," we are in effect compressing these distances symbolically, identifying ourselves with remotely related others *as if* they were literally our parents or children, our brothers or sisters. Nowadays, the word *family* stretches metaphorically to encompass virtually any community of people who care for each other and share a common bond.

From a poetic standpoint, the power of family metaphors resides in their capacity to call forth idealized and comforting images of warmth, safety, loyalty, and love. The word *family* seems to imply a dependable source of sustenance and stability, protection and mutual aid in the face of danger and hardship—in short, a haven in a heartless world (Lasch 1977). In reality, such family ideals are probably more often proclaimed than achieved, whether now or in the past. Such romanticized and selectively remembered versions of family life may represent, as Stephanie Coontz (1992, 1998) contends, "the way we never were" rather than the way we really are.

Yet so great is the poetic power of family metaphors that entire cultural systems have been built around them. Consider the traditional Jewish metaphor of the stern but loving God-as-father, watching over the children of Israel. Christianity, an offspring of Judaism, adopted and extended this central metaphor. Thus, in traditional Christian theology, God-the-father begets Jesus-the-son. Jesus takes the church as his holy bride and she becomes Mother church. In Roman Catholicism, clerical "fathers," earthly representatives of the Father in Heaven, govern the church, with the pope (*papa* in Spanish) serving as the supreme *pater familias* of the faith. One may argue that familial metaphors do not merely describe the social structure of the church; in some measure they constitute it.

Feminist critics of this traditional metaphorical system are quick to note that its paternalistic imagery serves the ideological function of bolstering patriarchal power structures here on earth, which have traditionally relegated women to second-class status in church and society (e.g., see Ruether 1987, 1989; Daly 1973, 1985; Fiorenza and Copeland 1996). Feminist theologians have typically favored more maternal metaphors of the sacred, conceiving images of the goddess or God-as-mother as an alternative to traditional male imagery. Despite their differences, however, masculist and feminist theologians alike have relied upon family metaphors to depict the divine.

Family metaphors are commonplace in contemporary culture. Consider the variety of social contexts in which nonsiblings address each other as "brother" and "sister," implying familial bonds of warmth and mutual obligation. We find the language of fictive kinship in some segments of the African American community (Liebow 1967; Stack 1974), as well as in "brotherhoods" of trade unionists, in college fraternities and sororities, among monks and nuns in Catholic religious orders, in fundamentalist Protestant congregations whose members still address each other as brother and sister, and among feminists for whom "sisterhood is powerful."

In general, sibling metaphors such as these suggest a more egalitarian, less hierarchical image of social relations than do vertical metaphors based on the parent–child relationship. The poet and culture critic Robert Bly (1996), in his book *The Sibling Society*, complains that American culture has become entirely too caught up in the horizontal imagery of siblinghood and is in danger of losing the crucial vertical distinctions (as between parent and child) that once defined adult authority and responsibility. Bly yearns for a return to a more hierarchical way of life, although he acknowledges that such hierarchies have often been brutal and repressive in practice.

It should be clear from these examples that family metaphors are often politically and ideologically charged, pitting hierarchical conservatives against egalitarian liberals. George Lakoff (1996) notes that while both conservatives and liberals employ the metaphor of the family as a model of society, they tend to embrace very different images of ideal family life. While conservatives tend to idealize a traditional patriarchal (i.e., vertical) family form, liberals tend to envision a more democratic (or horizontal) family model. Lakoff contends that these fundamental differences in the way we think about families lead to very different metaphorical conceptions of the good society and very different notions of how to achieve it politically.

In political rhetoric, kinship metaphors, both vertical *and* horizontal, are frequently mobilized to strengthen bonds of group solidarity, as when we refer to a nation-state as the "motherland" (or in Germany, the "fatherland"), or when diplomats invoke the image of a "family of nations." Kinship metaphors echo again in idealistic appeals on behalf of "universal brotherhood," the "power of sisterhood," or concern for the well-being of the "human family."

Such images have no doubt helped to promote many worthy ideals. But family metaphors also have a more dangerous and sinister side. In some instances, such metaphors are wielded rhetorically to confer privilege on one group while pointedly excluding others, creating an implied condition of we versus they, and thereby pitting one metaphorical clan (such as the Ku Klux Klan) against its imagined adversaries. In other instances, family metaphors may express a childlike desire to surrender oneself to strong, paternalistic leadership, with its notorious potential for authoritarian abuse by regimes of both left and right. The political record of the twentieth century—the century of Adolf Hitler, Benito Mussolini, and Joseph Stalin (known affectionately to his followers as "Papa")—reminds us that mass longings for strong political father figures can lead to ruin. George Orwell (1949) was alert to the dangerous side of family metaphor in his political novel *1984* when he gave absolute authority the slyly ironic name of "Big Brother."

None of this is to say that the ideal of the nurturant family should not serve as a metaphorical model upon which to build healthy and nurturant communities and societies. It is only to say that family imagery should not be invoked naively or uncritically, lest the metaphorical families we create turn out to be severely dysfunctional ones.

Society as Organism

Family metaphors have been more influential in general public discourse than among social theorists per se. The single most influential biological metaphor in social theory is surely the image of human society as a living organism—a system of interdependent parts working together to produce a vital and functioning whole.

The organismic metaphor has animated social theory at least since the time of the ancient Greeks. Robert Nisbet (1969) goes so far as to say that the image of society as a developing organism has been the dominant metaphor in Western social thought since classical antiquity. We encounter the metaphor in Plato's image of the ideal republic as a social body in which a pain felt in one part of the community is felt throughout the whole community ([ca. 370 B.C.E.] 1979: sec. 462d,e). We find the metaphor again in Aristotle's notion of the city-state as the "body politic," in the Christian view of the church as the symbolic "body of Christ," and in cognates of the words *organization* and *corporation* (from the Latin *corpus* or body). More recently, we find the Internet described as a kind of electronic organism, an emerging global nervous system capable of growing and learning as it coordinates vast arrays of informational stimuli (Ostman 1996). The social organism is, it seems, a metaphor that refuses to die.

Functionalism

Organic metaphors invite us to imagine that human societies, like biological organisms, are complexly structured systems composed of innumerable subsystems, each performing one or more vital functions for the system as a living whole. Hence their proponents have been called structural-functionalists, or simply functionalists (Parsons 1951; Merton [1948] 1968; Abrahamson 1978; Alexander 1985). The metaphor of the organism also underlies much of modern systems theory (e.g., Buckley 1967; Luhmann 1982; Bailey 1994), which views society as a set of interconnected and mutually interacting elements, and whose development is closely intertwined with the development of functionalist theory.

The analogy between societies and organic systems is typically elaborated as follows. In an organism, cells combine to form tissues, tissues to form organs, and organs to form the organism as a whole. Similarly, in societies individuals combine to form associations based on shared characteristics, associations combine to form institutions, and institutions combine to constitute society as a whole. Just as the organs of the body (heart, lungs, liver, etc.) are mutually interdependent, so too are the major social institutions (politics, economy, education, etc.), each serving important functions in maintaining the social system. The functioning system, like the functioning organism, must be well integrated and well coordinated if it is to avoid dysfunction or social paralysis.

Notice that the organismic analogy, conceived in this way, is immediately open to criticism. For example, while the individual cells that form the human body are generally specialized to perform functions within a single organ (the heart, the brain, the kidney, etc.), the individuals who compose society are almost always members of more than one social "organ" simultaneously and may perform many different functions in many different associational and institutional contexts (home, workplace, political and religious organizations, etc.). It is as though social individuals were versatile floating cells, moving from one location in the social body to another with the generalized capacity to learn and perform a multitude of specialized and context-dependent functions.

Despite numerous problems of this sort, analogies between biological organisms and social organization have figured prominently in modern social theory. Such analogies appear in the sociological writings of the French theorists Claude-Henri de Saint-Simon and Auguste Comte in the early the nineteenth century (Turner and Beeghley 1981: 31–53) as well as in Emile Durkheim's ([1893] 1947) famous analysis of the "organic" solidarity of complexly differentiated societies arising from the interdependence of their parts. We find similar imagery in the allusion by Jane Addams ([1907] 2000: 162) to the family as a social organism whose members learn to perform domestic functions in coordination with each other.

Organic analogies were developed most systematically in the late nineteenth century by the British social philosopher Herbert Spencer, whose biologically inspired theories of society enjoyed an enormous popular following in his day. "What is a society?" he asked. "Society is an organism" ([1876] 1906: 447, 449). Spencer noted that both organisms and societies share the organic properties of growth and development. As they grow, both tend to display increasing complexity and differentiation of structure, accompanied by a corresponding specialization of function. The parts of society, like the parts of the body, are mutually dependent, so that a change in one part may result in changes in other parts. Proceeding in this manner, Spencer pursued the organismic analogy in considerable detail.

Unlike many analogists in social theory, Spencer took care to note the negative as well as the positive side of the analogy. Organisms and societies are
disanalogous, Spencer observed, insofar as the individuals composing a society
are physically dispersed, communicate through language and symbol, and are
conscious, unlike the individual cells of an organism (Spencer [1860] 1972; Turner
and Beeghley 1981: 79; Peel 1972: xxvi–xxvii). But it is the organismic analogy,
not the disanalogy, for which Spencer is better remembered.

Social Homeostasis

Among twentieth-century social theorists, the structural-functionalist Talcott
Parsons is particularly notable for his organismic view of society. Parsons (1951)
argued that social systems, like organic systems, have certain functional prereq-
uisites that they must meet in order to survive. Parsons' early version of functionalism (as distinct from his later evolutionary theorizing) has often been criticized for allegedly promoting a static or changeless view of social reality (Demarath
and Peterson 1967; Gouldner 1970). It has been criticized in particular for importing the biological concept of homeostasis uncritically into the analysis of social
systems.

In biology, homeostatic processes are cybernetic or self-regulating mechanisms
(analogous to the mechanism of a thermostat) that operate to maintain an organism in a state of stable equilibrium. Homeostatic processes in the body include, for instance, the physiological mechanisms that maintain the body's temperature at a relatively constant 98.6 degrees Fahrenheit. The biological concept
of homeostasis was developed by Parsons' Harvard colleague, the physiologist
Walter B. Cannon (1932), who proposed that such processes, analogous to managerial or administrative processes in society, represent the unconscious "wisdom
of the body" in its remarkable capacity to maintain a stable internal environment. It was actually Cannon himself, during the turbulent instability of the Great
Depression, who initially advocated the notion of social homeostasis as a stabi-
lizing process in human societies (Cross and Albury 1987).

Borrowing Cannon's notion, Parsons suggested that when the relatively stable
equilibrium of human societies is disrupted, social processes analogous to homeostasis come into play to restore the system to its "normal" state of balance (Parsons 1961; Buckley 1967: 11–17). Thus, to offer an example of our own, if a
"deviant" political ideology arises to threaten the stability of a social order, we
might expect the established system and its leaders to mobilize homeostatic responses in politics and public opinion, neutralizing the ideology's effects by em-

ploying propaganda, appeals to patriotism, threats of force, and the like to combat disruptive elements and to restore the system to equilibrium.

Social Pathology and the Medical Model of Deviance

It is only a small step from this homeostatic analogy to the social pathology analogy, based on a medical model of behavior that regards many forms of social deviance, including sexual, religious, and political nonconformity, as illnesses potentially in need of therapeutic treatment. According to this view, social institutions and actors, like biological organisms, become "sick" when they depart from what is presumed to be their natural or normal state of order. When this occurs, social systems naturally respond to ward off disease, sometimes with the assistance and intervention of the social-scientist-as-physician. Thus, Parsons' Harvard colleague George Homans, not usually given to functionalist analysis, remarked that a "society is an organism and . . . like all organisms, if a threat be made to its mode of existence, a society will produce antibodies which tend to restore it to its original form" (in Gouldner 1970: 149). In this instance, the "disease" to which Homans referred was the growing influence of Marxism in the United States during the 1930s.

A hidden assumption in the organismic model is that a system's true nature resides internally. Thus, "foreign" influences that enter the system from the outside are alien to its nature and threatening to its integrity, like antigens that stimulate the body's production of defensive antibodies. In actuality, however, it is quite normal for societies to interact with and to be influenced by each other. The United States in particular is a society whose culture is a syncretic and dynamic blend of diverse elements, most of them borrowed from elsewhere in the world. The organismic analogy implies that outside influences are contaminating and dangerous, when in fact they may in many instances be invigorating and revitalizing.

Another hidden assumption in the organismic analogy is the premise that harmonious order is the natural state of society. Like the healthy body, the healthy society is presumed to be one in which each part functions smoothly with each other part to ensure the well-being of the whole. Thus the British anthropologist A. R. Radcliffe-Brown (1935: 397) spoke of the "functional unity" of a society, "a condition in which all parts of the social system work together with a sufficient degree of harmony or internal consistency, i.e., without producing persistent conflicts which can neither be resolved nor regulated."

The image of the good society as a harmonious organic unity appears in ancient Greek philosophy, in the feudal ideals of Confucian China and medieval

Europe, and even today in the social encyclicals of the Roman Catholic church. This image of perfect social harmony is still powerfully appealing to many, especially in an age marked by tumultuous change and harsh conflict. But while every society surely requires some degree of harmony and integration if it is not to disintegrate, one may doubt whether a society founded on absolute harmony and the attendant suppression of dissent and conflict would be ultimately desirable even if it were possible. As Lewis Coser (1956) and many others have observed, a certain measure of conflict in any society is almost certainly inevitable and may, indeed, be valuable and "healthy" when channeled in constructive ways.

As the sophisticated functionalist Robert Merton has noted, the degree of harmony and integration in human societies (or for that matter, in biological organisms) is highly variable. Merton contends that functionalist analysis, properly understood, does not assume a "functional unity" in society. It acknowledges harmony where harmony exists, but it also examines candidly the internal and external stresses, strains, and conflicts that may engender system change. Good functionalist analysis does not assume that every structure in a given society serves some positive function for the whole, nor does it assume that every structure is indispensable or irreplaceable by some alternative structure (Merton [1948] 1968: 79–91). Finally, good functionalist analysis does not assume that "functional" necessarily means "good" or that "dysfunctional" necessarily means "bad." The underground resistance movement in Nazi Germany may well have been dysfunctional within the frame of reference of the Third Reich, but it does not follow from this that the movement was "pathological," or that the goals of the Third Reich were "healthy."

A diagnosis of social pathology clearly reflects the moral judgments and political commitments of the diagnostician. Thus in *Citizen Cohn*, a film depicting the McCarthy era of the 1950s, we hear a fierce anticommunist describe the enemy's system as "an evil and malignant way of life. It reveals a condition akin to a disease that spreads like an epidemic. And like an epidemic, a quarantine is necessary to keep it from infecting the nation" (Franzoni 1992). Conservative social critics today speak of the toxic or pathological social effects of liberalism, or of cultural decay or decomposition (e.g., Bennett 1994; Horowitz 1993), while those on the left inveigh against the sickening effects of racism, sexism, extreme inequalities of wealth and power, and other "social diseases." Those on the right have been known to disparage the poor as social parasites, draining the health of the nation, while those on the left have been equally convinced that the rich are parasitic, living off the underpaid labor of their employees. (In either case, the metaphor of the parasite conveniently dehumanizes the enemy.) Those on the religious right warn of a growing moral cancer in the body politic (cancer being virtually the only kind of growth that has negative connotations in American culture), while those on the environmental left worry about the cancer of un-regulated urban growth and industrial development. Ideologies across the political spectrum thus mobilize organic metaphors rhetorically in the service of their divergent interests and objectives.

Bound up in the pathology metaphor is the notion that ideas and behaviors may spread rapidly like epidemic diseases. This epidemiological analogy is currently getting serious attention from cultural analysts studying phenomena ranging from crime epidemics to the spread of fads, fashions, and philosophies (Gladwell 1996, 2000; Lynch 1996; Brodie 1996). There is no denying that ideas and behaviors do sometimes spread rapidly, somewhat analogous to cancers in a body or virulent contagions in a population. Indeed, one of the earliest approaches to crowd behavior relied upon "contagion theory" to explain crowd phenomena such as mobs and riots (LeBon 1896). Anyone whose computer has come down with a virus will appreciate the potential power of the epidemiological analogy. But we must beware when such analogies are used rhetorically to induce social panics or to promote cultural bigotry, as when African influences in American life (such as in music and dance) are described as though they were cultural infections in need of containment or cure. Barbara Browning (1998: 107) suggests that such racist thinking, reflecting "fear of a foreign element infiltrating this country," is itself a kind of contagion. Finally, we should not assume uncritically that a phenomenon is insidious just because it spreads rapidly from person to person. Perhaps there is, after all, such a thing as the contagion of virtue.

Closely related to the pathology metaphor are metaphors of cultural purity and contamination widely observed by cultural anthropologists (Douglas 1966) and historians. Puritanism, for example, sought to cleanse and purify church and society of their corrupt elements. Reform movements in general aim to clean up metaphorical dirt—whether the polluted object in question be muddy politics, filthy song lyrics, or toxic ideologies. Unfortunately, the cure of purification in many instances may be worse than the real or imagined disease it aims to eradicate. Attempts at racial and ethnic "cleansing" in Nazi Germany and more recently in Bosnia and Kosovo testify that in some instances the social pathology metaphor may itself have toxic effects.

The pathology metaphor implies a medical model of society in which the social system is the patient and the social analyst the physician, equipped with the sophisticated conceptual tools of social anatomy and physiology, and perhaps even prepared to perform social surgery if necessary to excise unwanted pathogens (such as sexual, religious, or political deviants) and restore society to health. Beneath the rhetoric of medicine, the social pathology analogy conceals a cultural struggle between competing visions of what constitutes a good society and what its "normal" state of affairs ought to be—conflicting visions that are probably beyond the adjudications of science.

Homeostatic and pathological analogies tend to imply that a human society has a normal and unchanging ideal state, analogous to the medical ideal of a healthy body. But this "back to normalcy" assumption is clearly flawed, for it fails to acknowledge that social change is itself normal and even necessary for survival in many circumstances. Natural social processes may be at work not only in the restoration of previous equilibria, but also in the dynamic search for new and more viable equilibria (Buckley 1967: 15).

While remaining keenly aware of the dangers and pitfalls of social pathology metaphors, one may still cautiously argue that some social arrangements are indeed healthier for human beings than others. Anthropologist Robert Edgerton (1992), for example, has made the case for a transcultural ethics, contending that some societies, even at comparable levels of technological development, do a better job than others of fostering the well-being of their members and may therefore be judged "healthier" societies. Edgerton freely acknowledges that every society, including his own, falls short of the ideal. His argument thus manages to avoid both the hazards of ethical relativism (which in its extreme forms undermines all standards of ethical judgment) and, at the other extreme, the ethnocentric arrogance of supposing that one's own social institutions necessarily constitute the standard against which others must be measured.

Elsewhere we have similarly argued that ethics is fundamentally an inquiry into the conditions that nurture human well-being, and that all social arrangements are not equally conducive to such well-being (Rigney and Kearl 1994; Kearl and Rigney 1995). If we define ethics in this manner, then we may conclude that a society that affords all of its members decent access to food, clothing, shelter, medical care, education, and opportunities for meaning and fulfillment is, other things being equal (e.g., at similar levels of economic and technological development), a better or "healthier" society than one that does not. Marc Miringoff and Marque-Luisa Miringoff (1999) proceed from similar assumptions in their report, *The Social Health of the Nation*, wherein they attempt to track empirical indicators of the quality of life in the United States, in somewhat the same manner that a physician keeps a medical chart to track the vital signs of a patient, in order to monitor and promote the overall health and well-being of the society.

Arguments appealing to the metaphors of social health and illness continue to be intuitively appealing to many. Such arguments must, however, be made carefully and with due attention to the numerous hazards previously noted. In light of these dangers, it is understandable that some social theorists would prefer to avoid the idiom of social pathology altogether.

Social Life Cycles: Growth and Decay

Critics of functionalism have sometimes complained that its organismic image of society is essentially static—i.e., that by assuming homeostasis, it is incapable of offering an explanation of social change. This is not quite true. The organismic analogy does allow for the possibility of change if we are prepared to think of change embryologically, as a succession of developmental stages in an organism's life cycle (Nisbet 1969).

Aristotle long ago observed that the acorn contains within itself the mighty oak tree. By analogy, human societies have at times been thought to unfold according to their own internal principles, growing and passing away in a series of well-defined stages of development. From this organismic analogy the ancient Greeks derived a cyclical view of humanity and society. Societies, like individuals, were believed to experience cyclical development, for "a thing in growth has not only its genesis and development, but also its decay and, eventually, its termination: to be followed then by another cycle of genesis and decay, ad infinitum" (Nisbet 1969: 30).

Most cyclical or "rise and fall" theories have their origins in this organic conception of social life wherein newly born societies are seen to pass through stages of youthful vigor and productive maturity to eventual decadence and death (Appelbaum 1970: 99–116). Edward Gibbon's ([1776–88] 1974) classic history of the decline and fall of the Roman Empire, Oswald Spengler's (1926) romantically pessimistic *The Decline of the West*, and historian Arnold Toynbee's (1934–54) grand theory of civilization as a recurring cycle of challenge and response all imply cyclical models of social change. Karl Marx's and Friedrich Engels's ([1848] 1955; Marx [1859] 1970) theory of history is also in certain respects a cyclical theory, according to which each new mode of production grows in the womb of the old, leading finally toward a return to communism—not the primitive communism of prehistory but communism at a much more advanced level of technology.

Some developmental models are less cyclical and more linear, suggesting a progressive line of development with no return to previous forms. Thus, Spencer, in his essay, "Progress: Its Law and Cause," suggested that "the series of changes gone through during the development of the seed into a tree, or an ovum into an animal, constitute an advance from homogeneity of structure to heterogeneity of structure" and that "this law or organic progress is the law of all progress" (in Nisbet 1969: 164). We may note a hidden internalist bias in this embryological view of social change, a tendency to view societies as unfolding according to an inborn and predetermined program analogous to the genetic program that governs the development of biological organisms. There are difficulties in this internalist view, however, for even the development of biological organisms is powerfully influenced by external factors. Thus, two genetically identical acorns, planted in different soils and given differing amounts of sun, water, and nutrients, will result in two very different trees.

From time to time we encounter developmental analogies in public discussion, as when someone refers to the United States as a young nation or, alternatively, as a nation currently experiencing decadence, decay, and even the death of democracy (Goldberg 1999) and discourse (Slayden and Whillock 1999). At various times in our history, illnesses such as tuberculosis, cancer, and AIDS have served as metaphorical symbols of cultural decline and death (Sontag 1989). But in fact, while societies inevitably change, they rarely "die." The ancient Roman Empire may be gone forever, but Romans continue to inhabit the Eternal City and to enjoy a civilization in many respects more advanced than the one whose metaphorical death Gibbon mourned. In the end, the image of society as an acorn that grows into an oak and eventually withers and dies is poetically powerful but empirically weak. The future of real societies is not nearly so neatly preordained or internally dictated as this ancient metaphor would lead us to suppose. Neither, for that matter, is the future of an acorn.

Society as Evolutionary Process

Despite its many limitations, the metaphor of the social organism lives on. It lives, for example, in the corporate rhetoric of Bill Gates (Gates and Hemingway 1999) and the Microsoft Corporation. Consider these passages from a website promoting Microsoft business products, entitled "The Digital Nervous System." Microsoft Chairman Bill Gates is quoted as saying:

> In a Darwinian business world, the quality of an organization's nervous system helps determine its ability to sense change and quickly respond, thus determining whether it dies, survives, or thrives. . . . This analogy is apt . . . and important. In biological organisms, the nervous system automatically controls the basic systems—respiratory, circulatory, digestive—that make life possible. It also receives sensory stimuli, transmits them to the brain, and instantly triggers a response. In higher organisms, the nervous system makes it possible to think and plan with foresight and creativity. To meet the demands of the digital economy, organizations must be able to behave more like organisms. This will give them better "reflexes" for reacting to stimuli, a more efficient "metabolism" for managing daily operations, and a sharper "mind" for guiding plans and actions more intelligently. (Microsoft Corporation 1998)

So far, the analogy is between the communication and control system of an organization and the nervous system of a single organism. But the Microsoft narrative goes on to tell the story of the *evolution* of organizational nervous systems, from the introduction of paper and print technologies to the advent of the personal computer. This transition from organismic to evolutionary metaphor parallels the transition from organismic to evolutionary thinking in nineteenth-century social thought. Prior to Darwin's theory of evolution, biologically minded social theorists tended to compare human societies to individual organisms. After Darwin, they began increasingly to explore intriguing parallels between the evolution of species and the evolution of societies (Buckley 1967: 13).

Although social theorists such as Spencer and his American counterpart William Graham Sumner often employed both organismic and evolutionary analogies in their writings, the two analogies are in fact markedly different in their implications. The evolutionary analogy, with its emphasis on the continual adaptation of systems to changing environments, offers a more dynamic image of society than does the organismic analogy, with its focus on internal stability and programmed development. While the development of an individual organism is, at least to some degree, predictable in its stages of growth, the outcomes of evolutionary processes are more radically open ended and potentially more varied. Thus, while the physical development of a human infant is somewhat predictable, the future course of the evolution of humanity is much less so. If we imagine that a society is a developing organism, we will tend to imagine social change as unfolding according to some predetermined direction of development (or *telos*), whereas if we imagine society as an evolutionary process, its future direction will seem considerably less certain or predictable and, at the same time, richer with alternative possibilities.

Social Darwinism

While Charles Darwin himself did not propose the concept of social evolution (Nisbet 1969: 161; Degler 1991: 5–6), his theory of natural selection, published in *On the Origin of Species* in 1859, did inspire the rise of evolutionary theory in nineteenth-century social thought (Hofstadter 1944; R. J. Wilson 1989). Spencer ([1876] 1906) and Sumner (1883) were particularly influential as popularizers of Darwin's theory. Going well beyond Darwin's original intent, they attempted to apply the principles of natural selection to the study of human societies in a manner that has since been widely discredited. Their ill-fated venture has come to be called "social Darwinism."

It was actually Spencer, and not Darwin himself, who coined the phrase "the survival of the fittest" to describe Darwin's view of life as a struggle for survival (Sills and Merton 1991: 47, 221). The core insight of Darwin's theory, expressed in his own words, was as follows:

> [A]ny variation, however slight and from whatever cause proceeding, if it be in any degree profitable to an individual, . . . will tend to the preservation of that individual, and will generally be inherited by its offspring. The offspring, also, will thus have a better chance of surviving . . . . I have called this principle, by which each slight variation, if useful, is preserved, by the term of Natural Selection. (Darwin [1859] 1964: 61)

In briefer terms, evolution is the selective preservation of variations in a reproducing population (Campbell 1965).

Spencer and Sumner, in a caricature of Darwinian principles, depicted evolution as a fiercely competitive struggle for survival within and among species. In retrospect, this represents a partial distortion of Darwin's theory. By emphasizing competition as an evolutionary process, Spencer and Sumner understated the evolutionary value of cooperation within and among species as a means of survival (Singer 1999). While their reading of Darwin stressed individual competition over social cooperation, we know that in nature, social species (including our own) have frequently evolved strategies for working together in ways that enhance the prospect of mutual survival. This is not to deny that Darwin's world is rife with competition and conflicting interests, but only to say that cooperation is often the winning strategy.

By emphasizing individual competition at the expense of social cooperation, social Darwinism served to justify as natural (and therefore inevitable) the fiercely competitive aspects of unrestrained laissez-faire capitalism. The business elite found in Spencer's celebration of natural competition a welcome legitimation of their economic system, and of their own success. No less a titan of commerce than John D. Rockefeller declared to a Sunday school class that the "growth of large business is merely a survival of the fittest" and that this "is merely a working-out of a law of nature and a law of God" (in Hofstadter 1944: 45).

Spencer's notion of the survival of the fittest was widely misinterpreted to imply the moral superiority of the wealthy, the powerful, and those of northern European ancestry over the poor, the powerless, and the colonized. Thus, Spencer's misreading of Darwin, compounded by the public's misreading of Spencer, produced an ideology that justified doctrines of class and racial supremacy and imperial expansion, while fostering a callous indifference or hostility toward those who failed to thrive in the ruthless struggle for survival. Social Darwinism, although influential in commerce and popular culture, has long since been condemned by biological and social scientists as a dangerous and pseudoscientific ideology (Hofstadter 1944; Degler 1991). Some say, however, that the ghost of social Darwinism, with its justification of remorseless competition, still haunts our political and economic culture to this day.

Stage Theories of History

Distinct from the social Darwinism of Spencer and Sumner are various theories proposing the existence of historical stages in the evolution of human societies. Auguste Comte, for example, stated as a "fundamental law" that human societies have evolved in three major historical stages, from a primitive religious or "theological" stage, through a transitory philosophical or "metaphysical" stage, and continuing upward and onward to an advanced scientific or "positive" stage ([1830–42] 1998: 71–72). Karl Marx, Emile Durkheim, and many others have proposed their own distinctive stage theories of social evolution (Appelbaum 1970: 15–64). When we examine these theories closely, however, we find that they often owe more to the metaphor of society as a developing organism than to the metaphor of society as an evolving system. Hence, stage theories typically imply that human history is unfolding according to a series of relatively fixed and pre-ordained developmental stages, much in the way that the acorn becomes the oak or the larva the adult, leading inexorably to us, and perhaps continuing onward toward some even more advanced level of social development.

Evolutionary theorists now recognize that the course of history is not nearly so unilinear or straight-lined as this. Evolution is now understood to be *multilinear*, such that societies (like species) may evolve along a wide range of alternative pathways. These pathways may diverge unpredictably depending on the unique internal characteristics of particular societies and the unique environmental contingencies they face, producing a unique history for each society. Thus the presumption that developing societies must necessarily follow the same path of economic development that Western societies have trod probably says more about the hubris of the West than about the imperatives of social evolution.

While social Darwinist and unilinear stage theories are generally discredited today, several more defensible forms of evolutionary thought have survived in the social sciences. Linguists, for example, have long traced the evolutionary "family tree" of languages in ways clearly analogous to the tracing of species lineages in evolutionary biology (Lakoff 2000: 233–36). Striking parallels between organic and sociocultural evolution have intrigued numerous social and biological scientists as well (e.g., see Gerard, Kluckhohn, and Rapoport 1956; Campbell 1960, 1965; Miller 1978; Swanson 1983). Among the surviving strains of neoevolutionary thought are sociobiology, technological evolutionism, VSR (for Variation/Selection/Retention) models of cultural evolution, memetics, and computer simulations of evolution. Let us consider each of these in turn.

Sociobiology and Evolutionary Psychology

Pioneered by the entomologist E. O. Wilson, sociobiology attempts to apply the explanatory tools of evolutionary biology to the behavior of social species, including ants (Wilson's own specialty) and other social insects, together with many species of fish, birds and mammals. This would not seem an especially controversial undertaking in itself. However, the publication of Wilson's *Sociobiology* in 1975 and subsequent works (e.g., Wilson 1978) set off a howl of protest among many social scientists. In the closing chapter of *Sociobiology*, Wilson had threatened to invade large expanses of academic territory by suggesting that the humanities and social sciences might be viewed as "specialized branches of biology" (1975: 271). Wilson drew what many regarded as unwarranted analogies between nonhuman social species and human beings. In response, social scientists raised their hackles in a counteroffensive reminiscent of the defense of marked territory among animal species in the wild.

In his early formulations, Wilson had seemed to suggest that the myriad complexities of human behavior are reducible to biological principles. Many social scientists and even some biologists objected vociferously to Wilson's seemingly imperial pronouncements (e.g., Sahlins 1976; Caplan 1978; Lewontin, Rose, and Kamin 1984). More recently, however, Wilson and other sociobiologists (Lumsden and Wilson 1981; Wilson 1998) have moderated the rhetoric of reductionism somewhat, preferring now to speak of the "consilience" (literally, the jumping together) of scientific and humanistic understandings of life, and of the "coevolution" of biological and cultural systems. Cultural systems are now seen to interact with biological systems in complex and subtle ways, such that the evolution of one may influence (without strictly determining) the evolution of the other. With this more modest and disarming formulation, sociobiology and its close kin, evolutionary psychology (Buss 1998), now appear to be gaining ground in the social sciences, expanding the perimeters of their intellectual territory into areas of investigation (such as ethics, aesthetics, and religious studies) once reserved almost exclusively for humanistic and cultural analysis.

Sociobiology, unlike other forms of social evolutionism, is not based on a metaphor between organic and social evolution. Rather, sociobiologists believe that certain general forms of social behavior, such as altruism, loyalty, dominance, territoriality, and aggression, are *literally* shaped, in large measure, by the selective pressures of organic evolution and are encoded in our genes. Sociobiologists readily acknowledge, however, that genetic traits, including behavioral predispositions, may manifest themselves differently in different social environments—a principle biologists call the "norm of reaction" (Wilson 1998: 149–51). This principle undermines the widespread misconception that sociobiologists advocate a strict genetic determinism. Asking whether genetic heredity or environment determines behavior is a little like asking whether latitude or longitude determines the position of an object on the earth's surface.

Perhaps sociobiology's most important contribution to the social sciences will be to expand our field of vision to include *all* social species, and not merely the human species, in our understanding of the social (Machalek 1992; Turner 1998: 131–34). A truly comparative sociology would study societies across species, from ant to elephant, including societies without culture. In short, a truly comparative sociology would study both wasps and WASPs, and with as much attention to their similarities as to their differences.

Technological Evolutionism

A very different variety of neoevolutionary theory emphasizes the social and cultural impact of technological change. Technological evolutionists typically regard technology as a distinct third level of evolutionary analysis, operating alongside organic and cultural evolution and potentially influencing both. Representatives of this approach have included Marx ([1859] 1970), who viewed technological change as a driving force in history, and William Ogburn (1922), who argued that modern technologies tend to change more rapidly than their surrounding cultures can adapt to them, creating what he termed "cultural lag." On the contemporary scene, Gerhard Lenski and Jean Lenski (1987) and Stephen Sanderson (1990) continue to speak for this approach to the study of social change, viewing a society's technology as a fundamental determinant of its way of life.

While technological evolutionism, like sociobiology, is sometimes accused of being reductionist—i.e., of seeking to reduce the complexities of social life to a single explanatory factor—it need not be so. According to subtler forms of technological evolutionism, technology does not strictly determine social forms, but merely expands or constrains the range of options available to a society. Thus, societies at similar levels of technological development (e.g., Japan, France, and the United States) may still retain significant cultural differences. Those who worry that an exclusive emphasis on technological factors implies a crudely materialist philosophy of history should find reassurance in the fact that every technology is first an idea (and indeed, that materialism itself is an idea). History emerges out of the complex interplay (or dialectic) of ideas and material conditions. Neither determines the course of social evolution by itself. Thus, it would be just as great a mistake to understate the power of technological factors in history as to exaggerate them.

Many contemporary observers (e.g., Bell 1973; Toffler and Toffler 1995; Thurow 1996) believe that we are now, for better or worse, in the throes of a technological revolution comparable in scope to the transition from hunting and gathering to agriculture, or from agriculture to industrialism. The rapid pace of technical innovation in postindustrial societies, and its disorienting impact on global commerce and culture, suggest that social evolution is now occurring at an accelerating rate of speed. As technological evolutionists might have predicted, this rapid evolution (or "r-evolution") is driven largely by spectacular advances in computer and communication technologies. Whether this evolutionary lurch is leading us to new heights of civilization or merely hastening our extinction as a species (or both) remains an unanswered question.

VSR Models

A third strain in current evolutionary thought, termed VSR (Variation/Selection/Retention), adopts the logic of Darwinian evolution to explain social and cultural change without attempting to reduce social evolution to biological or technological factors. From a VSR perspective, biological and social evolution are merely two particular manifestations of the same general evolutionary principles. Proposed by Donald Campbell (1960, 1965, 1975) and others, this approach has been used to study subjects as diverse as the evolution of organizations (Aldrich 1979) and the evolution of scientific concepts (Toulmin 1972).

VSR may be described as a three-phase evolutionary process (Aldrich 1979: 33–35). In the first phase, a variation or innovation occurs in some biological, psychological, or social system, such as a genetic mutation in a population of organisms. (It makes no difference whether the variation is planned or unplanned, predictable or random.) In the second phase, factors in the system's environment consistently select for or against the new variation, either extinguishing it or allowing it to survive. Finally, those variations that have been systematically selected by the environment are preserved or retained so that they may be repeated or "reproduced" (as through biological reproduction) on future occasions. Wherever this three-phase process operates, whether in biological, psychological or social systems, it naturally tends to produce an improved fit between the system and its environment.

To take an example from the social world, consider the decision by a corporation to introduce a new product in the marketplace. The new product or variation (V), if selected (S) often enough by consumers, will be retained (R) in the company's product line and reproduced. Most new products fail, just as most genetic mutations fail, being either useless or harmful to the system in which they reside. However, those biological mutations or commercial innovations that enhance the fitness of the species or the corporation are selected and kept. The logic of evolution is the same in either case, whether the system in question is biological or social.

Further examples are easy to generate. Consider the politician running for office who seeks to distinguish herself from her opponents by varying (V) from her opponent's positions in such a way as to be differentially selected (S) by voters and retained (R) in office. Or consider the baby in the crib who babbles various sounds (V). Those sounds that resemble sounds in the parent's language are selectively rewarded (S) and are more apt to be retained (R) in the child's linguistic repertoire and reproduced on future occasions (Aldrich 1979: 33–35).

Social evolution is, in Campbell's view, the result of countless instances such as these, accumulating and building upon one another over long periods of time. Notice that we may interpret such instances through the Darwinian concepts of variation and selective retention without reducing social evolution to biological evolution, or even referring to biology at all. For it is the basic logic, and not the substance, of Darwinian biology that VSR models seek to capture. The same basic principles of evolution operate at the biological, psychological, and social levels simultaneously, and they are not the exclusive property of any one discipline.

Perhaps the most impressive and ambitious attempt thus far to apply Darwinian concepts to the study of social practices is W. G. Runciman's sprawling *Treatise on Social Theory* in three volumes (1983/1989/1997). In a manner similar to Campbell's, Runciman treats aspects of the history of Europe, and of twentieth-century Great Britain in particular, as cases of institutional evolution, applying concepts such as mutation, selection, competition, recombination, replication, and reproduction in their analysis.

Memetics

In a closely related variation on the evolutionary theme, biologist Richard Dawkins (1976, 1989) has proposed an approach to cultural evolution based on an analogy between genes, the basic units of biological reproduction, and "memes," his term for the basic units of cultural reproduction. This proposed new science of the meme, known as memetics, has gained widespread popular interest in recent years (Lynch 1996; Brodie 1996), including an avid following in Internet newsgroups, although it remains something of a curiosity in established academic circles.

Memes are units of imitation. As examples of memes, Dawkins offers "words, music, visual images, styles of clothes, facial or hand gestures, skills" (Dawkins 1982: 109)—indeed, any bit of behavior that can be imitated. "Just as genes propagate themselves by leaping from body to body in sexual reproduction, so do memes propagate themselves by leaping from brain to brain via imitation" (1976: 206). We may also speak of memes colonizing or "parasitizing" brains in the manner of viruses, just as a biological virus parasitizes the body or a computer virus parasitizes a disk. The principle is the same whether the host is a body, a mind, or a machine (Dawkins 1989: 329–30).

Dawkins takes the orthodox Darwinian position that "all life evolves by the differential survival of replicating entities" (1976: 206). In organic life, the gene or DNA molecule is the replicating entity. Dawkins maintains that we (or our bodies at any rate) are "survival machines—robot vehicles blindly programmed to preserve the selfish molecules known as genes" (1976: ix). Just as the gene is the organic replicator, so is the meme the replicator of culture, "achieving evolutionary change at a rate which leaves the old gene panting far behind" (1976: 206). Dawkins chose the name *meme* for the cultural replicator because it sounds a bit like *gene*, but also because it suggests the Greek word for "imitation" and the French word for "memory" (1976: 206). He might have added that the selfish meme, like the selfish gene, seems to cry out "me!me!"

Memes are born, live, migrate, reproduce, and die like the members of human populations, and thus can be studied, we would suggest, within the conceptual framework of demography. According to Dawkins, cultural evolution occurs as new memes become dominant in a population, taking over the minds of their hosts, while older memes are gradually forgotten and eventually go extinct. Dawkins contends that memes compete with each other for memory space in much the same way that files in a computer compete with each other for scarce disk space (Dawkins, 1976: 211). Memes also compete for the time, energy, and attention of their hosts and, in the external environment, for media time, billboard space, shelf space, and the like. Moreover, they seem to link up with other memes in ways analogous to genetic linkages (or "coadapted gene complexes") in gene pools. Thus, a meme for belief in God is culturally linked to certain forms of ritual, music, art, architecture, and the like, each promoting the survival of the others.

Many social theorists, not directly influenced by Dawkins's memetics, nonetheless speak of the *reproduction* of social and cultural forms through time, a process vaguely akin to biological reproduction, although operating through entirely different mechanisms. Thus, Nancy Chodorow (1978) writes from a psychoanalytic perspective of the "reproduction of mothering" from one generation of women to another. Perhaps we may also speak of the *hybridization* of memes—the combination and recombination of memes from diverse sources to produce entirely new meme complexes. In this postmodern era of rapidly expanding global travel and communication, and with more memes available to combine and recombine than ever before, cultural elements from around the world and across historical eras are constantly mixed and matched to produce exotic cultural hybrids, ranging from new machines to new cuisines.

Dawkins carries the gene-meme analogy to considerable lengths. To his credit, however, he candidly acknowledges the disanalogies as well as the analogies between biological and cultural evolution (1982: 109–13; 1989: 322–32). He concedes that in certain respects memes are *not* like genes. Genes are capable of making more or less exact copies of themselves which can be transmitted with high fidelity to succeeding generations. Memes, on the other hand, are often fuzzy and inexact; something is lost or gained in transmission from person to person, as in the passing around of a joke. Moreover, it is not clear where the boundaries of memes are to be drawn (1982: 112). Dawkins asks: If a tune is a meme, then how many memes are in a symphony? In a piece of music, should the unit of memetic analyis be a bar? a chord? a symphonic movement? Here Dawkins concludes, somewhat vaguely, that a unit is a meme if it is "sufficiently distinctive and memorable to be abstracted from the context of the whole" (1976: 209–10).

While Dawkins is often associated with sociobiologists, he diverges from them in several important ways. First, he suspects that cultural evolution may be largely independent of biological evolution. For example, it is difficult to discern any genetic advantage in the practice of priestly celibacy; yet this meme continues to survive in the meme pool of some religious traditions. Moreover, while Dawkins (1987) joins other biologists in denying that organic evolution proceeds teleologically, according to some purposeful design, he acknowledges the possibility that cultural evolution is at least partially intentional due to the remarkable human capacity for conscious foresight or purpose. This capacity to simulate possible futures in our minds and to work toward realizing imagined goals gives us some measure of freedom, he suggests, from the tyranny of both selfish genes and selfish memes (1976: 215). It seems that conscious human choice introduces an element of *artificial* selection into the evolutionary equation. Thus, human cultural evolution is not entirely blind, but only vision impaired.

Dawkins's concept of the replicating meme, the "gene" of culture, may prove to be a fruitful analogy. Others have proposed similar analogies in recent years, giving a variety of names to their proposed units of cultural selection: "mentifacts" or "sociofacts" (Aldous Huxley, in Swanson 1983: 91), "mnemotypes" (H. F. Blum, in Swanson 1983: 91), "i-culture" (F. T. Cloak, in Dawkins 1982: 109); "culturgens" (Lumsden and Wilson 1981), and sociogenes (Swanson 1983). In a similar vein, Bernard Campbell (1966; Swanson 1983: 92) has proposed that "ritual is, as it were, the DNA of society . . . the encoded informational basis of culture."

By whatever name, "meme" may be a meme whose time has come, judging from the widespread notice it has received (e.g., Swanson 1983; Lewontin, Rose, and Kamin 1984; Calvin 1990; Casti 1989; Dennett 1991) from a variety of audiences. Might the discovery of the meme represent an evolutionary break-through in the study of cultural evolution itself? Only time and artificial selec-tion will tell.

Computer Simulations of Evolution

Evolutionary theory continues to evolve and to branch out not only in the social sciences, but in other fields as well. Borrowing Darwinian concepts from biology, computer scientists and engineers have developed *genetic algorithms* or problem-solving procedures that simulate the evolutionary mechanisms of genetic muta-tion, natural selection, and reproduction (nature's own problem-solving proce-dures). Genetic algorithms are essentially computer programs that create a Darwinian competition among a population of possible solutions to a given prob-lem. They have been used to arrive at more optimal solutions to problems rang-ing from robotic design to stock market prediction (Levy 1992: 153–87; Goldberg 2000). A related development, called *artificial life*, consists of computer programs that, from a small set of initial rules, are able to simulate the birth, transforma-tion, and death of very simple life forms on a computer screen. These geometric games, which are readily accessible on the World Wide Web, have the capacity to create elementary "societies" of artificial objects and to track their patterns of evolution through time (Levy 1992). *Artificial neural networks* are still another mathematical simulation of biological systems. These programs simulate the struc-ture and learning abilities of natural nervous systems, and even have the capac-ity to evolve (Pinker 1997: 177–79). It is safe to predict that in the coming de-cades, researchers will discover a multitude of new ways to apply genetic algorithms, artificial life, neural networks, and other emerging approaches to problems in the social sciences. Evolutionary analogies are thus increasingly likely to find their way into the social sciences through the gateway of computer simu-lation. One prescient observer (Wright 2000: 339–43) forecasts that we will soon be seeing on-screen computer simulations of human cultural evolution.

Society as Ecosystem

Social theorists have likened human societies not only to individual organisms and to evolving species, but also to entire ecosystems. The notion that societies are like ecosystems first flourished in the "Chicago school" of human ecology in the 1920s and 1930s. Although this school of thought has receded in recent decades, new forms of ecological thinking have come to the fore with the dramatic rise of the environmental movement in the late twentieth century. Let us briefly examine the history of this vital metaphor.

The Chicago School

Ecology as a scientific concept is a relatively recent invention. The German biologist Ernst Haeckel defined the term (from the Greek root meaning "household") in 1870 as the "body of knowledge concerning the economy of nature— . . . the study of all the complex interrelationships referred to by Darwin as the conditions of the struggle for existence" (in Kormondy 1976: x). Haekel's notion of an "economy of nature" suggests parallels between socioeconomic systems and biological systems. Thus, biologists sometimes refer to the niches that species fill as their "occupations" in the ecological economy. One early zoologist described ecological systems as hierarchies ordered by rank, with dominant species enthroned at the top, by analogy to the social and economic hierarchies of feudal Europe (Wolfe 1993: 92–93). We make similar projections of human social structures onto the natural world when we describe beehives and ant "colonies" as communities composed of "workers" in service to their "queen."

Soon after biologists borrowed the concept of ecology from economics, social scientists began borrowing it back. Ecology was still a new branch of biology in the early decades of the twentieth century when a group of University of Chicago sociologists (Robert Park, Ernest Burgess, R. D. McKenzie, and others) began to apply its basic tenets to the study of societies, and to urban life in particular. They made good use of their own urban environment, using the city of Chicago as a living laboratory for their investigations.

Chicago sociologists used the term *ecology* broadly to refer to the intricate web of interdependencies that exist within and among human communities, and they soon set out to investigate urban communities as ecological systems. They examined the tendency of urban growth to radiate outward from the center of a city in concentric circles. They tracked the territorial movement of economic classes and ethnic groups. Applying ecological concepts such as competition, dominance, succession, and symbiosis, Chicago sociologists sought to explain the spatial configurations of cities and the continual transition of land use from one residential or commercial use to another (Theodoreson 1961). In short, they viewed the city as a kind of radiating, pulsating, dynamic living ecosystem. Meanwhile, in anthropology, a new breed of ethnologists known as cultural ecologists began to view societies and cultural systems as complex adaptations to their natural environments.

The Green Wave

By the 1960s, ecological concepts had begun to make their way into the popular culture. Rachel Carson's best-selling *Silent Spring* (1962) sounded an alarm against the hazards of synthetic pesticides. Paul Ehrlich's *The Population Bomb* (1968) and Barry Commoner's *The Closing Circle* (1971) were also best-selling books during this period, raising public awareness, if not dread, about the problems of overpopulation and environmental degradation. In general, these books and others like them challenged the atomistic view of human society as a collection of autonomous individuals, offering in its place an ecological image of society as a complex web of interdependencies. Popular slogans from the period sent a clear message: "Everything is connected to everything else," "We're all in this together," and "Nature bats last."

The ecological movement gained momentum with the publication in 1972 of *The Limits to Growth*, a controversial study by a group of MIT demographers (Meadows et al. 1972) who used computer forecasting models to project global trends in population growth, environmental deterioration, and the depletion of nonrenewable resources. The authors grimly concluded that past growth trends were *unsustainable*. Unless industrial and industrializing nations radically altered their course, exponential population growth and its environmental consequences would culminate in global catastrophe at some point in the twenty-first century. While the authors' assumptions were sternly challenged by critics, their message was enormously influential and has continued to provoke research and debate (Meadows et al. 1992).

By the 1980s, the environmental or "green" movement had grown too large to be ignored, particularly in advanced industrial nations. The movement posed a serious challenge to the mechanistic worldview that had come to dominate Western societies since the sixteenth century. Physicist Fritjof Capra (1982), in *The Turning Point* (on which the intellectually provocative film *MindWalk* is based) described the transformation as follows. Before 1500, the dominant metaphors in Western (and other) societies had been organic. "People lived in small, cohesive communities and experienced nature in terms of organic relationships, characterized by the interdependence of spiritual and material phenomena" (Capra 1982: 53). The medieval church, integrating Christian theology and ancient Greek philosophy, reinforced this conceptual framework in the West.

But this organic worldview changed dramatically in the sixteenth and seventeenth centuries with the rise of the scientific Enlightenment. "The notion of an organic, living and spiritual universe was replaced by that of the world as a machine, and the world-machine became the dominant metaphor of the modern era" (1982: 54). The scientific empiricist Francis Bacon articulated this changing view of nature when he wrote of the need to bind and enslave nature and to "torture nature's secrets from her." Domination and control of nature's machine became the watchwords of scientific progress.

Capra maintains that in the twentieth century we approached the limits of the mechanistic metaphor and were evolving toward a more ecological worldview. Many within the scientific community itself are turning away from crudely mechanistic thinking and toward more holistic approaches to the study of nature. The green movement represents the cultural and political arm of this emerging ecological perspective.

Despite limited success in influencing legislation and public opinion, the green movement has had its share of critics—not only among industrialists, deforesters, and developers (whose economic motives are plain enough), but also within the scientific community itself. Some critics have noted, for example, a naive tendency in popular environmentalism (as distinct from environmental science) to paint an idealized picture of nature, imagining ecosystems as peaceable kingdoms in which harmony and mutual cooperation reign, and in which hierarchies of domination within and among species are rare (e.g., Sale 1991). Environmental scientists are apt to regard this image of nature as a romantic fantasy, as partial and incomplete as the opposing image of nature "red in tooth and claw." There is also in some green literature a tendency to romanticize life in hunting-and-gathering or simple agrarian societies, and to dream of a return to an idyllic preindustrial way of life.

Wolfe (1993) finds a different sort of difficulty in green thinking. Ecological metaphors, he notes, challenge us to see the world holistically—to respect the whole, and not merely its individual parts. But this holistic view has some deeply disturbing implications. It leads us to conclude that the human species, as merely one among millions of species, has no special value. The deeper implications of deep ecology, Wolfe fears, are profoundly antihumanistic, undercutting the possibility of an ethics that cherishes human life.

Yet despite its limitations, the ecology movement has succeeded in challenging many of the taken-for-granted assumptions that underlie industrialism as a way of life. Ecofeminist writers, for example (e.g., Merchant 1990; Plant 1991), have explored the relationship between patriarchy and the compulsion to dominate and control nature. Others have sought to explore the spiritual implications of environmentalism (e.g., Schumacher 1973; Spretnak 1986; Berry 1988), while still others have challenged the mentality which assumes that every problem in the world is amenable to a "techno-fix" (Trainer 1991: 204). By challenging the ideologies of unrestrained growth, material accumulation, and technological domination, the green movement is causing us to rethink some of our culture's most deeply rooted assumptions.

Are Societies Alive?

The ecological metaphor offers a view of human societies as living entities nested within a still larger system of living things, the world biosphere. Several prominent scientists in recent years have controversially suggested that human societies or cultures may actually be *literally* alive—a claim not to be confused with the even more controversial Gaia hypothesis (Lovelock 1979), which proposes that the earth's entire biosphere is a single living and self-regulating organism.

The pioneer ethologist Konrad Lorenz, for example, renowned for his studies of animal behavior in natural habitats, has proposed that we interpret culture as a living system (1977: 177–96). The evolutionary biologist Dawkins is also willing to take seriously the possibility that cultural memes are not just metaphorically but technically alive (1989: 192). Similarly, the biologist James G. Miller (1978), whose major work constitutes the most thorough and systematic exploration to date of analogies between biological and social phenomena, explicitly advocates the view that human societies are living systems.

Miller examines living systems on eight distinct levels (cell, organ, organism, group, organization, community, society, and supranational system). At each level he finds the same fundamental processes of life operating. Living systems reproduce themselves. They maintain boundaries that protect them from their environments. They ingest matter and energy, storing these inputs or converting them into more usable forms and distributing them among subsystems. Living systems receive and process information. They produce outputs and extrude wastes. We may observe these and other basic life processes at every level of life, Miller argues in great detail, from the micro-level of the cell to the macro-level of the international system. Miller maintains that a human society does all of these things and more. If we define life with reference to these criteria, he concludes, we must acknowledge that a society is a living being.

Has Miller succeeded in establishing that societies are living systems? Critics may object that the boundaries of social and cultural systems are too porous and ambiguous, their units of replication too imprecise, and their modes of reproduction too different from those found in organic systems to justify the claim that societies are alive. Yet the intriguing resemblances that Miller finds between biological and social systems must also be fairly considered. In the end, the question may be largely a semantic one, hinging on precisely how we choose to define the meaning of "life."

More than a century ago, Spencer described human societies as vast "superorganic" living systems. He has often been ridiculed for this view. Now we are asked to consider the possibility that Spencer, wrong-headed in so many other ways, might have been on to something. Many scientists would no doubt cast a skeptical eye on the literal truth of Spencer's claim. Yet metaphorically, the image of society as a living being has considerable aesthetic power. Certainly most of us would find it more poetically absorbing than the competing image of society as a lifeless machine, to which we will soon turn our attention. The image of society as a living system suggests that we are an organic part of something much larger than ourselves, which has a life and being all its own. In the memorable words of Darwin ([1859] 1964: 490), describing the general process of evolution in lyrical language, "there is grandeur in this view of life."

CHAPTER THREE

~

Society as Machine

A culture's metaphors commonly reflect its technological way of life. Thus, agrarian cultures, closely attuned to the rhythms of nature and farming, typically conceived social life in organic terms, as though society were a kind of living thing. But with the rise of modern science and industrial technology, new social metaphors began to emerge. Among the most formidable of these is the distinctly modern image of society as a mechanical system, for in modern societies the machine has served as both tool and metaphor (Haken et al. 1993). Mechanical metaphors suggest the powerful poetic image of a social world driven by impersonal forces, whether these be natural forces beyond our control or social forces of our own making. The image of society as a system of impersonal forces suggests in turn the need for a social science to explain these forces, and for a social engineering to direct them.

From a mechanistic perspective, a social system is an apparatus composed of integrated parts whose operation yields more or less predictable outcomes. In comparison to earlier organic metaphors, mechanistic metaphors tend to present a rather cold, rigid, and lifeless image of social structures. Such metaphors are often invoked to describe the relatively routine, uniform, and standardized features of social life. (Thus we may hear a large educational institution described as an "assembly line" or a "diploma factory," a governmental organization as a "bureaucratic apparatus," or an army as a "green machine.") Mechanistic metaphors are less well suited, however, to capturing the unpredictable and improvisational aspects of social life. For while an army marching in military formation in peacetime may resemble a well-oiled machine, the same army thrown into the chaos and confusion of battle will likely not.

We find two major strands of mechanistic imagery in social theory. The first sees human societies as *natural mechanisms* governed by social laws of nature, analogous to physical laws such as gravitation, which are thought to be discoverable through scientific investigation. Those embracing this version of the machine metaphor have long dreamed of the possibility of a "social physics"—an explanatory science of society as rigorous as the physical sciences. The second strand of mechanistic imagery pictures human societies as *artificial mechanisms,* analogous to technological inventions, which can be designed and redesigned to accomplish human goals. Those who embrace this version of the metaphor are inclined to imagine the possibility of "social engineering" that would enable us to harness nature and society toward desired ends. Although these two strands of mechanistic thought are intertwined, they are nonetheless distinct. In the end, as we shall see, they point in rather different directions.

The Dream of Social Physics

Mechanistic metaphors first came to prominence during the scientific Enlightenment of the seventeenth century as René Descartes, Francis Bacon, Isaac Newton, and others ushered in what has come to be called the modern era. Physicists and astronomers of the period, drawing metaphors from the advanced technology of their time, began to imagine nature as a kind of divinely crafted clockwork (Rifkin 1980: 15–30; Capra 1982: 52–74). They sought to reveal the inner workings of the cosmic clock by means of scientific methods, making careful observations and subjecting these observations to rational and systematic analysis. Applying mechanistic images of nature to human societies, the political philosopher Thomas Hobbes ([1651] 1964: xxvii) proposed that the human body is a machine composed of mechanical subparts, and that the state or "body politic," as a gigantic artificial social body, is likewise a machine. Thus emerged the image of society as a complex mechanical device made of cogs within cogs and gears within gears—in short, something akin to a *social* clockwork imbedded within the larger clockwork of nature (Rifkin 1987: 201–8).

Nineteenth-century social theorists, impressed with the achievements of the physical sciences of their time, dreamed that human societies could be investigated with the same precision and rigor that physical scientists had applied successfully to the study of matter. The French theorist Auguste Comte wrote in 1822: "We now possess a celestial physics, a terrestrial physics, either mechanical or chemical, a vegetable physics and an animal physics; we still want one more and last one, social physics, to complete the system of our knowledge of nature" (in Coser 1971: 28). Comte envisioned a social science, analogous to the natural sciences, that would achieve nothing less than "positive" knowledge of the natural laws governing society and history (Comte [1830–42] 1998; Turner and Beeghley 1981: 40, 52). His intellectual descendants have ever since been known as *positivists.*

In 1835, the Belgian statistician and scientist Adolphe Quetelet reinvented Comte's term, proposing the creation of a new discipline also to be named "social physics," whose task it would be to search for statistical uniformities in human behavior. Believing that Quetelet had stolen his original term, Comte reluctantly decided to rename his new discipline "sociology" instead (Coser 1971: 3, 28–29). While the term *social physics* is no longer in use, long since replaced by the more general term *social science*, the influence of analogies to physical science is still felt today.

Following Comte, positivists generally adopted the classical mechanistic view that everything in nature, including human societies, is governed by deterministic and non-negotiable laws. Ironically, the scientific notion that the physical universe is "governed" by natural "laws" is actually a metaphor that physical scientists first borrowed from the social realm of jurisprudence. Physical phenomena do not, after all, obey laws in any literal legal sense, or go to jail for their violation. In this mechanistic or billiard-ball model of the universe, all natural (including social) phenomena are conceived as systems of invariant and law-governed causes and effects. Natural laws, operating on a given set of initial conditions $(a,b,c, \ldots n)$, should always produce the same outcome (o). Moreover, if we vary the initial conditions, the outcomes should vary in regular and predictable ways. In a mechanistic universe, it should therefore be hypothetically possible for the perfectly informed scientist, equipped with a knowledge of the relevant natural laws and initial conditions, to predict future events with impressive precision.

The rhetoric of positivism suggests that natural laws governing society and history, like laws of physics, operate whether we like them or not, and hence that it is futile to resist them. The locomotive of history will follow its determined course whether we resist it or not. Indeed, even our resistance is determined and demanded by the laws of nature. Humanistic critics are quick to respond, however, that such a strict determinism erases the possibility of human freedom and responsibility, reducing social actors to human pinballs, propelled and shunted about by forces entirely beyond their control. Following the existentialist philosopher Jean-Paul Sartre, Peter Berger (1963: 143) has deemed this sort of mechanistic fatalism "bad faith," or the refusal to take responsibility for one's choices by pretending that one could not have chosen otherwise. Most social scientists today would reject both extreme social determinism *and* the equally extreme opposing view that human freedom is entirely unconditioned and unconstrained by the actor's social circumstances (as though starving children freely chose their own starvation). At the former extreme, the strictly deterministic worldview adopted by early positivists is no longer current even in the physical sciences, having been called into question by developments in quantum mechanics and the emerging sciences of chaos (Gleick 1987) and complexity (Waldrop 1992). Although the physics that Comte dreamed of emulating in the early nineteenth century no longer exists, his intellectual descendants still look to the physical sciences of our own day for inspiration and guidance as they continue their search for natural laws governing society and history.

Theorists in the positivist tradition have sought to model the social sciences after the physical sciences in at least two ways: first, by attempting to emulate the logic and methods of the physical sciences, and second, by borrowing substantive concepts and vocabularies from their more scientific neighbors. Let us consider each of these ways in turn.

The Logic of Scientific Inquiry

The logic of scientific investigation is often visualized as a circular and self-correcting process (e.g., Wallace 1971). According to an idealized description of what scientists do, an investigator begins by carefully observing, measuring, and recording data pertaining to some object of study. The investigator looks for nonrandom patterns in the data. To this point, the logic of scientific inquiry is inductive, proceeding from particular observations to empirical (i.e., observation-based) generalizations.

Having identified general patterns in the data, the scientist then seeks to explain them. In a creative leap of imagination, the scientist proposes a theory, either verbal or mathematical, to explain or interpret what has been observed. (Here metaphors and analogies often come into play as imaginative sources of creative insight, as discussed in the postscript.) Some philosophers of science (e.g., Popper 1963) contend that a theory is not truly scientific unless it is in principle falsifiable. That is to say, a theory is not scientific unless it permits the logical derivation of specific hypotheses (statements of what one expects to observe), formulated in such a way that they are capable of being tested and possibly proven false by further observation. The logical derivation of specific hypotheses from a general theory is a process of deductive reasoning, proceeding as it does from the general to the particular. If a hypothesis derived from a general theory is then tested against empirical observations, and if these observations are found to be consistent with the theory, our confidence in the theory grows.

Strictly speaking, a theory is never "proven" with absolute certainty. Even if all previous evidence is consistent with the theory, tomorrow we may encounter inconsistent or anomalous evidence, as has often happened in the history of science (Kuhn 1972). When evidence is inconsistent with our hypothesis, we must either reexamine the adequacy of the evidence or presume that the theory from which we derived the hypothesis is deficient, in which case we may either refine and retest the theory or abandon it altogether and go in search of a better theory.

Now the process has come full circle—from observation to empirical generalization (the inductive side of scientific reasoning) to theory to derived hypothesis (the deductive side) and back to observation. This circular process is presumed (rather optimistically) to be self-correcting. Positivists hope that by continually refining our social theories and testing their derivative hypotheses against further evidence, we will achieve increasingly adequate scientific knowledge of the social world.

This description of the scientific process is, to be sure, highly idealized and excessively tidy. Real scientists rarely work in such a "cookbook" fashion. Actual scientific work is almost always messier and more ridden with ambiguities than this picture would suggest (Latour and Woolgar 1979), and some philosophers of science (e.g., Feyerabend 1978) contend that a single uniform "scientific method" does not even exist in actual scientific practice. Nonetheless, this idealized portrait of science (or something resembling it) has been embraced by positivists since the time of Comte as a physical science model for the development of the human sciences.

Objectivity and Value-Neutrality

In their efforts to emulate the success and reap the prestige of the physical sciences, positivists have often invoked the rhetoric of "objectivity" to justify their work to the scientific community and to the larger public. They have insisted that scientific inquiry must strive to be "value-neutral," describing and explaining the world as it really is without making moral judgments about how the world ought to be. This insistence on the separation of fact and value has been attributed especially to the German sociologist Max Weber ([1918] 1958), who articulated the principle in his famous essay on science as a vocation. The neoclassical economist Ludwig von Mises ([1949] 1966: 10) stated his own version of the principle when he asserted that theoretical science "abstains from any judgment of value. It is not its task to tell people what ends they should aim at. It is a science of the means to be applied for the attainment of ends chosen, not, to be sure, a science of the choosing of ends." The choosing of ends is, Mises insisted, "beyond the scope of any science."

The belief that scientific facts can be examined independently of moral values did not originate with Weber. It was expressed much earlier in the writings of the seventeenth-century scientist Francis Bacon, who advocated building "a true model of the world, such as it is in fact, not such as man's own reason would have it to be" (in Rifkin 1980: 20). The attempt to drive a wedge between facts and values appears even earlier in the writings of political philosopher Niccolò Machiavelli ([1532] 1981: 56), who observed that "the way men live is so far removed from the way they ought to live that anyone who abandons what is for what should be pursues his downfall." True to his own advice, Machiavelli proceeded to analyze the cold realities of politics without reference to moral ideals. Of course, Machiavelli's analysis was not really value-neutral. It tacitly affirmed the values of power and conquest. But that is another story.

Critics of positivism typically regard the doctrine of value-neutral science as philosophically and politically naive. It is increasingly apparent that the social sciences (and for that matter, the physical sciences) could not be value-neutral even if they wished to be. Science itself rests upon certain value-commitments, including commitment to the values of honesty, open communication of results, freedom of inquiry (and the political institutions that make it possible), rigor, prediction, control, and the like (e.g., Popper 1950; Merton 1973; Sjoberg and Nett 1997). Critics note that because the very act of doing science is drenched in value judgments, the notion of scientific value-neutrality is self-contradictory and therefore untenable.

Critics further observe that value judgments and assumptions enter into every stage of the scientific process, from the selection of *what* to study and *how* to study it (often dictated by the economic, political, or military objectives of those who fund research) to decisions about *how, when,* and *to whom* findings will be disseminated (Gouldner 1970; Sjoberg and Nett 1997). Science does not exist in a social and political vacuum, and it never has. Scientific work has been intensely politicized since before the time of Galileo, who was prosecuted by the religious authorities of the seventeenth century for publicly professing the heretical belief that the earth revolves around the sun (Ronan 1974). The trials of Galileo and, in the twentieth century, the scientific research efforts that eventuated in the dropping of atomic bombs on Hiroshima and Nagasaki, are vivid reminders that scientific knowledge and its applications are, for better or worse, rarely neutral in their social effects. We must continually ask the questions, "For whom, and for what, is scientific knowledge produced?" (Lynd 1939; Lee 1978).

Scientists, as human beings, are inevitably motivated by more than a purely disinterested desire for knowledge. (Witness the fierce political competitions that occur within the scientific community for Nobel Prizes.) Scientists and their institutions have political interests of their own, since they must compete with other scientists and other social institutions for scarce and valued resources such as funding, prestige, and political power. In our own time, scientific institutions are powerful political players in their own right (Aronowitz 1988). All of these moral and political considerations should cause us to reconsider popular images of science as a morally and politically "neutral" endeavor.

Reductionism

Another ideal held by many (though by no means all) mechanistic theorists is the goal of reducing social or cultural explanations of human behavior to more fundamental psychological, biological, and ultimately physical levels of explanation. Mechanistic metaphors since the time of Hobbes have typically assumed that societies, as machines, are composed of and reducible to their constituent parts (i.e., individuals), which are reducible to smaller machines (e.g., biological organs), which are in turn reducible to still smaller machines (cells, molecules, and atoms, etc.). George Homans (1964) exemplifies this turn toward reductionism in his controversial remark that the "institutions, organizations and societies that sociologists study can always be analyzed, without residue, into the behavior of individual men."

Critics of reductionism have responded that while wholes are doubtless composed of parts, they are more than *merely* the sum of their parts. Wholes contain not only parts, but also the relations among these parts, and these relations are not contained within the parts themselves. Thus, if we disassemble an automobile on a shop floor, the parts of the automobile taken separately do not add up to a working automobile. In place of atomistic reductionism, some propose a "holistic" view (e.g., Koestler and Smythies 1969; Hampden-Turner 1981: 162–65) in which systems are seen to display emergent properties and relations at each higher level of organization. Thus, organs display attributes not found in atoms and molecules; individuals display attributes not found in their constituent organs; and societies display attributes not found in their constituent individuals taken separately. As the *non*reductionist positivist Emile Durkheim put it, a society has a reality *sui generis*—a reality of its own kind. In place of a reductionist agenda, which seeks to analyze higher-level systems "downward" to their parts, holists propose an agenda that investigates the "upward" evolution of emergent properties in higher-order systems.

We may take a step toward resolving the seemingly endless debate between reductionists and holists (or emergentists) if we think of explanation as a two-way street, with legitimate investigations proceeding in both the "downward" and "upward" directions. Thus, while reductionists may continue to analyze the constituent parts of higher-order systems, holists may continue to investigate the emergent relations among these parts as they combine to form larger wholes. Either strategy, by itself, gives us only half of the picture, for the view going up the street may be rather different from the view going down.

Prediction and Control

Those in the positivist tradition have generally sought explanations of social phenomena that would permit human beings to predict and (where possible) control their own, or each other's, behavior. Behaviorist psychology, for example, has spawned a form of social technology known as behavior modification, involving the strategic application of rewards and punishments to shape human behavior in desired directions. This desire to predict and control behaviors and environments is not unique to science and engineering. Don't we *all* seek some measure of predictability and control in our everyday lives? Yet the desire for control, pushed to extremes, poses certain hazards.

First, the goal of total predictability, taken as a political imperative, would demand that we create and maintain perfectly tidy and tightly ordered social systems that will not behave (or *mis*behave) in unexpected and unforeseeable ways. Building a perfectly predictable society would require the suppression of innovators, dissidents, eccentrics and other such heralds of complexity and uncertainty, whose activities would threaten to disrupt the smooth operation of the social machinery and to make social prediction more difficult. In short, the desire to render human behavior as predictable and controllable as possible may conceal hidden tendencies toward a crushing authoritarianism.

This is not to say that every attempt to control human behavior (through law, custom, economic incentive, and the like) is unduly authoritarian or illegitimate. A certain measure of social control is necessary to the survival of any society and its members. The danger resides in elevating order and social predictability to the level of supreme values at the expense of other worthy human values, as authoritarian regimes of both right and left have done at great human cost in the past century. Political and moral issues of this kind—including issues pertaining to the ethics of social research itself (Sjoberg 1967)—tend to fall outside the positivist field of vision precisely because positivism's commitment to value-neutrality tends to suppress awareness of its own moral and political context. In fairness, we should note, however, that some theorists in the positivist tradition (e.g., Lundberg 1961) have made sincere efforts to reconcile political and moral concerns with the dream of a positivist science.

Despite its many detractors, the positivist dream of a social physics is still alive in some sectors of the social sciences today, and perhaps especially in experimental social psychology and economics. In sociology the dream of a rigorous and naturalistic science of society still has its capable defenders (e.g., Turner and Beeghley 1981; Turner 1991; Collins 1975, 1988; Gibbs 1989; Bailey 1994). Collins, for example, insists that "sociology can be a successful science and that it is well on its way to becoming so" (1975: 1). Yet even defenders of the dream acknowledge a widespread loss of faith among social theorists in recent years concerning the existence and/or discoverability of scientific laws of society (Collins 1988: 494; Turner 1991: 28). With a touch of mournful nostalgia, Jonathan Turner and Leonard Beeghley (1981: 551–52) describe the decline of Comte's vision of a social physics as a "great intellectual tragedy," the loss of a common vision of what social theory "can and should be." They conclude that sociology must strive to "rekindle the vision of Comte and begin [once again] to seek and articulate the abstract laws of the social universe."

This clarion call for a return to the dream of a social physics does not, at this moment, seem to be winning the day. Many social theorists are now more inclined to turn to historical and literary studies than to physics and chemistry for inspiration. The positivist faith in a mechanistic social world governed by preexisting natural laws is undermined by a growing sense that we have the capacity, through language and symbol, to *create* social realities according to rules and laws of our own choosing, and that while we may be constrained by natural laws of society and history—if, indeed, such laws exist—we are not mechanically determined by them.

Whether new developments in the natural sciences, such as breakthroughs in chaos or complexity theory, can breathe new life into the dream of a social physics is an open-ended and uncertain prospect. Chaos and complexity theory examine the ways in which orderly and coherent patterns emerge out of randomness and apparent disorder in nature. The capacity of natural systems for spontaneous self-organization is a matter of increasing interest among organizational theorists in search of relevant analogies between physical and social phenomena (Morgan 1997: 261–74). But if the dream of a social physics is rekindled by these emerging new sciences, the social physics of the future will bear as little resemblance to the social physics of Comte's time as the physics of the future bears to the physics of Newton's time.

Borrowed Vocabularies

The influence of the physical sciences on social thought may now be waning, but their historical mark is undeniable. Social scientists have borrowed not only the logic and methods of the physical sciences, but their concepts and terminology as well—often in ways that must make physical scientists wince. The vocabulary of the social sciences is piled high with allusions to physics, chemistry, geology, and mathematics. Social scientists borrow the language (if not the substance) of physics when they speak of "social forces," as when urban theorists speak of the centripetal forces of urbanization that concentrate populations in central cities versus the centrifugal forces of suburbanization that disperse populations outward from the urban center. One urban theorist (Stewart 1948), an astronomer by training, had some success in predicting the economic and social flow of traffic among cities by borrowing from physics the mathematical equation used to measure the gravitational force between objects. Thus, he found, as the gravity equation predicted, that the larger and closer together two cities are, the greater is the strength of their interaction.

Other concepts taken loosely from the physical sciences include references to social pressures, stresses and strains, friction, attraction and polarization, social movements, social momentum and inertia, atomistic individuals and nuclear families, push and pull factors in migration, ripple effects, social pendula, balances of power, scales of justice, social equilibria, social circulation, social entropy (Adams 1975; Rifkin 1980), critical masses, threshholds, and "tipping points" (Gladwell 1996, 2000) that trigger sudden accelerations or changes of direction in system behavior. The psychologist Kurt Lewin, trained in the physical sciences, constructed an entire theory of personality out of the language of physics and topology. His writings are strewn with references to force fields, valences, gradients, and the like (Lewin 1951; Black 1962; Hall and Lindzey 1970). Similarly, Marx ([1867] 1967), in the preface to *Capital*, paid homage to Newtonian physics when he declared that his ultimate aim was to "reveal the economic laws of motion in modern society." Contemporary economists employ physical metaphors in their public rhetoric at every turn (McCloskey 1985, 1990, 1994; Samuelson 2000), referring to inflation and deflation, expansion and contraction, overheating and cooling, economic take-offs and soft (or hard) landings, soaring and plummeting stocks, and the like, as though economic abstractions were physical objects.

Social scientists employ the language of chemistry when they speak of social cohesion (Durkheim [1893] 1947) or bonding, or of the formation of stable social compounds. (Such metaphors, in rhetorical use, may themselves have socially solidifying and catalytic effects, as in the case of the Polish trade union, Solidarity.) In popular parlance we speak of the "chemistry" of personal and group relationships. Vilfredo Pareto ([1916] 1935) had a rather different sort of social chemistry in mind when he transposed his theory of social equilibria directly from the theory of chemical equilibria advanced by chemist J. Willard Gibbs.

Social scientists adopt the vocabulary of geology when they refer to stratification (i.e., the unequal distribution of rewards among social strata, visualized as though they were layered like rock strata), the sedimentation of cultural customs, the erosion of traditions, groundswells of public support, the trickle-down of economic prosperity, social earthquakes, and the volcanic eruption of revolutions. In this vein, Lester Thurow (1996: 11) likens current global economic shifts to profound geological events such as the tectonic shift of plates on the earth's mantle, by means of which whole new continents have been formed.

Psychologists in the Freudian tradition employ physical metaphors when they picture the human psyche as a kind of hydraulic system, with the flow of psychic energies being blocked here and channeled there. Other psychologists have referred to the river or stream of consciousness (James [1890] 1950: 239) and the flow of experience (Csikszentmihalyi 1990). Friedrich Engels ([1878] 1970: 138–39) likewise invoked water metaphors when he likened the revolutionary transformation of society to the qualitative transformation of ice into water and water into steam. The metaphor of steam appears again in the historian Frederick Jackson Turner's (1920) thesis that migration to the American frontier served as a kind of "safety valve" in early American history, reducing social pressure and thus avoiding social explosions.

Conventional moralists employ physical metaphors when they speak of the deterioration or decomposition of our moral life, the erosion of moral standards, or the unraveling of the social fabric. Especially commonplace are architectural references to the pillars of the community, and to imagined moral foundations that are feared to be crumbling. Those who resist conventional morality also invoke physical metaphors when they complain of the repressive, constricting, or stagnating effects of tradition, or of the suffocating pressures of conformity.

Mathematics, the language of science, has been a common source of imagery in social theory. Jeremy Bentham spoke of the arithmetic or calculus of pleasure and pain that social actors employ when making choices. Georg Simmel ([1908] 1955) spoke of the geometry of social forms, and Giovanni Arrighi (1978) of the geometry of imperialism. Sociologists of knowledge (e.g., Mannheim 1936) draw analogies to the geometry of perception when they observe that one's position in social space largely determines one's perspective or point of view. Geometric forms are also implied when we speak of social hierarchies or pyramids, or of trajectories of social change, or, indeed, whenever we represent social relations spatially in the form of diagrams. (Organization charts, for instance, are spatial analogies depicting formal relations of authority that are physically invisible.) Geometric metaphors are also implied in such terms as "upper" and "lower" class (as though the former were spatially above the latter), vertical and horizontal mobility, center and periphery (Wallerstein 1974/1980), and cultural lag and cultural lead (Ogburn 1922; Zurcher 1972). In a broader sense, all mathematical models of social phenomena may be understood as elegant analogies between the formal properties of number systems and the empirically observed properties of social systems.

The use of physical and mathematical imagery in the social sciences implies that social systems are in certain respects like natural phenomena, and are thus subject to mechanistic laws similar to those that govern the physical world. Comte's dream of a social physics may be dying, but the vocabulary of the physical sciences lives on, largely beneath the level of conscious awareness, in the routine discourses of the social sciences.

The Dream of Social Engineering

Thus far we have considered mechanistic metaphors that depict human societies as *natural* mechanisms whose properties, like the properties of molecules or solar systems, can be *discovered* scientifically. Yet other mechanistic metaphors imply that societies are more like *artificial* machines or social technologies, *invented* by human beings and open to continual redesign. The metaphor of social engineering, in contrast to the metaphor of social physics, shifts our focus to human freedom, creativity, and imagination. While technological metaphors affirm that natural constraints limit the range of possible social designs, they also imply that many alternative designs are possible within these constraints. In this sense, mechanistic metaphors borrowed from the world of technology point in a rather different and more open-ended direction than do mechanistic metaphors borrowed from the world of the natural sciences. They introduce a *teleological* or goal-seeking dimension into social analysis, a dimension largely missing from analyses based on the assumption that human behavior is driven entirely by natural laws.

Consider another automotive analogy. Suppose that a team of engineers is commissioned to design a vehicle that is as fast as a race car, as safe as a tank, as fuel-efficient as a compact, and as inexpensive as a bicycle. In the language of engineering, they are asked to optimize these four values with as little compromise to each as possible. The team must work within the natural constraints of physical laws and the physical properties of available materials. They must also operate within the social and economic constraints imposed by the specifications. But within these constraints the team is free to imagine and build a range of possible prototypes, consistent with external constraints but not strictly determined by them, which meet each specification to a varying degree.

Similarly, a society may be viewed, from an engineering perspective, as a kind of design problem. The challenge is to design and maintain a working system that rationally and efficiently fulfills the specifications (i.e., the needs, desires, or values) of its members. The task of the social engineer is to work within natural and cultural constraints to design systems that optimize these values. Something like this occurs in the actual practice of social engineering, from the design of highway traffic systems to the construction of corporate, governmental and military policies—although in real-life social engineering it is not always the needs and desires of the whole society that are served, but rather the needs and desires of its most politically and economically powerful segments.

In ideological rhetoric, the term *social engineering* is sometimes used in a pejorative way to denote governmental attempts to redirect the course of society. But social engineering clearly is not an exclusively political or governmental activity. Corporate policies, practices, and advertising campaigns seek to direct social and cultural changes just as surely as do public laws. Indeed, every attempt to control human behavior may be viewed, for better or worse, as a kind of social engineering project.

Social scientists often simultaneously play the role of social engineer, participating not only in the design of governmental and corporate policies and programs, but also in the day-to-day maintenance of social systems. In engineering parlance, they provide decision makers with "instrument panels" of strategic data tracking the performance of economic and other social systems through time. Such indicators are indispensable sources of information for modern decision makers (Bauer 1966). Thus, economists and other policy scientists function increasingly as navigators, if not copilots, in the decision-making cockpits of industrial and postindustrial societies.

Technological Metaphors Through Time

Historically, machine metaphors in the social sciences have evolved in tandem with the technologies of their times. Thus, early Enlightenment thinkers likened social systems to preindustrial machines such as clocks. Later, with the rise of the industrial revolution, theorists drew mechanistic metaphors from newly emerging industrial technologies such as the factory machine and the assembly line, picturing modern organizational systems as vast people-processing machines. Today, social theorists look increasingly to postindustrial technologies such as the computer and the hologram for poetic inspiration. Let us take a closer look at the relationship between emerging technologies and the metaphors they inspire.

Social philosophers during the Enlightenment often incorporated technological images into their social designs. The Founders of the American republic, for instance, were modern social inventors (and in the cases of Benjamin Franklin and Thomas Jefferson, technological inventors as well) who proposed a mechanically inspired system of "checks and balances" among the branches of government, based on Enlightenment notions propounded by John Locke and Charles-Louis Montesqieu, to prevent excessive concentrations of political power. Early modern social inventors often displayed an engineer's penchant for efficiency and control. These themes are evident, for instance, in British philosopher Jeremy Bentham's eighteenth-century proposal for the design of a modern prisonhouse (Foucault 1977). Bentham called his proposed prison the *panopticon* (meaning "total vision") because it would permit guards to conduct total 360-degree surveillance of prisoners housed in a circular structure around a central control tower. The lighting of the panopticon was such that while guards could observe the prisoners in silhouette, prisoners could not see their guards. As Drew Leder (1993: 33) observes, the "privilege of being in power is that you get to be invisible, whereas the people subject to the power are made visible." We find such architectures of power in today's prisons, employing technologies of social control based on one-way surveillance and loss of privacy. Similar control systems have appeared in other institutions as well, including schools, hospitals, mental asylums, and military organizations (Goffman 1961a; Foucault 1977; Leder 1993).

With the coming of the industrial revolution in the eighteenth and nineteenth centuries, new technologies began to suggest new images of society. As literary critic Leo Marx (1964) acutely observes in his influential analysis of American writings during the transition to industrialism, the agricultural metaphor of the garden gave way rather suddenly in nineteenth-century literature to harsher industrial metaphors of American life. Henry David Thoreau's reverie on Walden Pond was rudely shattered by the scream of a locomotive whistle. The signal was clear: there was now a machine in the garden, and no amount of nostalgia would bring back the pastoral past. Social observers began to view society itself as a great industrial machine, and social engineers began to design social systems by analogy to industrial production systems. Public schools built to train a more literate labor force were designed to resemble factories (Bowles and Gintis 1976), preparing students for the discipline and regimentation of real factory life that soon awaited them.

Industrial metaphors were increasingly important in organizational theory and management practice during this period (Morgan 1997: 11–31). Max Weber, in his classic essay on bureaucracy, explicitly likened the pure or "ideal-type" bureaucratic organization to a gigantic machine. Contrary to the current view of bureaucracies as inherently inefficient, Weber ([1922] 1958) believed that bureaucratic forms of social organization (in private corporations as well as in governmental and military organizations) were in fact the most efficient modes of social organization ever devised—so efficient, in fact, that by Weber's time they had largely eliminated and replaced more traditional organizational forms. Weber remarked that the "decisive reason for the advance of bureaucratic organization has always been its purely technical superiority over any other form of organization. The fully developed bureaucratic mechanism compares with other organizations exactly as does the machine with non-mechanical modes of production" ([1922] 1958: 214).

Carrying the analogy a step further, Weber compared modern bureaucratic legal systems to automated machines. "The conception of the modern judge" he noted, is that of "an automaton into which the files and the costs are thrown in order that it may spill forth the verdict at the bottom along with the reasons, read mechanically from codified paragraphs" ([1922] 1958: 219). It is as though the justice system were a kind of vending machine. The facts of the case are inserted, the lever of legal reasoning is pulled, and out comes the judgment.

Weber understood that bureaucracy is "a power instrument of the first order—for the one who controls the bureaucratic apparatus" ([1922] 1946: 228). Weber's insight would later be taken up by the radical American sociologist C. Wright Mills (1956) in his trenchant analysis of the American power elite. Mills examined the small and socially interconnected elite who occupy the command posts of powerful corporate, governmental, and military bureaucracies in the United States. Such bureaucracies, he argued, are like massive social machines—powerful tools designed to get big jobs done, whether producing steel, enforcing laws, or fighting wars. Mills stirred up controversy during this rather placid period in American history when he contended, following Weber, that the interests served by these bureaucratic behemoths were not the interests of the public at large, but rather those of the power elite themselves.

Weber well understood that the experience of those at the privileged pinnacle of the bureaucratic machine is quite different from the experience of those who toil deep within its boiler rooms. Weber characterized the bureaucratic functionary as a kind of beast of burden who "cannot squirm out of the apparatus in which he is harnessed" but who is "chained to his activity . . . a single cog in an ever-moving mechanism which prescribes to him an essentially fixed route of march" ([1922] 1946: 228).

Not all organizational theorists agreed with Weber that bureaucratic organizations, however dreary, are inherently efficient. By the late nineteenth century, some management theorists were looking for ways to enhance the productivity of the social machinery. The most influential of these was undoubtedly the American engineer Frederick W. Taylor (1911), who pioneered the "scientific management" approach to improving organizational productivity. Taylor maintained that every task in the workplace may be broken down into its smallest constituent parts. Each industrial work routine may then be analyzed as a series of physical movements that can be measured objectively with the aid of a stopwatch. Taylor contended that time-and-motion studies of this sort could dramatically improve worker productivity by removing wasted motion from each component of each task, thus standardizing the workers' movements and rendering them as efficient as humanly possible. Principles of scientific management or "Taylorism" have been widely employed in the United States throughout this century despite criticism from organized labor and human relations theorists that they dehumanize and roboticize the worker (Perrow 1979).

Closely allied with Taylorism is Fordism (Jary and Jary 1991: 173–75), an approach to industrial production named in memory of Henry Ford, a creator of the modern industrial assembly line. The invention of the assembly line permitted managers to control the pace of work mechanically, forcing workers either to keep up or to give up. Karl Marx seems to have anticipated Fordism in his comment (Marx and Engels [1848] 1955: 16) that in industrial capitalism the worker becomes merely an "appendage of the machine." This pessimistic image of the modern industrial worker is brilliantly depicted in a Charlie Chaplin classic, Modern Times (1936), and more recently in Godfrey Reggio's remarkable Koyaanisqatsi (1983), two films which suggest that in the process of mechanizing the world we have mechanized ourselves as well. The more machines resemble people, Marshall McLuhan (1951: 99) observes, the more people resemble machines.

In Modern Times, Chaplin plays a factory worker who, controlled by industrial machines all day long, comes to behave like a robot himself. Among occupations available to workers in industrial societies, few produce lower levels of work satisfaction than assembly-line jobs. While Ford's large-scale, centrally controlled, and mechanically standardized mode of organization has certainly transformed the process of industrial production, vastly expanding the quantity of industrial goods available for mass consumption, it has done so at a great human cost.

Taylorism and Fordism were pieces of a much broader social engineering movement that emerged in the late nineteenth century and continued well into the twentieth century in the United States and other industrial countries. Its leading American advocates were a diverse lot, each representing a different view of how an engineering approach should be applied to the solution of societal problems. Such figures as Lester Frank Ward, Thorstein Veblen, Frederick Taylor, John Dewey, Herbert Hoover, and Franklin D. Roosevelt would hardly have agreed on every issue, but they all inclined toward the hope that an engineering approach to problem solving, with its focus on controlled cause and effect, could help to bring about the rational reform of society (Jordan 1994). Science, rationality, planning, efficiency, and control were the watchwords of the technocratic movement. Together they formed the conceptual infrastructure of what John M. Jordan calls "machine-age ideology."

Other core values of the modern machine age have been seen to include order and predictability, speed and precision, standardization, and centralization (Toffler 1980). In this system of values, reason becomes a crucial tool in the achievement of goals. Bentham's panopticon, Taylor's scientific management, and Ford's assembly line are all exemplars of *instrumental reason* at work in social engineering—i.e., the use of reason to achieve goals efficiently. Despite the many benefits that instrumental rationality has produced, it also harbors certain hidden dangers. Purely instrumental reasoning is strictly amoral. It represents a kind of ethical anti-intellectualism that seeks the most efficient means of achieving ends without inquiring very deeply into the ends themselves (Rigney 1991). In the extreme case, it is the mentality of those who designed and built efficient gas chambers in Nazi Germany (or who design and build weapons of mass destruction in our own time) without serious reflection on the larger consequences of their actions (Arendt 1963). This "engineering mentality," focusing on the efficient achievement of narrow goals but neglecting to question the goals themselves or the consequences of achieving them, is captured in Tom Lehrer's (1965) musical satire of the German rocket scientist: " 'I make them go up. Who cares where they come down? It's not my department,' says Wernher Von Braun."

This sort of instrumental rationality, Jürgen Habermas (1970) and others have argued, is one of the dominant ideologies of our time, and doubly dangerous because it is largely invisible to those who practice it. This is not to say that attempts to engineer efficient solutions to human problems are always wrong. It is only to say that such efforts are dangerous when they are undertaken in the absence of ethical reflection. The technocratic ideology that accompanied the rise of industrialism survives today in various high-tech and postindustrial versions. (We're now running Technocracy 7.1, with an upgrade available early next year.) Yet in the present age of nuclear and environmental peril, we no longer can afford to be quite so trusting of technology as a social panacea as we once were, nor so naïve as to accept uncritically the technocratic optimism or "techno-fix" mentality that predominated just a few decades ago.

Some industrial metaphors still survive in the postindustrial era. Edward S. Herman and Noam Chomsky (1988), for example, describe contemporary public opinion figuratively as a kind of engineered or "manufactured" product. The authors contend that powerful corporate, governmental, and mass-media organizations control not only the information available for public consumption, but also the interpretation (or "spin" as we now say) given to such information. Similarly, David C. Berliner and Bruce J. Biddle (1995) argue that certain national "crises," such as the "crisis in our public schools," are like manufactured products, created by special interests to serve private agendas. The manufacturing metaphor suggests that public opinion is effectively shaped and molded like a piece of plastic by those who can most effectively control the production, distribution, and interpretation of data. Thus, Edward Bernays, the founder of modern public relations, spoke candidly of the hidden manipulation of public opinion as the "engineering of consent" (Bernays 1947; Ewen 1996: 373–98).

Another prominent engineering metaphor, fashionable in business and managerial circles in the 1990s, was the popular term *reengineering*. Management theorists spoke of reengineering corporations from the ground up, restructuring business organizations around their central functions in order to achieve greater efficiency and effectiveness. Michael Hammer's and James Champy's (1993) *Reengineering the Corporation*, one of the most influential business best-sellers of the decade, made explicit use of engineering metaphors to describe the task of redesigning corporate social systems to achieve greater efficiency and adaptability.

Along with *reengineering*, the term *reinvention* became a popular buzzword in the 1990s. The image of the social engineer as an inventor and reinventor of social systems was featured in the title of David Osborne's and Ted Gaebler's important policy-reform manual, *Reinventing Government* (1992), which gave impetus to the federal "REGO" (reinventing government) program to streamline governmental agencies in the United States through experimentation and competition. This modern notion that the social world is a human invention—and therefore, that we may choose to reinvent and reengineer it—remains a popular idiom in contemporary culture. In this view, a society is not so much a fixed structure as it is an ongoing social construction, always being built but never finished.

Mechanistic Metaphors of the Future

We make our tools, McLuhan (1964) observed, and thereafter our tools make us. Technological innovations of the past have often shaped their surrounding culture, including the culture's dominant metaphors. As we make the transition from an industrial to a postindustrial information society (Bell 1973; Toffler 1980; Toffler and Toffler 1995), we may expect our social metaphors to change accordingly. As new postindustrial technologies come into view, what fresh metaphorical images of the social world might they inspire? How might they reshape the way we think and talk about social life?

Metaphors derived from electronic technology are already common in daily parlance. Technical terms such as *input, output, interface, parameter, feedback*, and *glitch* turn up figuratively in conversations having nothing to do with computers. Such graceless terminology is now commonplace in the technical (or pseudotechnical) language of administration and management. (Indeed, I must confess that I myself have prioritized an interface parameter or two in a previous life as a university administrator.)

Electronic metaphors are also increasingly prevalent in the cognitive and social sciences. Psychologists, for example, have spent several decades developing elaborate models of cognition based on analogies between human minds and computers (Lindsay and Norman 1977). The computer metaphor highlights the ways in which the mind stores, retrieves, and processes information. While this model of the mind has generated enormous bodies of research, Rosenblatt (1994: 23) notes that it has serious limitations. The computer metaphor "obscures intuitive processes, the ways in which input is multiple, chaotic, fluid, or out of control, and the instability and multiple transformations of what is stored in human thought." Yet despite their limitations, information-processing models of cognition have been increasingly prominent in psychology in recent years. If each of us is a data processor, can the image of society as a network of interfacing processors be far behind? (We are already halfway there, actually. The image of society as a non-electronic network is already well developed in sociological theory. See Turner [1998: 520–30] and David Willer [1999].) In the age of the Internet, everything in sight begins to look like an information-processing system. Why did we not see this before?

As psychologists and social scientists borrow images from the world of computing, computer scientists in turn borrow metaphors freely from the psychological and social domains. Thus, computer scientists speak anthropomorphically of computers as having memories, making decisions, talking to each other, and the like. One pioneer in the field of artificial intelligence (Minsky 1985) relies explicitly upon social metaphor when he speaks of natural and artificial minds as "societies" of simultaneously operating and interacting routines and subroutines. Thus, Marvin Minsky proposes not that a society is like a computer, but rather that a computer and its programs are like a society.

The origins of computer metaphors in social theory can be traced to a series of dramatic developments in mathematics and engineering in the 1940s: John von Neumann's and Oskar Morgenstern's mathematical game theory (1944), Claude Shannon's and Warren Weaver's information theory (1949), and especially Norbert Wiener's theory of cybernetics (1948), which spurred the development of modern computer technology. Cybernetics (from the Greek root *kubernetes*, the helmsman who steers the boat) is the study of control and communication systems in machines and animals. More specifically, it is the study and use of information systems to regulate energy systems (Trask 1971: 9–14). A cybernetic system regulates energy in relation to the system's external environment through the operation of feedback loops. Feedback may be either negative (tending to moderate system output toward the achievement of some goal state) or positive (tending to amplify system output, and sometimes causing the system to spin out of control). Note that this usage is rather different from the way these terms are used in psychology and in popular speech. A simple example of a cybernetic system is a thermostat, which regulates a heating or cooling system through negative feedback, with the programmed goal (the designer's goal, not the machine's, really) of maintaining a room at a given temperature. More complex examples of cybernetic systems include the software programs that regulate the operation of machines and the human central nervous system that regulates various physiological functions of the body.

Cybernetics has influenced the social sciences in a variety of ways in recent decades (see Heims 1993). Several social theorists during the 1960s conceived human society itself as a kind of self-regulating cybernetic system that harnesses and directs animate and inanimate energy and other material resources toward the achievement of culturally defined goals (Parsons 1966; Buckley 1967; Etzioni 1968). Thus, Talcott Parsons envisioned human society as a four-tiered cybernetic hierarchy in which the society's culture and values direct the energies of "lower" social, personal, and organismic systems, in somewhat the same way that a washing machine's control box (high in information, low in energy) directs electrical current (low in information, high in energy) and other resources toward the achievement of system goals.

If we want to know what technological metaphors are likely to gain currency in the twenty-first century, we would do well to keep an eye on new technologies being developed in the research laboratories of today. The development of virtual reality systems (Rheingold 1991; Gelernter 1991), for instance, offers some intriguing metaphorical possibilities. Virtual reality systems are computer-generated simulations or illusions so convincing that they are, in principle, virtually indistinguishable from conventional reality. Interesting parallels can be drawn to human culture. We are reminded of anthropologist Clifford Geertz's (1973: 90–91) famous essay on religion as a cultural system—an artificial symbol system that creates vivid conceptions in the human mind, "clothing these conceptions with such an aura of factuality [that they] establish powerful, pervasive and long-lasting moods and motivations [that] seem uniquely realistic." Geertz's description of a cultural system now sounds surprisingly like a virtual reality program.

As cybernetic and other postindustrial metaphors gradually surpass industrial metaphors in the social sciences, the industrial image of society as a "hardware" device may gradually give way to more subtle "software" metaphors that draw our attention away from the machines themselves and toward the abstract and creative programs that run them. In high-tech industries, software programmers are coming to be regarded not merely as technicians, but as creative artists and designers (Rifkin 1987: 208–18). Accordingly, the mechanistic images of the postindustrial future may be considerably less harsh and more flexible, fluid, and creative than the machine metaphors of the industrial past. And in contrast to the traditionally "masculine" tenor of industrial metaphors, the aesthetics of postindustrial metaphors seem more gender neutral and inclusive in their appeal (Turkle 1984: 109–19; 1995: 50–66).

Interest in technology and its metaphors is turning up unexpectedly across the humanities in disciplines not generally known for their technological orientation. Postmodern philosophers such as Jean Baudrillard (1983, 1988) and Jean-François Lyotard (1984), for example, have invoked high-tech metaphors to describe our peculiar times. Baudrillard in particular is fascinated with the sleekness and speed of advanced technologies, with their mutability and volatility, and with their capacity to create artificial or simulated realities (or what Baudrillard calls "simulacra"). The creation of artificial realities seems at times to put the status of real life (RL) in doubt. As one young cybernaut puts it: "RL is just one more window . . . and it's not usually my best one" (in Turkle 1995: 13).

Few theorists have explored the impact of high technology on our culture more perceptively than Sherry Turkle, whose position as a sociologist and psychologist at MIT gives her an insider's view of the emerging cyberculture. In *The Second Self* (1984: 306) Turkle argues that the computer is "the new mirror, the first psychological machine" in whose digitized reflection we see images of ourselves. To vary the analogy, the computer is a kind of Rorschach ink blot test into which we project our deeper fears and hopes (1984: 14). In our interactions with this strange new creature we are challenged to reconsider fundamental questions about machines, about ourselves, and about the relation between the two. Where does the machine end and where do we begin? Are we ourselves anything more than "a collection of programs," as one of Turkle's informants cheerfully remarks? Can a computer be in some sense "alive," like the infamous HAL aboard the Jupiter mission in Arthur C. Clarke's (1968) popular novel and film, *2001: A Space Odyssey*? In what subtle and unexpected ways does the transformation of our technology simultaneously transform us and our culture?

Turkle pursues these questions further in *Life on the Screen* (1995), an exploration of the Internet as an imaginary space whose anonymous inhabitants experiment freely with alternative identities in such venues as the open-ended and interactive role-playing worlds known as MUDs and MOOs. The Internet mirrors a postmodern culture in which social identities are manifold, fluid, and free-floating, in contrast to the more unitary and fixed identies of the past. "In the emerging culture of simulation, the computer is still a tool," she observes, "but less like a hammer and more like a harpsichord" (1995: 61), with a vast and largely unexplored potential for complex, creative, and improvisational play.

We have seen that machine metaphors, like machines themselves, undergo evolutionary and even revolutionary transformations through time. From clock-works to assembly lines to cyberworlds, technologies have offered us changing images of ourselves and our societies. Each new technological breakthrough is, for better or worse, a potential generator of new images of humanity and social life. The hologram is invented, and soon the mind and society are seen to resemble a hologram (Pribram 1971; Morgan 1997: 100–115). The Internet comes into being, and suddenly the planet is perceived to have an electronic nervous system. One wonders what technologies not yet dreamed of will inspire the cultural metaphors and societal images of the future.

CHAPTER FOUR

⌒

Society as War

As these words are written, the sound of semiautomatic gunfire can be heard in the distance. Rival street gangs know what conflict theorists have long professed: that a society is like a war fought by opposing forces for control of scarce and valued resources such as territory, power, and glory.

The notion that society resembles a war may seem self-contradictory on the face of it. What could be more *anti*social, after all, than the savageries of battle? Are wars not waged with the intent of damaging and even destroying societies? If so, war would hardly seem a fitting metaphor for society, inasmuch as it connotes social disintegration and chaos rather than social organization and order. Yet there is a certain ugly truth lurking in this metaphor. Paradoxically, war has a double aspect in human societies. While damaging or destroying social relations in some respects, war may fortify and revitalize them in others. The destructive aspects of warfare are obvious enough, especially in this age of biological, chemical, and nuclear weaponry. Less obvious but nonetheless disturbing are its socially constructive aspects.

Consider, for example, the contribution of war to social solidarity. As the German sociologist Georg Simmel ([1908] 1955) noted nearly a century ago, and as many others have testified since then (e.g., Coser 1956; Sherif 1966; Collins 1975), the bonds of group solidarity are often strengthened by the threat of a common enemy. If we were to express this insight mathematically we might hypothesize that, in general, the degree of internal cohesion in a group is directly proportional to the degree of external threat. Many political leaders have conjured real or imagined external enemies in order to quell internal dissent and increase solidarity within their own ranks. This strategy may backfire, however, when a war proves unpopular, for then leaders are faced with two wars—one abroad and another at home.

Emphasizing the social benefits of war, some theorists have seemed almost to celebrate the gory glories of combat. German historian Heinrich von Treitschke

([1898] 1965: 244–45) wrote rhapsodically of the "greatness of war" which, "with all its brutality and sternness, weaves a bond of love between men and men, linking them together to face death." Similarly, Robert Nisbet (1973: 13) has observed that despite its carnage and devastation, warfare calls forth such social virtues as heroism, courage, discipline, and sacrifice, forging powerful bonds of community among compatriots. Whether or not we share Nisbet's apparent enthusiasm for the military ethos, we cannot deny his claim that the winds of war have had a powerful influence on the course of social theory. Nisbet argues convincingly (1973: 11–90) that the relationship between war and society has been a central theme in Western social philosophy since its beginnings in strife-torn ancient Greece. Many of the greatest achievements in social theory, from Plato onward, were forged during times of war and revolution, when questions about the nature and future of society assumed a special urgency. It should not surprise us, then, that the imagery of warfare has been a recurring theme in social thought through the centuries.

Military Models of Society

The power of military metaphors is revealed in the fact that entire societies have been organized around them. Ancient Sparta is perhaps the clearest historical example. Built upon the warrior virtues of strength, stringent discipline, loyalty, and sacrifice, Sparta was the most formidable military power of its day. Spartan society did not merely have an army; one may almost say that Sparta *was* an army. Many societies and organizations since Sparta have been designed at least partially along military lines, including (ironically) Sparta's principal rival, ancient Athens (Nisbet 1973: 28–34). Contrary to the popular image of ancient Greece as a peaceable kingdom devoted to refined talk and the disembodied contemplation of eternal truths, historic Athens was a cauldron of internal and external conflicts. To bring order out of tribal chaos, the sixth-century B.C.E. military commander Cleisthenes found it necessary to enact an explicitly military social order, rich in the ritual and symbolism of war (Nisbet 1973: 28–34). Plato preserves elements of the military model in his own formulation of the good society, *The Republic*, which envisions a hierarchy of well-defined ranks with a class of self-selected philosopher–rulers at its pinnacle. Stationed one step below, a spirited cadre of military auxiliaries stands ready to impose order upon the enemies of wisdom.

Nisbet notes that in societies organized along military lines, violence achieves the status of a heroic act. Societies that celebrate heroic violence typically celebrate other moral values associated with war; for "valor, heroism, courage, and sacrifice are admired by us all, and it is in time of war that these qualities are likely to be vividly manifest" (Nisbet 1973: 16, 17). The customs of medieval knighthood, for example, clearly romanticized military virtues (Bloch 1964; Nisbet 1973: 45–53), as did the code of the Samurai in traditional Japanese culture. In each of these instances, the code of military conduct was imbued with sacred religious significance, giving divine blessing to the warrior class's military adventures.

Military organizations are in some respects the prototype of modern bureaucracies. They display nearly all of the characteristics identified by Max Weber ([1922] 1958: 196–244) in his classic essay on bureaucratic structure, including well-defined hierarchies of authority, complex specialization of functions, elaborate rule systems, and the like. In a bureaucratized world, organizations of every kind, from business corporations to governmental agencies, tend to resemble military organizations in these respects. This is especially so in societies with strongly authoritarian states, whether of the left or right. Stalinism in the Soviet Union, Maoism in China, Nazism in Germany, and fascism in Italy, despite their numerous differences, shared at least this feature in common. Governed by strongly authoritarian state bureaucracies, these societies were ordered along quasimilitary lines.

Modern capitalist corporations also resemble military organizations in certain respects, displaying the same top-down authority structures and the same drive toward strategic conquest (of competing firms) and domination (of markets) that characterize traditional military bureaucracies. Inspirational management literature (e.g., Hubbard 1899; Roberts 1985) has often invoked military imagery to spur its corporate officers and their troops toward the conquest of competitors and the control of markets.

Social order and unity are supreme values in military-model organizations, so it is not surprising that such organizations should firmly seek to suppress conflict, by force if necessary, within their ranks. Yet we know that in actual practice there is no such thing as a perfectly harmonious organization, military or otherwise. Efforts by officers to control each other and their underlings are apt to meet with underground resistance, backroom intrigues, turf protection, foot-dragging, and other forms of organizational subterfuge—especially in organizations whose members are not there by choice. Authoritarianism breeds counter-authoritarian resistance to total control. In the end, the totalitarian dream of a perfectly ordered military society, even if it were desirable, would be unrealizable. *Some* measure of conflict is inherent in all social institutions. This is the core insight of conflict theory, to which we now turn our attention.

Early Conflict Theorists

The image of society-as-army that we have been considering thus far is actually a very different metaphor from the image of society-as-war. Odd as it may seem, these two military metaphors are directly opposed to each other; for although the military organization epitomizes rigorous social *order*, war is the *disorder* that results from the clash of two or more such orders. Conflict theorists have frequently invoked the latter metaphor, perceiving society as a figurative battlefield upon which contending social factions struggle for control of scarce resources such as wealth and power. Here we will consider the works of three early conflict theorists in particular—Niccolò Machiavelli, Thomas Hobbes, and Karl Marx—who, despite their considerable differences, all lived in times of turmoil and came to view conflict as a central dynamic of human history. To describe these thinkers as conflict theorists is not to imply that they advocated social warfare as an end in itself (although certainly there have been those who relish the fray.) On the contrary, we shall see that each, in his own way, sought the transcendence of conflict and the eventual achievement of one or another form of social peace. We will return to more detailed discussions of Hobbes in chapter 5 and of Marx in chapter 6.

Images of war recur throughout the writings of the sixteenth-century Florentine diplomat Niccolò Machiavelli. Living in a time of bloody conflict among the warring city-states of southern Europe, Machiavelli portrayed social reality as a brutal struggle for survival driven by natural human passions for the accumulation of wealth, power, and glory. He dreamed of the day when a fierce and shrewd Florentine prince, with Machiavelli at his side, would unify the warring states of Italy under a single military command the likes of which Europe had not seen since the fall of the Roman Empire more than a millennium before. That day of glory never came for Machiavelli, but his legacy of political cynicism lives on today. His most renowned work, *The Prince* ([1513] 1981), is a compendium of political and military strategies addressed to the Medici ruler whose favor he sought.

Machiavelli advised the prince to be as ruthless as necessary (but no more so) in the pursuit of strategic objectives. An advocate of the use of strong force at decisive moments, Machiavelli observed that "all armed prophets have succeeded and all unarmed ones have failed" ([1513] 1981: 27). But he emphasized that brute force alone is not sufficient to ensure victory. Force must be tempered with cunning and the clever manipulation of appearances. The great leader must be both a lion *and* a fox. In the tradition of the Greek Sophists, Machiavelli drove a wedge between ethics and practical action. "I deem it best to stick to the practical truth of things rather than to fancies," he counseled, adding that "the way men live is so far removed from the way they ought to live that anyone who abandons what is for what should be pursues his downfall rather than his preservation" ([1513] 1981: 56). In this connection, Daniel Donno (1981: 6) asserts that "Machiavelli's chief contribution to political thought lies in his freeing political action from moral considerations." Just how this represents a contribution, and to whom, remains unclear. Sophisticated defenders of Machiavelli (e.g., Barzun 2000: 255–59) argue that his writings must be understood within the context of his own time and place in history—a context of chaotic violence, treachery, and deceit. If Machiavelli proposed to fight evil with evil and violence with violence, Jacques Barzun contends, it was with the noble aim of bringing a measure of stable order into a morally chaotic world.

Machiavelli nonetheless remains a disturbing figure. Underlying his view of life is the cynical assumption that our nature as human beings inclines us to be relentlessly self-serving in the pursuit of our own gain. Although it is possible to act otherwise, Machiavelli warned that "a man who strives after goodness in all his acts is sure to come to ruin, since there are so many men who are not good" ([1513] 1981: 56). Machiavelli's grim view is understandable within the context of the violent and dangerous times in which he lived—times that many perceive to resemble our own. Yet the cynical assumption that selfishness is inescapable, taken as a guide to action, may readily take the form of a self-fulfilling prophesy. If we assume the worst of others, we ourselves are likely to become, in turn, more wary, hostile, and self-protective. The resulting loss of basic trust among members of the community thus degrades the community as a whole, to the detriment of all of its members. To this day we designate as "Machiavellian" those who, by acting without scruple and assuming that others will do likewise, create a more unscrupulous world.

The seventeenth-century British social philosopher Thomas Hobbes advanced an equally pessimistic view of human nature and society in his classic work *Leviathan* ([1651] 1964). Living during the tumult of the English civil war between the Stuart monarchy and the Puritans under General Cromwell, Hobbes took warfare to be the natural state of human affairs. Human life, he observed, is "solitary, poor, nasty, brutish and short." Driven by appetite and fear, humanity is condemned to a state of perpetual battle—a condition of all against all—unless some greater power can be summoned to prevent individuals from tearing each other limb from limb. To transcend the war of all against all, Hobbes envisioned the creation of an absolutely powerful state authority constituted by common agreement or *social contract* for the mutual benefit of society's members. This powerful giant, whom Hobbes named the Leviathan, would wield the "publick

Sword" against the forces of chaos, thus ensuring social order and lifting humanity above the state of nature. Order and the authority to maintain it were, for Hobbes, supreme social values.

If Hobbes's brutish state of nature is meant to describe the way "primitive" societies have actually lived, his anthropology is dubious at best. The limited evidence we possess from hunting and gathering societies suggests that these groups are by no means universally violent. On the contrary, they must have evolved cooperative strategies with each other and with neighboring groups merely to survive. Although skirmishes and rivalries have no doubt always existed within and among human communities, warfare is probably less characteristic of hunting and gathering societies than of societies of other types (Lenski and Lenski 1987; but for a contrary view, see Keeley 1996). Gregory Leavitt (1977) finds, for example, that although warfare is common or perpetual in only 27 percent of hunting and gathering societies for which good evidence exists, it is progressively more common in societies that cultivate crops, rising to an incidence of 82 percent among advanced horticultural societies. At the very least, such evidence demands that we qualify the Hobbesian assumption that war is the natural human state. Kinds and degrees of warfare vary markedly among societies at various levels of technological development, but among human societies closest to what Hobbes believed to be our natural state, warfare is by no means pervasive.

Hobbes also can be criticized for his "atomistic" view of society as a loose collection of disconnected and self-serving individuals. The Hobbesian image of society as an individualistic and competitive struggle is a distinctly modern notion, probably more reflective of the assumptions that underlie individualistic cultures than of anything universal to human nature. Aristotle, in his *Politics* (ca. 330 B.C.E.), was probably nearer the mark when he observed that we are by nature communal creatures. Rooted in our tribal origins as hunter-gatherers, we are irrevocably joined in relations of interdependence by the bonds of kinship, custom, common interest, and the need for cooperation and mutual aid. Aristotle's view implies a more cooperative and less warlike understanding of human relations than the view advanced by Hobbes.

We must concede, however, that wars have been frequent and recurrent in horticultural, agrarian, and industrial societies marked by the accumulation of wealth and the formation of extreme class inequalities. Thus, Karl Marx and Friedrich Engels could offer the sweeping generalization, with reference to societies in *recorded* history (i.e., history since horticulture and the invention of writing), that the "history of all hitherto existing society is the history of class struggles" ([1848] 1955: 9). Marx, like Machiavelli and Hobbes before him, described previous human societies as battlefields whereon social adversaries contend fiercely for scarce and valued resources. But for Marx this struggle is not primarily a war among city-states or principalities (as for Machiavelli) or among individuals (as for Hobbes), but rather a war among economic classes. The main characters in Marx's war story are freeman and slave, lord and serf, capitalist and factory worker:

> . . . in a word, oppressor and oppressed [who, having] stood in constant opposition to one another, carried on an uninterrupted, now hidden, now open fight that each time ended, either in a revolutionary reconstitution of society at large, or in the common ruin of the contending classes. (Marx and Engels [1848] 1955: 9)

Whereas Machiavelli and Hobbes envisioned the possibility that social warfare could be transcended through the creation of a powerful and ruthless central authority, Marx envisioned the possibility of transcendence through a revolutionary struggle that would culminate in a more equitable social order. In Marx's historical scenario, a revolutionary class of industrial laborers, the proletariat, would fight fire with fire and meet violence with violence until the fire of class warfare had been put out once and for all. Marx expected that the revolutionary triumph of the working classes would result in a temporary "dictatorship" of, by, and for the proletariat. He believed, however, that this rule by the proletarian majority would eventually make possible a "withering away of the state." An oppressive state would no longer be needed, because the historical function of the state as an instrument of class domination would no longer be necessary in a classless society. Marx optimistically envisioned the proletarian revolution as a class war to end all class wars, ushering in an epoch of peace and mutual cooperation. But in his revolutionary optimism, Marx failed to anticipate that oppressive forms of state socialism might emerge, in which state authority acting in the name of the people would pursue political and economic interests of its own, distinct from the interests of the society it was constituted to serve. In short, Marx failed to anticipate Joseph Stalin. His analysis of economic class conflict nonetheless remains too formidable to ignore, for one would have to be historically illiterate to deny that such conflict has been a recurring theme in human history. The collapse of the Soviet Union and the winding down of the cold war have hardly diminished economic inequities in the world; on the contrary, inequalities both within and among societies have only grown wider in recent years, with potentially destabilizing social and political consequences. Thus, reports of the death of Marxian analysis are premature, although such analysis would have to be considerably revised and updated to take account of emerging global trends in economy and technology.

Marx's optimistic view of the human prospect sets him apart from Machiavelli and Hobbes, who represent what might be called the *cynical tradition* in social theory. A cynic (in the modern, not the ancient, sense of the term) regards human nature as fundamentally selfish and oriented toward the accumulation of wealth, power, and glory. Others in the cynical tradition might be said to include the philosopher Friedrich Nietzsche ([1885] 1954) and the psychoanalyst Alfred Adler (1930), both of whom regarded the "will to power" and the drive toward superiority (often, though not always, expressed through domination of others) as fundamental human attributes. We find cynicism again in the philosophy of the Prussian military strategist Karl von Clausewitz ([1834] 1962), who famously remarked that war is a continuation of politics by other means. Similar views can be found in non-Western traditions as well, as in the writings of the ancient Chinese military strategist Sun Tsu, whose Art of War ([ca. 500 B.C.E.] 1963) inspired the corporate villain Gecko in the popular film Wall Street. In our own time we find pervasive evidence of cynicism not only in contemporary North American culture (e.g., Kanter and Mirvis 1989; Goldfarb 1991), but in other postmodern cultures as well (Sloterdijk 1987), reflecting widespread disillusionment and loss of trust in the dominant social institutions of the postindustrial world.

Although Karl Marx, in his fierce critique of capitalism, may at first appear to stand in this cynical tradition of Machiavelli and Hobbes, his position was rather different from theirs. Marx was not cynical toward human nature per se, for he regarded our nature or "species being" as open-ended and full of positive possibilities, developing in step with developments in the material or technological base of society. Marx turned a critical eye instead toward what he regarded as oppressive social systems invented by privileged classes in the service of their own interests. Thus, he regarded dominant ideologies (including moral ideologies) as weapons of class warfare with which privileged classes have historically conquered and controlled subordinate classes. (Curiously, Nietzsche took the very opposite view, regarding conventional moralities as self-serving ideologies created by the weak to fend off the strong.) Marx believed that by transforming oppressive systems, human beings can create the conditions necessary for the fuller development of their potentials. Our best natures are most fully realized, he believed, in a return to communism—not the primitive communism of hunters and gatherers, but a communism built on a dramatically more advanced base of technological development.

Despite their differences, Machiavelli, Hobbes, and Marx share at least this much in common. Each identified conflict as a central theme in human history, and each held out the hope that destructive conflicts could be transcended. Machiavelli hoped that conflict would be quelled by a strong prince capable of unifying vast territories through force, cunning, and surgical violence. For Hobbes, conflict would be quelled by the impersonal state apparatus of the Leviathan, crushing dissent and disorder wherever they might arise. For Marx, social peace would arrive when a revolutionary class, the creator of a humane socialism, rendered class warfare obsolete. Paradoxically, all three theorists recommended organized violence, under specified circumstances, as a means of bringing their preferred forms of peace into the world, although none sought violence as an end in itself.

Contemporary Conflict Theory

The image of society as a battlefield lives on in sociology today in various current versions of conflict theory. Contemporary conflict theorists, especially those who locate themselves within Marxist traditions, continue to regard economic struggles over scarce resources as a central dynamic of history. Yet today's conflict theorists rarely confine their interests exclusively to economic class conflict. Their interests frequently extend to include political, racial and ethnic, gender, religious, and other social conflicts as well. Although such conflicts nearly always have an economic dimension, they are rarely reducible to economic factors alone, as some cruder versions of Marxism have seemed to imply. Weber ([1922] 1958: 180–95), in a classic critique of economic reductionism, argued that the dimensions of economic class, social status, and political power are at least to some degree independent of one another, such that a social group's status and political power are not entirely explained by its control of economic resources. Weber's objections to economic reductionism are now generally acknowledged in the writings of contemporary conflict theorists (e.g., Collins 1975; Zeitlin 1981: 159–63; Dahrendorf 1988).

Conflict theorists employ a multitude of quasimilitary concepts in their analysis of relations among groups. They examine the strategies and tactics (both offensive and defensive) of conflicting groups, the stockpile of resources that each can mobilize, the shifting alliances that form in response to common threats, the propaganda campaigns that are waged to protect and promote partisan interests, and the battles, negotiations, and eventual settlements that determine the gains and losses of the respective sides. This approach to the study of social movements and social conflicts is often called *resource mobilization theory.*

Conflict theorists are naturally interested in the role that violence plays in helping groups to gain and maintain social advantages over their adversaries. Their interest is not confined to literal physical violence, however, but extends to include forms of figurative violence as well. Conflict theorists often discern subtle forms of economic, political, and psychological violence occurring in the routine operations of social institutions. These invisible aggressions, sometimes called "systemic" or "structural" violence, may be every bit as destructive of human well-being as literal or physical violence. For example, market systems, despite their economic efficiencies, often inflict "hidden injuries" (Sennett and Cobb 1993) upon those who lose out in the struggle for competitive advantage, such as displaced workers and their families. Class and race discrimination in health-care delivery systems may be as lethal as bullets to those deprived of adequate access to medical treatment. Systemic forms of violence such as these often go unrecognized because they are not easily attributable to particular individuals. They are "just the way things work out" in a given system, and so they often go unquestioned, especially by those who benefit from the system's routine operations. In such instances, it is difficult to say just where metaphorical violence ends and literal violence begins.

Contemporary conflict theory came to prominence in American sociology during the turbulent decade of the 1960s, when strong voices rose to challenge the prevailing orthodoxy of the period, structural-functionalism, and its leading proponent, Talcott Parsons. Among the most influential conflict theorists of this period were C. Wright Mills (1956, 1959) and Alvin Gouldner (1970), two sociologists on the political left who took seriously Marx's dictum that the point of intellectual labor is not merely to interpret the world but to change it. Their combative personal styles, reflected in writings sharply critical of both the American political establishment and the structural-functionalist establishment in sociology, drew a large following among young political activists in the civil rights and antiwar movements during this period. Mills, Gouldner, and other conflict theorists largely succeeded in toppling the functionalist orthodoxy in sociology and establishing in its place, in some quarters at least, a counterorthodoxy that viewed social life as a battlefield and theorists as active participants, on one side or another, in the political fray.

Another major influence in contemporary conflict theory has emanated from a group of German theorists known collectively as the Frankfurt school of critical sociology (Connerton 1976; Dreitzel 1979; Arato and Gebhardt 1990; Agger 1998: 78–98). The first generation of Frankfurt theorists, including Max Horkheimer, Theodor Adorno, and Herbert Marcuse, challenged the rising tide of Nazism in Germany during the 1930s, eventually seeking exile in the United States. There they continued to challenge fascism from a neo-Marxist perspective, analyzing Nazi anti-Semitism and propaganda in *Dialectic of Enlightenment* (Horkheimer and Adorno [1944] 1990) and exposing the psychological dynamics of fascism in *The Authoritarian Personality* (Adorno et al. 1950). But in the United States they encountered a propaganda apparatus at least as sophisticated as those they had seen in Europe, which they called the "culture industry." They warned that the culture industry, which organized the distribution of films, phonograph records, and other popular media in the United States, was effectively manipulating the tastes and opinions of the American people in accord with the political and economic interests of capitalism (Horkheimer and Adorno [1944] 1990; Marcuse 1964). Marcuse's *One-Dimensional Man* in particular exerted a major influence on the student left of the 1960s in its analysis of the subtle forms of psychological and social repression that exist in nominally "free" societies. Critical theorists today continue to be interested in what Antonio Gramsci (1971) called "hegemony," or the ideological control of populations through dominant cultural institutions such as the mass media. We will return to a fuller discussion of the Frankfurt school in chapter 9 when we meet its most prominent contemporary figure, Jürgen Habermas.

Another important variant of conflict theory is world-systems theory (e.g., Wallerstein 1974/1980; Chase-Dunn 1989; Frank 1993), which focuses on international conflicts between dominant capitalist societies at the center of the world system (such as the United States) and less developed societies at the periphery. Those at the center of the world system, they contend, richly benefit from the relative powerlessness and dependency of developing nations, exploiting the latter as sources of cheap labor and raw materials, and subjecting them to economic, cultural, and, in some instances, military penetration. We will encounter these theorists again in chapter 6, when we examine the metaphor of the marketplace.

Warfare, as a recurring metaphor in conflict theory, stands in sharp contrast to the functionalist metaphor of the social organism discussed previously in chapter 2. The organismic metaphor suggests that the "normal" or "natural" state of society is a smoothly functioning homeostatic equilibrium. Conflicts within the system disrupt this equilibrium and are therefore seen as inherently dysfunctional or pathological. The war metaphor, by contrast, invites us to view conflict as a natural and pervasive phenomenon. Conflict theorists examine the positive as well as the negative consequences of conflict (Coser 1956), arguing that social antagonisms are essential and sometimes even beneficial to society. Consider the fact that virtually every major social reform or innovation in modern times has met with staunch opposition from groups whose interests were threatened by the proposed change. It is doubtful, for example, that the abolition of slavery and subsequent advances in civil rights would or could have occurred through entirely peaceful means. Conflict theorists contend that without such social confrontations, unjust institutions would go unchallenged and societies would stagnate. Sometimes a war must be fought to achieve a more just peace. Only the purest pacifist will renounce absolutely the ways of war.

War Metaphors in Public Discourse

The metaphor of war is prevalent not only in social theory, but in public discourse at large. Metaphors that surface in public discussion can tell us a great deal about a culture's deepest assumptions (Lakoff and Johnson 1980; Lakoff 1996).

Thus Deborah Tannen (1998: 3) perceives in American culture a "pervasive warlike atmosphere that makes us approach public discourse . . . as if it were a fight." In politics, for instance, we speak of candidates for office filling their war chests and gathering ammunition as they prepare to fight tough electoral battles. Meanwhile, political speechmakers routinely promise to wage war against poverty, or drugs, or crime.

The term *culture wars* emerged during the 1990s to describe political conflicts between liberals and conservatives over issues related to religion, law, family, art, and education (Hunter 1991; Whitehead 1994). On radio talk shows and television programs such as the aptly named *Crossfire*, representatives of competing political camps attacked each other ferociously with words as their weapons. Partisan strategists on the right (e.g., Horowitz 1999) openly advocated political warfare as they escalated the rhetoric of violence against their enemies. Confrontations of this sort are what Robin Lakoff (2000) calls "language wars," fought by ideological combatants who aggressively maneuver to spin and frame public issues in ways that serve their interests. Meanwhile, antigovernment groups calling themselves "militias" and modeling themselves after military organizations waged not only verbal but in some instances literal warfare against police and paramilitary governmental agencies. James Davison Hunter (1991) contends that these heated cultural battles constituted nothing less than a struggle to define the nation's cultural identity.

Military metaphors permeate our economic culture as well. We speak of "price wars" between competing firms or "trade wars" between competing national economies. Corporate campaigns employ warlike strategies and tactics to conquer and defend market shares, planning "hostile takeovers" and sending out "corporate raiders" to deplete the ranks of their adversaries. Business books with titles like *The Corporate Warriors* (Ramsey 1987) and *Leadership Secrets of Attila the Hun* (Roberts 1985) fight their way up the best-seller lists.

Meanwhile, wars of ideas are fought in the groves (or trenches) of academe, giving the lie to the popular but naive view of academic life as a cloistered retreat from the struggles of life in the "real" world. Mary Douglas (1980: 1–6) describes the case of a young philosopher caught in a war of worldviews between metaphysicians and materialists. When the young scholar showed an interest in the social sciences, his metaphysical colleagues perceived him to be "going over to the enemy"—not merely leaving the territory of metaphysics undefended but, like a traitor, "moving into a good position from which to prepare an attack on it." Intellectual conflicts of this sort are a kind of sublimated warfare in which cerebral combatants channel their aggressions through the medium of symbols. Tannen (1998: 256ff) finds this "adversarial approach to knowledge" operating at every stage in the educational process, from kindergarten through graduate school, which she describes as an academic boot camp.

Religious culture is also shot through with images of war. Traditional Christian doctrine, for example, is commonly framed as a great struggle pitting the forces of Good against the forces of Evil. We should not be surprised, then, that military metaphors are deeply imbedded in church history. Thus, the Jesuits, a Catholic religious order founded by a Spanish military officer, St. Ignatius Loyola, in 1540, is modeled after a military organization, with its highest officer holding the rank of Superior General. Among Protestant bodies, the Salvation Army is likewise organized along military lines. Protestant hymns are often well fortified and well armed. Martin Luther himself composed the lyrics of the hymn "A Mighty Fortress is Our God," and "Onward Christian Soldiers" remains a Protestant standard. Conservative Protestants may still be heard to issue calls for the "moral rearmament" of God's troops.

Even our recreations are inspired by war. Many popular games are simulations of battle. Chess, for example, simulates a battle between two medieval kingdoms, in which bishops, knights, and common pawns lay down their lives to protect royalty. Football, in its physical violence, comes considerably closer than chess to literal warfare. As comedian George Carlin (1997: 50–53) astutely observes, rugged teams clad in helmeted uniforms play in places with names like Soldier Field and War Memorial Stadium. Their quarterbacks are "field generals," launching "aerial assaults" with "deadly accuracy" in the face of enemy "blitzes." Running from the "shotgun" formation, they fire "bullet passes" and "long bombs" as they "march into enemy territory . . . punching holes in the front walls of the enemy's defense," and playing to "sudden death" if necessary.

Is it any wonder that war metaphors should flourish in a culture that romanticizes and celebrates organized violence? Young males in particular—not coincidentally the segment of society from which warriors are traditionally drawn—are the main market for commercial products such as violent films, television programs, and video and computer games. Military metaphors, with their subliminal appeals to toughness and strength, seem to resonate particularly among men formed in traditional molds. Yet, as we shall see, such metaphors are sometimes wielded by women as well.

Gender Wars

Metaphors have long shaped the ways in which we interpret relations between women and men. Early British feminist and sociologist Harriet Martineau ([1837]

1985; Yates 1985: 18), for example, likened women to slaves in view of their "political non-existence" in nineteenth-century American society. American feminist Charlotte Perkins Gillman ([1898] 2000) similarly decried women's status as virtual livestock in their roles as workhorses in the domestic economy (in Kivisto 2000: 154; see also Lemert 1997a: 15ff). Perhaps the most familiar metaphor describing gender relations in our culture, however, is the image of the "battle of the sexes," appearing in various forms in our popular social literature. Lillian Rubin (1990) offers a variation on the theme in *Erotic Wars*, a reflection on changing gender relations in the wake of the sexual revolution (a phrase which is itself a kind of war metaphor). Feminist writers Susan Faludi (1991) and Marilyn French (1992) also summon the imagery of the battlefield in their writings, both featuring a "war against women" in the titles of their books. Faludi's use of military metaphor is exceptionally well developed from a rhetorical standpoint, as a brief analysis will show.

In *Backlash: The Undeclared War against America Women*, Faludi begins by alluding to the "handful of small and hard-won victories" that the feminist movement has fought to achieve in recent years. She notes, however, that the decade of the 1980s "has seen a powerful counterassault on women's rights, a backlash" (1991: xviii) on the part of those whose interests are threatened by the advances of women. Religious conservatives have waged what they themselves term "spiritual warfare" on the women's movement. In her own analysis, Faludi takes up the militaristic rhetoric of the religious right and turns it against her adversaries. She describes the rank-and-file of the religious right as "fundamentalist soldiers" and "warriors" who "trooped to Washington" on "maneuvers . . . against what they saw as the dominant enemy—the proponents of women's rights." "Crusaders" with a sense of "mission" (terms with both religious and military overtones), they campaigned under the "banner" of family rights. While this pro-family "strategy allowed the New Right men to launch an indirect attack against women's rights, . . . they also went for the direct hit" (Faludi 1991: 237–39). Faludi thus skillfully paints an image of feminism under siege, presenting her subject as an embattled and endangered target of fanatical aggression. In the process, she appropriates her adversaries' rhetorical weapons and makes them her own.

Faludi's analysis also targets Allan Bloom, conservative classical scholar and author of the surprise 1987 best-seller, *The Closing of the American Mind*. Like the religious right, Bloom has mobilized military rhetoric in his campaign against the women's movement. "The latest enemy of the vitality of the classics is feminism," he has written, describing the women's movement as a "Reign of Terror" whose "object is nothing less than the destruction of the values, methods and goals of traditional humanistic study" (1987: 65–101). Faludi once again turns the rhetoric of war back upon her adversary. She describes Bloom as a shell-shocked "refugee from the feminist occupation," <u>hunkered</u> down in a "practically all-male <u>bunker</u>" (the Committee on Social Thought at the University of Chicago) and <u>rarely venturing out into the</u> "demilitarized zone" outside of his fortress (Faludi 1991: 291–92). <u>Thus does military imagery serve as ammunition on both sides of this war of words.</u>

Still another target in Faludi's sights is the manly poet Robert Bly, who alternately describes the effects of feminism as a "disease" (a standard organic metaphor) and as an "invasion" (Faludi 1991: 310). Although most of her criticisms are aimed at masculists like Bly, Faludi saves a few sharp points for her fellow feminists, including the pioneering author Betty Friedan (1963; 1981) and the influential moral psychologist Carol Gilligan (1982), whose positions are less militant than her own. Faludi is clearly a kind of warrior in her own right. Yet as a thoughtful writer she also recognizes the limitations of the war metaphors that she and her adversaries wield so effectively.

> Women's advances and retreats are generally described in military terms: battles won, battles lost, points and territory gained and surrendered. The metaphor of combat is not without its merits in this context and, clearly, the same sort of martial accounting vocabulary is already surfacing here. But by imagining the conflict as two battalions neatly arrayed on either side of the line, we miss the entangled nature, the locked embrace, of a "war" between women and the male culture they inhabit. (1991: xxi)

Thus Faludi acknowledges that the <u>war metaphor itself is vulnerable to attack</u>.

Whereas some feminists, including Faludi, enlist military metaphors in the service of their cause, others note that such metaphors tacitly appeal to traditional male assumptions regarding power and violence (e.g., Tannen 1998). Men are historically the warriors of society, and elements of the warrior cultures that have evolved through history are preserved in traditional male sex roles (Barash 1991; Boulding 1992). Nisbet (1973: 16–17) and others seem at times to romanticize the traditionally "masculine" values associated with the rigors of military life, as though virtues such as courage, discipline, and sacrifice were gender-specific and required the trigger of warfare to manifest themselves. While the rugged manliness of military metaphors may be appealing to some, others urge us to seek less destructive images of social life. We do not deny that the metaphor of the social battlefield has often been a fitting one in human history. The point, however, is to create a world that the metaphor no longer fits, sublimating both violence and its rhetoric by seeking nonviolent resolutions (insofar as possible) of the social conflicts that undeniably permeate social life. *This too is a kind of conflict theory*, in acknowledging social conflict as a central dynamic of history, but taking active nonviolent resistance, rather than war, as its core metaphor. It is the tradition advanced by such historic figures as Mohandas Gandhi and Martin

Luther King, who challenged not only social injustice but the rhetoric of warfare as well.

Race, Ethnicity, and Metaphors of War

In race and ethnic discourse, as in gender discourse, metaphors often shape the ways in which we visualize intergroup relations. Thus, the metaphor of the melting pot has often been invoked to suggest the fanciful image of American culture as a harmonious and homogenized blend of ethnic influences. Others have suggested that race and ethnic relations in the United States more nearly resemble a tossed salad or a stew, whose ingredients remain distinct even as their flavors intermingle. W. E. B. Du Bois ([1908] 1970), the leading African American intellectual of his day, chose a harsher and less idealized image of race relations when he wrote of the "race friction between black and white." Harsher still is the image of race relations as war.

The imagery of racial warfare became commonplace in public rhetoric during the height of the civil rights movement of the 1960s, and could be heard from militant groups on both right and left. White supremacist groups, on the one hand, adopted not only the bellicose rhetoric but also the organizational trappings of militarism, surviving to this day in the form of racist paramilitary "militias." Militant black groups of the 1960s, such as the Black Panthers and the Symbionese Liberation Army, also organized themselves around military metaphors in response to threats from hostile and heavily armed segments of the surrounding society. African American leaders of the time were internally divided with respect to the imagery of warfare. Malcolm X (1970) frequently invoked the rhetoric of revolutionary violence and militant self-defense in his earlier public pronouncements. Martin Luther King ([1963] 1970), by contrast, chose instead the language of peace and nonviolent reconciliation as the symbolic framework within which to pursue the dream of racial justice.

By century's end, the rhetoric of racial warfare had largely subsided in the mainstream culture, although it still survived among white supremacist fringe groups with a visible presence in cyberspace. African American leaders rarely invoked the imagery of race war except as a cautionary vision of what might yet happen if the achievements of the civil rights movement were allowed to erode further (Rowan 1996). Although the African American community still faces formidable problems (e.g., West 1993; Gates and West 1996; Wilson 1999), proposed solutions to these problems are now rarely couched in the language of the battlefield. Thus, William Julius Wilson (1999) now speaks of the need to build "bridges over the racial divide," uniting in common cause economically marginalized people of all racial and ethnic groups. The emerging metaphors of multiculturalism speak not of violent conflict, but of complementarity; not of revolution, but of patchwork quilts and rainbow alliances, to borrow two images popularized by Jesse Jackson. Meanwhile, African American women writers such as Toni Morrison, Alice Walker, and Maya Angelou draw upon metaphors of birth, mediation, kinship, and spiritual regeneration (Holloway 1992) to articulate their visions, in contrast to the traditional masculist metaphors of the warrior.

The metaphors we choose to use in our public discussions of race and ethnicity may tell us a great deal about the state of our relations. The advance and retreat of war metaphors in particular may serve as revealing indicators of how near or far we are from a state of literal warfare. As always, we must choose our metaphors with care. The ill-chosen metaphor may lead us down a spiralling path toward mutual destruction, while the right metaphor at the right moment may open our minds to new and hopeful possibilities. In either event, the future of racial and ethnic relations, both nationally and internationally, will be shaped by the metaphors we create to visualize them.

Beyond the War Metaphor

There is no denying that the metaphor of war is dramatic and poetically powerful. It aptly captures many of the harsher and more painful aspects of social reality, calling our attention to the pervasiveness of conflict in human relations. Yet just as the functionalist metaphor of the social organism tends to understate the degree of conflict that exists in real societies, the metaphor of the social battlefield may go too far in the other direction, overstating the degree to which societies are inherently conflict ridden. In reality, a society truly in a state of unremitting warfare could scarcely be called a society at all.

In the end, describing relations between women and men (or between blacks and whites, or young and old, or left and right, or any other binary opposition in the social world) as a "war" may conceal as well as reveal. By framing issues in the language of violence, this formulation of the problem can obscure opportunities for nonviolent conflict resolution, reconciliation, and the recognition of shared interests. Hence, the metaphor may potentially create a self-fulfilling prophesy (Merton [1948] 1968); for when social actors *define* warfare (whether literal or metaphorical) as necessary and inevitable, and act on that understanding, they increase the likelihood of destructive conflict. As U.S. diplomat and historian George Kennan (1977: 202) observed, a "war regarded as inevitable or even probable, and therefore much prepared for, has a very good chance of eventually being fought." Accepting the inevitability of violence may block our capacity to imagine nonviolent, win-win alternatives in situations involving conflict over scarce and valued resources.

Some theorists have sought to turn the metaphor of war to more constructive uses. The pioneering psychologist William James (1911: 263) proposed that young people be conscripted for a certain number of years to wage metaphorical warfare, not against other nations, but against the limitations imposed upon humanity by nature. James called this alternative to traditional warfare the "moral equivalent of war," the redirection of traditional military virtues in the pursuit of peaceful ends. Environmentalists have suggested that energies traditionally mobilized to fight wars among nations be redirected instead toward the defense of ecosystems. Others have proposed that the exploration of space or the pursuit of scientific discovery might serve as inspiring superordinate goals (Sherif 1966), uniting humanity in a common quest for shared victory. This was the spirit in which Gandhi proposed a war against war itself.

While war metaphors can perhaps be turned to constructive uses, it may be more constructive in the long run to go beyond the imagery of war in search of more life-giving images of social life. To give just one example, consider the recent movement in legal circles to expand the range of alternatives to the adversarial system of justice, which traditionally pits two sides against each other in courtroom "battles." The mediation movement, as an alternative to costly and destructive legal warfare, creates opportunities for negotiation, dispute resolution, and reconciliation between opposing parties (Folberg and Taylor 1984; Moore 1986; Fischer and Ury 1983; Dunlop 1984; Fischer and Brown 1988). In effect, the mediation movement goes beyond the war metaphor to a metaphor of diplomacy in the settling of social disagreements. Without denying or suppressing the stubborn reality of social conflict, it seeks to sublimate conflict in ways that are potentially constructive and mutually beneficial. Efforts such as these take us a step beyond the grim poetry of war. But such efforts will no doubt continue to meet resistance; for the metaphors of war are deeply entrenched in our culture, and will not be readily surrendered.

CHAPTER FIVE

~

Society as Legal Order

The image of society as a battleground may excite the passions of warriors. Most of us, however, would find life unbearable in a perpetual combat zone. While some measure of societal conflict is inevitable and even desirable, no society can endure for long in a state of intense and relentless strife. If we are to move beyond the metaphor of social warfare, we will need a more life-sustaining model of what societies are and what they can become.

Going beyond the image of society as a battleground, some theorists have proposed the more hopeful image of society as a community of shared rules and laws, including rules for mediating destructive conflicts. In this view, social life is not so much a war as it is a peace treaty or social contract among actual or potential adversaries, transforming the chaos of social warfare into life-preserving order. To those who embrace this metaphor, rules and laws are the very stuff of which human societies are constituted. Without them we would be mired forever in the trenches.

Imagining society as a system of rules or cultural norms has some important implications. It implies that we are governed not only by impersonal "laws of nature" over which we have no control, but also by laws and rules of our own making, opening the possibility that we may literally "rule" ourselves. It implies that our cultural capacities for rule making, rule interpreting, rule enforcing, and rule breaking lie near the very core of our nature as human beings.

Virtually everything we do is oriented in one way or another toward codes of expected conduct. Metaphorically, we all play the role of legislator, advocate, judge and juror, police agent, warden, and outlaw at one time or another in the varied venues of our lives. Every social institution—not just the legal system per se, but the family, the school, the place of work, and the place of worship as well—may be viewed as a kind of regulatory system, directing or restraining human conduct and guiding it toward desired ends.

Many important theorists, including Emile Durkheim, Max Weber, and

81

Sigmund Freud, have invoked the image of society as a system of rules or social norms regulating human energies and impulses. To imagine society as a normative system, it may be useful first to imagine its opposite: a society that is entirely normless (or *anomic*, as Durkheim would say). It is unimaginable that such a society could exist for long in actual practice. Indeed, it is doubtful whether such a thing could be properly called a society at all in the utter absence of social agreements of any kind. But as a thought experiment, let us imagine what such an antisociety might look like if it were to come into being, however briefly.

Anomia

In our hypothetical society—call it Anomia, from the Greek root meaning "without law"—inhabitants enjoy complete freedom to do just as they please without restraint. If one inhabitant builds a shelter, another may choose to take it by force or the persuasive threat of force, killing its prior occupant as the need arises. Acts of homicide, rape, theft, and deceit are commonplace in Anomia, because no established authority exists to thwart them. The strong survive (at least until they meet the stronger) while the weak either consent to the will of the strong or perish in the act of resistance. This is not the idyllic free society envisioned by the utopian anarchist P'etr Kropotkin ([1902] 1972), but something rather more sinister. It is the fearsome "war of all against all" that Thomas Hobbes ([1651] 1964) postulated as the natural state of human existence in his classic work, *Leviathan*. Something akin to the war of all against all is depicted in William Golding's novel, *Lord of the Flies*, in which a group of British schoolboys crashlands on a remote deserted island and must somehow reinvent social order among themselves. As the boys gradually lose the trappings of their home civilization, their world degenerates into a fierce and brutal struggle for survival. The strong prey freely upon the weak, and the only rule in effect is "might makes right."

Real-world examples of pure anarchy are hard to find. The Hobbesian state of nature certainly does not exist in most actual "primitive" societies, for these small hunting and gathering communities would never have survived if they had not evolved codes of conduct to restrain aggression, ensure cooperation, and resolve disputes. While anthropologists (e.g., Keesing and Keesing 1971: 356–59; Turnbull 1972) have occasionally reported cases of social disintegration in simpler societies, often brought on by contact with colonial powers, such cases appear to be relatively rare.

More complex civilizations have also occasionally witnessed episodes of severe disorder; but again, such episodes appear to have been more the exception than the rule. The collapse of the Roman Empire, the reign of terror that swept

Paris and the provinces in the latter days of the French Revolution, and the American "wild west" of the nineteenth century are mythic symbols of the breakdown or relative absence of public order, though even these episodes did not descend to the level of pure anarchy. There are reports of social disintegration in our own times as well (Kaplan 1994). In recent years, chaos has reigned in the killing fields of the Balkans and Cambodia, in regions of Africa and the former Soviet Union, and in the decaying interiors of major cities in the United States, as warlords and their gangs have preyed upon the populace in a vacuum of effective civil authority. Yet even in these chaotic circumstances, some measure of social organization persists and life goes on. Anomia, like utopia, exists nowhere in its pure form, but only in degrees. We are, after all, a species with a certain genius for organization. The state of nature postulated by Hobbes is a hypothetical, not an empirical, entity. Hobbes's essential point was that wherever human beings live together, it is in their mutual interest to establish strong rules of governance in order to head off the dreaded war of all against all; for without such rules we cannot survive, either individually or as societies.

How might the imaginary inhabitants of Anomia transcend the Hobbesian state of nature and establish a decent measure of social order? They might begin by joining together to protect their common interests. The powerless may find strength in their superior numbers. For while powerful individuals may easily prey upon powerless individuals, they will not prey so easily upon well-organized *groups* of such individuals. Hobbes argued that it is in the interests of the majority of individuals in society to agree among themselves, in an implicit social contract, to transfer some measure of personal autonomy to the transpersonal, centralized power of the state, a Leviathan or giant with the strength to prevent members of society from tearing each other apart. Hobbes himself was a staunch monarchist, and to this day his arguments remain the classic defense of strong centralized governmental authority.

The hidden danger in Hobbes's proposal is, of course, that those who control the apparatus of the state, with its virtual monopoly on force, might usurp its legitimate powers in the pursuit of their own interests. Totalitarian regimes of the right and the left, including fascism and Stalinism, represent extreme expressions of what we might call *hypernomie* or "excessive order"—the attempt to establish absolute order by authoritarian and repressive means. Such regimes commonly rule through terror, for as Hannah Arendt ([1951] 1979: 325) observes, totalitarian regimes are "never content to rule by external means," but also seek "means of dominating and terrorizing human beings from within."

One may argue from historical experience that the dangers of hypernomie are as grave as those of anomie. While hypernomie and anomie are in one sense opposites, they paradoxically resemble each other like fractal images at different scales of magnitude. In Anomia, the war of each against all is fought among individuals, and the strongest thug rules. In Hypernomia, the state (Hobbes's Leviathan?) is potentially a thug on a much larger scale, preying upon its own subjects and upon weaker states in a continuation of Hobbesian warfare, but this time transposed to a higher and more dangerous level. Following Hobbes's own reasoning, this new war of state against subject and state against state would occasion the need for an even larger Leviathan—perhaps a global state—capable of preventing rapacious states from terrorizing their own subjects and each other. But then what would prevent the world state, and those who control it, from abusing its awesome power? How are we to prevent the rule of thugs at any level?

John Locke ([1690a] 1965: 448) suggested one possible answer when he observed that "Where-ever Law ends Tyranny begins." An alternative to the rule of thugs, in short, is the rule of rules. The idea of a society governed by abstract and impersonal laws may seem unappealing until one considers the prospect of a society governed by the personal whims of its most powerful members. Political philosophers for centuries have sought solutions to the Hobbesian problem of order, focusing particularly on the proper scope and limits of law and the state as instruments for bringing order out of chaos. We will return to these issues toward the close of the chapter. But first let us ask some more preliminary questions regarding the nature of rules and their role in creating a viable social order.

Rules as Tools

What are these things called rules that we love to complain about but cannot seem to live without? Anthropologists offer a promising clue in their description of the human species as *homo faber*, the maker and user of tools (Tyrrell 1951). Through the centuries our ancestors have invented and used a multitude of tools to solve problems they have encountered in their diverse environments. We are by no means the only species in nature to manufacture useful artifacts. Ants and beavers are magnificent architects, and chimpanzees can assemble simple implements to secure food that lies beyond their grasp. But for better or worse, no other species on earth can match the variety and complexity of our technological inventions—from the sundial to the quartz watch, from the abacus to the computer, and from the bow and arrow to the terrible destructive power of the ballistic missile.

While our capacity to create material technology is certainly impressive, even more extraordinary is our capacity to invent tools made of nothing but symbols. Mathematical equations, cookbooks, repair manuals, editorials, and software programs are tools of this sort, each designed to solve its own peculiar sort of problem through the medium of language.

Rules are symbolic tools. A rule is a linguistically encoded instruction normally taking the form "Under condition X, do Y." Rules may prescribe ("thou shalt"), proscribe ("thou shalt not"), or merely permit ("thou mayest") a given mode of conduct. Yet every rule at its inception represents someone's attempt to solve a perceived problem, whether it be avoiding traffic collisions ("drive on the right side of the road and expect others to do likewise"), promoting health ("no smoking"), or protecting property ("thou shalt not steal").

Rules, like physical tools, come in a wide assortment of shapes, sizes, and types to fit the contours of the problems they are designed to solve. Some are extremely narrow in scope ("to open this child-resistant bottle, squeeze arrows, turn lid counterclockwise, and lift"), while others are more abstract and generalizable to a wider range of situations ("do unto others as you would have others do unto you"). Some rules (called informal norms) are unwritten and unspoken, while others (formal norms) are written and codified, having evolved in some instances from more informal folkways and mores (Sumner [1906] 1940). Some rules apply only to specific subpopulations, such as the members of a single age group or organization, while others are more inclusive in their jurisdiction. Some rules are temporary while others are long standing. Some are strictly observed while others are ignored, and so forth. It would be an exhausting task indeed to construct an exhaustive typology of rules.

Rule Systems

Rules rarely travel alone. They usually live in interrelated groups or systems. While some rule systems are designed to produce uniform and predictable results (such as the official procedure for making a Big Mac, whether in Boston or Beijing), the more interesting rule systems are those whose outcomes are potentially complex and unpredictable. The rules of chess, for instance, form a simple integrated system that permits a complex range of possible strategies and outcomes. Similarly, the system of basic grammatical rules governing the English language is simple enough to be learned in grammar school but complex enough to enable speakers to generate a nearly infinite number of novel but grammatical sentences, including sentences of poetry and physics.

Rule systems often exhibit a hierarchical structure, with general statements of mission, principle, or value at the top. These higher-order norms are presumed to govern the narrower and more specific norms, such as statutes and ordinances, that reside below them in the normative hierarchy (Parsons 1951). Constitutions are general statements of this sort, setting the boundaries within which more specific national, state, and local laws are made. In principle, such rule systems are rationally codified and internally self-consistent. In practice, however, they often contain tensions and contradictions that must eventually be adjudicated and resolved, whether through judicial deliberation, negotiation, political struggle, or even war.

Some rule systems are relatively fixed and permanent (such as the rules of chess) while others contain within themselves meta-rules (rules about making more rules or amending previous ones) which facilitate their continual transformation. The U.S. Constitution is an example of the latter, because it contains a mechanism in its provisions for making constitutional amendments (including, presumably, the power to amend the amendment provision). In general, rule systems that permit their own transformation have the evolutionary advantage of being more flexible than "frozen" or unchanging systems, and hence more readily adaptable to changing needs and conditions.

Rule Makers

The ability to make and apply rules is universal among human beings. We are all legislators in one sphere of life or another. Even small children are capable of inventing their own rule-governed activities and improvising new rules as they go along—rules that the parental supreme court must sometimes override. Rule making is a regular and essential process in every social institution, from the family to the workplace to the legislature.

The Social Construction of Rules

We create social order through the countless legislative acts of everyday life. As Peter Berger and Thomas Luckmann (1966) observe in their influential treatise, *The Social Construction of Reality*, we are by nature world builders, defining and organizing our worlds largely through the creation of social norms. Other species also create and recreate their worlds, as anyone knows who has ever tried to destroy a fire ant mound. But unlike other species, we order our worlds primarily through the medium of symbols. Each generation fabricates symbolic structures (or embellishes the ones it has inherited) and presents these as objective realities to each succeeding generation.

Berger and Luckmann observe that while we may initially confront rules as external, objective constraints imposed on us by others, such constraints are often subjectively internalized and become profoundly a part of who we are. We make our rules, and thereafter our rules make us. Without this crucial ability to externalize and internalize normative orders across generations, we would soon descend into social chaos.

The social world that we encounter as infants is already massively built up with rules and rule systems. Many of these social structures, like architectural structures, were in place long before we were born, and many will presumably survive, although not unchanged, long after we are gone. Rules have histories—often long and complex histories, as Norbert Elias ([1939] 1978) demonstrates in his studies of the evolution of etiquette. Like physical buildings, some social structures will crumble and fall during our lifetimes, while others will be restored or renovated, and still others built anew from the ground up.

These social structures are never entirely static. The creation, preservation, modification, and destruction of social structures is best conceived as a continual and ongoing process akin to what Anthony Giddens (1984) calls "structuration," wherein social agents, in their daily practices, actively make and remake the structures in which they live, and which in turn live in them. We are not totally constrained by the social structures in which we live, but neither are we purely voluntaristic "free agents" either, acting just as we please. In philosophical language, we may say that our lives emerge from the dialectical interplay of structure and agency.

The social structures we inhabit (and which also inhabit us) are made up largely of rules, which are so pervasive in our lives that we may scarcely notice them. This is particularly true of rules we have internalized so deeply that they constitute a part of our very being. We are scarcely conscious, for example, of the linguistic rules that govern our communications with others—phonological rules governing the production of the sounds we utter; grammatical or syntactical rules governing the ordering of words in sentences; semantic rules linking words with meanings; discourse rules determining the kinds of linguistic performances that will be deemed appropriate in any given social context; and myriad other interpretive rules and cultural procedures (sometimes called "ethnomethods") that we employ, often unconsciously, as we make our way together through daily life (Garfinkel 1967; Cicourel 1970). Often we become conscious of such rules only at those moments when their violation elicits the disapproval of others.

Rules and Rulers

While we all have the capacity to make rules, we are not all equally empowered to do so. The great German sociologist Max Weber ([1922] 1958: 180) defined power as the probability of realizing one's goals even against the resistance of others. In legalistic societies such as the United States, the ability to achieve goals often rests on the ability to make, enforce, or exploit rules, even against opposition, in the service of one's own interests. Entire professions, including the legal and political professions, are devoted largely to the business of manipulating rules in the service of private or partisan interests. Rules are not merely tools; they are often *power* tools.

This realization opens up a range of difficult questions. If rules are problem-solving tools, who will be empowered to define what constitutes a "problem" and what constitutes a "solution"? Who will make the rules and who will have to live with them? When competing rules are proposed, which rules will prevail and whose interests will they serve? These are profoundly political questions if politics is fundamentally about who benefits and who suffers from social decision-making (Lasswell [1936] 1951).

Rules typically reflect the interests of those who make them. And in general, those who make the most important and far-reaching rules in a society are those individuals and organizations that command the greatest resources. The golden rule of rule making, the cynic wryly observes, is that those who have the gold make the rules. (Who else can afford the best legislators money can buy?) A more sophisticated version of this view is expressed in Karl Marx's and Friedrich Engels's ([1846] 1947, [1848] 1955) theory of ideology, which holds that the ruling ideas of every age are the ideas of its ruling class. Economic power, they argue, is implicated in every other form of power, including the power to legislate. Laws may have the outward appearance of neutrality and fairness and yet conceal self-serving class biases. Thus Anatol France ([1894] 1991: 84) sharply observed that "the majestic equality of the law . . . forbids the rich as well as the poor to sleep under bridges, to beg in the streets, and to steal bread."

Powerful rulers throughout history have acted as laws unto themselves, enforcing their edicts through force or the threat of force. Indeed, as Weber ([1921] 1958: 78) noted, every political state, whether despotic or democratic, ultimately rests on the application or threat of force. But brute force is a messy and inefficient method of governing. Rulers everywhere prefer the willing compliance of their subjects and therefore seek to convince them that the laws are just, fair, and deserving of respect and obedience. This attempt to persuade the people to acquiesce to the leaders' exercise of power is an aspect of what Weber called the legitimation of domination, and what Antonio Gramsci (1971) called "hegemony." Domination may be legitimated by appeals to tradition (such as the medieval Christian doctrine of the divine right of kings), to the charismatic appeal of the leader, or to the rationality of the rules and laws themselves (Weber [1921]

1958: 79). But in each instance, leaders aim to turn raw power into the more refined form of legitimate authority.

Weber noted that in the modern world power is more often legitimated by secular appeals to reason than by appeals to charisma or sacred tradition. Modern rational systems of law, administered through the impersonal authority of the bureaucratic state, have largely replaced the personal authority of charismatic leaders and the traditional authority of religious leaders, although by no means everywhere. Remnants of charismatic and traditional authority have survived into the modern era—witness the charismatic leadership of Adolf Hitler in Nazi Germany and the divine authority of Emperor Hirohito in imperial Japan during World War II.

While traditional forms of social organization still exist, Weber was perhaps the first major social theorist to recognize the rising power and growing pervasiveness of bureaucratic organization in the modern world. Modern bureaucracies, in principle if not always in practice, are impersonal organizations governed by abstract rules. For better or worse, these abstract and rationally justified rules and laws are the protective but confining "iron cage," in Weber's famous phrase, within which most of us in the modern world now live out our existence.

Rule Interpreters and Rule Enforcers

We have noted that as human beings, we are by nature legislators or rule makers. But creating new rules is only the beginning of social regulation. Rules do not become fully real until they are interpreted, implemented, and enforced. As legal creatures, we are more than mere legislators. We are judges, executors, and enforcers as well.

Rules, after all, do not interpret and implement themselves. Even relatively unambiguous "black letter law" must first be read and construed before it can be put into effect. In the interpretation of rules, we often encounter dilemmas concerning whether a given rule or principle applies to a particular case or set of facts. Does the burning of a national flag constitute protected free speech? Is a fetus a citizen? Do private gun owners in the United States constitute the "well-regulated militia" stipulated in the Second Amendment as a condition of the constitutional right to keep and bear arms? Dilemmas such as these arouse fierce passions and interests in the purportedly rational interpretation of rules, not only in courts of law but in the courtroom of public opinion as well. As we try to interpret rules in our daily lives, we all find ourselves playing the role of judge.

Each of us, at one time or another, also plays the role of executor and enforcer of rules. As executors we administer rules; as enforcers we apply sanctions—rewards and punishments—to ensure compliance, for rules without sanctions are toothless and unenforceable. Sanctions need not be formal or official in order to be effective. Sometimes a simple facial expression of approval or disapproval is enough to ensure compliance with a rule, as every kindergarten teacher knows.

Anyone who has ever been in a position of authority, whether at home or in the organizational world, knows the experience of policing others. But from the standpoint of social control or the "policing" of society, the most important police sanctions may be those that we internalize and impose upon ourselves. Inducing social actors to police themselves is a far more efficient means of social control than maintaining massive judicial, law enforcement, and penal systems at great public expense. In the self-policing society there is no need for a cop on every street corner, because there is already one in every head.

Sigmund Freud called this internalized control system the "superego." In *Civilization and Its Discontents* (1930), Freud made a convincing case that such internalized constraints are a necessary and universal condition of social life. In Freud's three-part model of the human psyche, the formation of a strong *ego* (the rational, calculating processes of the human psyche) and *superego* (the moralistic processes that punish us with a guilty conscience when we fail to live up to our learned ideals) are necessary to tame the wild and wooly *id* (representing the biological demands of the body, including our sexual and aggressive impulses). If the id were unleashed, social order would soon collapse in a riot of unrestrained passion. It might be fun while it lasted, but it would not last for long. Civilization itself would soon disintegrate.

Freud observed that we pay a high psychic price for civilization. The drives and demands of the id resist restraint. Thus, the biological demands of the body and the moral constraints of society are in a constant state of internal warfare. This seething cauldron of psychic conflict is mediated by the ego, the "executive of the psyche," whose difficult task it is to reconcile the competing demands of id, superego and external reality. The price we pay for civilization is paid in internal conflict, guilt, anxiety, frustration, and discontent. But the price of civilizational collapse would be even higher. It is in our rational interest, Freud insisted, to pay the price for the sake of our individual and social survival. Members of society who have failed to internalize effective restraints on their sexual and aggressive impulses are termed sociopaths. Their absence of internal restraint often makes necessary the external restraint of prison bars.

At the opposite extreme from sociopaths are those so thoroughly *oversocialized* (Wrong 1961) and internally controlled that they resemble programmed robots, incapable of spontaneity and joy. Most of us live our lives between the extremes of oversocialization and sociopathy, acting neither as robots nor as beasts but as some peculiar hybrid of the two.

To pursue the legal metaphor a bit further, we may imagine Freud's superego as a kind of internalized justice system. It includes not only a police agency monitoring compliance with codes of expected conduct, but also a judicial agency rendering self-judgments and a penal agency capable of inflicting internal punishments (such as guilt and self-loathing) for the violation of moral codes. External courts, police organizations and prisons provide a back-up system in the event that these internal controls prove ineffective. But a society that must rely *primarily* on external controls to ensure compliance with the law is in serious trouble, for this signifies a massive cultural failure to inculcate habits of self-control in the populace at large.

Freud took a pessimistic view of human nature, and particularly of the beastly and unruly id. Other social philosophers, by contrast, have romanticized human nature and have regarded civilization as a repressive and corrupting influence on the natural development of our innate goodness. "Man is born free," Jean-Jacques Rousseau remarked in the opening lines of *The Social Contract*, "and yet we see him everywhere in chains" ([1762] 1973). Others, such as John Locke ([1690b] 1959), have regarded human nature as essentially neutral, a *tabula rasa* or blank slate upon which experience inscribes its lessons. But Freud saw instead a natural perversity in human nature, requiring civilized restraints to channel or "sublimate" its potentially destructive energies in socially constructive directions. As Talcott Parsons once remarked, every new generation born into the world represents a kind of barbarian invasion. From a psychoanalytic perspective, the principal challenge of childhood socialization is to channel the wild energies and impulses of the young, through the formation of the superego, in ways that promote rather than destroy civilization.

Rule Breakers and Rule Changers

Thus far our discussion has implied that conformity to rules is socially beneficial, since it is essential to the survival of society. No society can endure unless its members respect some common set of rules or social norms. This is not to say, however, that every rule is equally worthy of respect. On the contrary, most of us can agree, upon reflection, that in some circumstances it is better to violate a rule than to obey it.

Deviance, from a Latin root meaning "away from the path," is the rather unfortunate term sociologists have given to the violation of social norms, whether formal or merely customary. For purposes of social analysis it is crucial to understand that the term *deviant* does not necessarily mean "evil" or "wrong." Deviance is always contextual, and so we must always remain clear about the frame of reference within which a given act is socially defined as either deviant or conformist. Members of the underground resistance in Nazi Germany were certainly deviant from within the framework of the Nazi system, but it does not follow from this that they were morally wrong to resist.

Some libertarian philosophers, such as John Stuart Mill ([1859] 1986) and Henry David Thoreau ([1849] 1983), have emphasized the innovative contributions that nonconformists (a less stigmatizing word than "deviants") have made to social progress—even to the point of challenging existing laws in acts of civil disobedience when necessary. A society without dissent, according to their view, would be stagnant, suffocating, and incapable of adapting to changing circumstances.

Cultural innovators throughout history—Socrates and Jesus, Albert Einstein and Mohandas Gandhi, Susan B. Anthony and Martin Luther King—were all deviant within the established frames of reference which they rose to challenge. Thus, the deviants of one age may be the heroes of the next. Thoreau himself was jailed for an act of civil disobedience in his lifetime and commemorated on a postage stamp only after he was long and safely dead. Charismatic deviants throughout history have been major agents of cultural change, repealing rules in the very act of breaking them—often in the name of a higher and more just law.

Of course, historical instances of heroic deviance do not thereby render every act of deviance heroic. While "deviant" does not mean "evil," neither does it necessarily mean "good" or "right." Rule breakers include not only great innovators but also great charlatans, not only harmless eccentrics but also heinous criminals. Our own culture seems at times to romanticize certain deviant types uncritically. We romanticize, for example, the defiant outlaw, from Jesse James and Billy the Kid to Rambo and the Godfather; yet a society composed entirely of outlaws would be uninhabitable. We admire rugged individuals who do not seem to care what other people think; but a society composed entirely of such boorish types would be unbearable in practice. We admire those who march to the beat of their own drums; but a society composed entirely of different drummers would be a drum wreck.

Whether any particular act of deviance is beneficial or destructive, some measure of deviance in a society is normal and natural. As long as there are human societies there will be rules of conduct; and as long as there are rules of conduct there will be those who deviate from them. Durkheim ([1895] 1958) went further to suggest that every society *needs* some deviant members in order to establish the limits of permissible behavior (by making examples of those who cross the line) and to strengthen the solidarity of the group in the face of perceived threats. It is often said that if deviants did not exist, we would have to invent them. And indeed, we do invent deviants by definition when we create the rules and categories that define what is deviant and what is not. In every society there will be those who draw lines in the sand to mark the boundaries that separate acceptable from unacceptable behavior. And in every society there will be those who transgress those boundaries. Durkheim seemed to suggest that we need both.

Postmodern Anomie

Social definitions of what constitutes deviance vary widely from culture to culture and may fluctuate markedly through time. As the cultural sands shift, old moral boundaries are erased and new ones are drawn. Behaviors in American society that were once socially accepted (such as slavery and child labor) are now prohibited, while behaviors once prohibited (such as abortion) are now permitted. The meanings that we attach to behaviors are also in constant transition. What was once called "corporal discipline" is now culturally redefined as "child abuse," and those who were once labeled "bums" are now known more charitably as "homeless."

Daniel Patrick Moynihan (1993) contends that we have "defined deviancy down" in recent decades by reducing the stigma that we once attached to social behaviors such as vandalism and teen pregnancy. But one can argue that in some respects we have also "defined deviancy up," rendering less socially acceptable such acts as telling racist or sexist jokes, smoking in enclosed public spaces, wearing fur, producing unsafe and unhealthy products, and despoiling the environment. Even as some social restraints are loosened, others are tightened.

Postmodern is the name now commonly given to this era of cultural flux in which rules and meanings are constantly in motion, and traditional out-of-bounds markers seem to shift and blur even as the game is in play. Participants in the game of postmodern culture play according to conflicting rules in the pursuit of conflicting goals, and there is no agreed-upon system of scoring. The rhetoric of deviance and traditional respectability now competes with the rhetoric of legitimate difference, diversity, and tolerance of alternative lifestyles. Indeed, the very notion of deviance loses much of its meaning in a world in which there are fewer clearly defined and widely shared rules of acceptable conduct. Durkheim ([1897] 1966: 253) termed this social condition anomie—a moral "state of de-regulation [in which] traditional rules have lost their authority," occurring especially in times of rapid change and social dislocation such as our own. In his notion of anomie, Durkheim seems to have anticipated much of what we now call postmodernity.

Thinking in organic metaphors, Durkheim ([1893] 1947) regarded anomie as a kind of social sickness. Not everyone would now agree. While the flux and social vertigo of postmodern life are deeply disturbing to some, others seem to revel in the multitude of new choices and novel opportunities that a postmodern culture affords. (For example, see Turkle's 1995 account of the myriad forms of imaginative play on the Internet.) Postmodern life, like a carnival ride, is terrifying to some but exhilarating to others.

Whose Order? *Which* Values?: Three American Ideologies

Even those who find the loosening of traditional cultural restrictions liberating and stimulating do not normally desire the *complete* disintegration of social order. We all envision the need for social order of some kind and in some degree. We simply cannot agree among ourselves concerning just what sort of social order we want. Whose vision of the good society shall we seek to achieve? What core values shall we strive to uphold? Answers to these questions seem to vary widely according to the ideological orientation of the observer. Indeed, questions of this kind are at the very heart of the culture wars (Hunter 1991; Gates 1992) currently waged in the United States over issues ranging from sexuality and school prayer to environmental protection and gender equality.

While the disputants in these cultural debates are usually described with reference to a simple one-dimensional ideological continuum ("conservatives" at one end versus "liberals" at the other), we believe it is more insightful to conceptualize American ideological discourse as a triangular exchange among three distinct ideological positions, which we will call traditional conservatism, libertarianism, and social democracy. Each of the corner positions in this ideological triangle is defined by its own distinctive core values. Most Americans, because they hold multiple and sometimes contradictory values, fall somewhere among the extremes. Let us consider each of the three "primary colors" that, mixed in various proportions, produce the American ideological palette (see Fine 1996 for a similar analysis).

1. *Traditional conservatism* embraces, above all the values of social order, authority and tradition. Arising in part as a reaction to the excesses of the French revolution (Nisbet 1986), conservatism's historical roots reach back to the feudalism of the Middle Ages, when aristocracies and religious officials ruled Europe, and still further back to classical and biblical sources originating more than two millennia ago. Echoing themes from Plato's *Republic* and ancient scriptures, traditional conservatives affirm the need for social hierarchy and respect for superior wisdom as the foundations of a stable social order. They typically embrace traditional religious beliefs and venerate the military values of discipline, law and order, pa-

triotism, patriarchy, and respect for authority. The religious and military right represent contemporary versions of this ideology in American society.

2. *Libertarianism*, also known as classical or nineteenth-century liberalism (not to be confused with twentieth-century liberalism), is a more modern ideology, with its young roots in the scientific Enlightenment and the rise of capitalism in the West. Its core values are individual liberty and individual responsibility. Libertarianism has two aspects—economic and civil. *Economic* libertarians, in the spirit of the Scottish economic philosopher Adam Smith ([1776] 1937), advocate laissez-faire ("let it be") capitalism with minimal state interference in the workings of the free marketplace, contending that such interference impedes individual initiative, efficiency, and innovation. Civil libertarians, classically represented by the British philosopher John Stuart Mill ([1859] 1986), advocate rights of free expression, including freedom of speech, press, and religion, against what they perceive to be the undue constraints of tradition and state authority. The "true" libertarian embraces both the economic and civil tenets of this ideology.

3. *Social democracy is* the third primary color on the American ideological palette. The core value of social democracy is the achievement of greater political and economic equality in American life. While social democrats do not claim that absolute equality is possible or even entirely desirable, they regard the extreme degree of existing inequalities, both nationally and globally, as morally intolerable, since such inequalities produce vastly different levels of real opportunity for well-being and advancement among different segments of national and world society. With historical roots in organized labor movements, egalitarian religious movements, and democratic political revolutions, social democrats typically pursue strategies designed to redistribute wealth and power from the top of society downward (in contrast to conservative and libertarian ideologies, which are generally hostile toward the ideal of equality and tend to justify concentrations of social advantage at the top). Social democrats commonly defend the interests of groups that have been historically suppressed or marginalized, including the poor, women, and racial, ethnic, and cultural minorities.

Those who call themselves conservatives in the United States today usually represent a blend of traditional (or "true") conservatism and economic libertarianism, with religious and military conservatives tending toward the former and business interests toward the latter. Similarly, those who call themselves liberals today are typically torn between the ideology of social democracy and the more individualistic ideology of libertarianism (particularly civil libertarianism). Most Americans borrow elements from all three primary ideologies and thus hold intermediate views (largely unconscious and unexamined) of various shades and hues.

How do each of these primary-color ideologies interpret contemporary social life in a postmodern age? Traditional law-and-order conservatives typically regard the current cultural situation with alarm, perceiving a general breakdown of social order, authority, and morality. Conservative social critics (e.g., Bennett 1994; Kilpatrick 1992; Bloom 1987) decry the widespread failure of our culture to inculcate virtuous habits in the young, reflected in statistics on juvenile crime, unplanned pregnancy, illegal drug use, and the like. The more pessimistic among them warn that this cultural failure signals the very real prospect of civilizational collapse.

Traditional conservatives typically contrast our present age with previous eras in which, they believe, absolute and objective standards of moral conduct were more widely acknowledged and respected. According to this view, moral standards have eroded steadily until they are now largely matters of personal or subcultural taste. Traditional conservatives fear that moral relativism (i.e., skepticism toward the existence of absolute, objective, or universal moral truths) and the "moral anarchy" that flows from it have been loosed upon the land (Johnson 1983: 4), and that Western societies, having lost their moral bearings, are now careening down a slippery slope toward a grim and perilous future.

Critics of this view respond that there never was any such golden age of morality, and that the traditional and authoritarian moralities of the past have too often served to justify or conceal economic, racial, sexual, religious, and other forms of bigotry and oppression. Libertarians, and to a lesser degree social democrats, appear to be more at home with the flux and ferment of postmodern culture, but for differing reasons. Libertarians see in the postmodern situation unprecedented opportunities for the exercise of individual freedom to live as one likes without the constraints of tradition or state coercion. They may be inclined to cultivate what Michael Sandel (1996) has critically termed the "unencumbered self"—a self free of the binding ties of social responsibility and communal identity. There is indeed evidence that the majority of Americans embrace elements of a libertarian view. A strong majority agree, for example, with the statement that morality "is a personal matter and society should not force everyone to follow one standard" (Rigney and Kearl 1994; Kearl and Rigney 1995).

Social democrats, like libertarians, generally welcome the postmodern tolerance of cultural differences and the freedoms that permit marginalized groups to define and redefine their identities on their own terms in a multicultural society. However, they are strongly critical of libertarian tendencies toward extreme individualism in American culture. Social democrats sometimes join conservatives in arguing that extreme forms of moral individualism (itself a kind of ethical relativism in which each of us is a moral law unto himself) are potentially disastrous in their social consequences. Social democrats emphasize the value of social (as against merely individual) responsibility and fear that the "everyone-for-himself" society, reminiscent of the social Darwinism of the late nineteenth century, represents a step away from civilization and toward the Hobbesian war of all against all.

The Communitarian Movement

In the decade of the 1970s, numerous social critics of varying ideological persuasions began to warn of the dangers of libertarian individualism and to affirm the value of community. Tom Wolfe (1976) offered his famous critique of the "me decade." Christopher Lasch (1978) wrote of a disturbing "culture of narcissism," and Daniel Bell (1976) called into question hedonistic tendencies in the culture of consumer capitalism. More recently, Robert Bellah, Richard Madsen, William Sullivan, Ann Swidler, and Steven Tipton (1985, 1991) have exhorted Americans to seek deeper moral commitments that transcend narrow self-interest. We do not live separately from our social institutions, they rightly argue, but rather in and through them, and thus our personal well-being is ultimately inseparable from the well-being of our communities and societies.

By the 1990s, a communitarian movement led by Amitai Etzioni (1993) and others had formed in opposition to the perceived excesses of libertarian individualism. Mary Ann Glendon (1991) controversially explored the limits of individual rights in American jurisprudence, arguing that rights imply corresponding responsibilities, and that to speak of rights without responsibilities is irresponsible. Robert Putnam (1995, 2000) took "bowling alone" as a metaphor for what he believed to be the declining sense of social connectedness in the United States, while Jean Bethke Elshtain (1995) and Sandel (1996) warned of the breakdown of civic virtue and the malfunction of democracy in an excessively individualistic society. Meanwhile, Charles Taylor (1989) and James Collier (1991) explored the historical sources of self-centered individualism. The communitarian movement, although neither ideologically "left" nor "right," has blended elements of both traditional conservatism and social democracy in its challenge to what it views as an increasingly dominant libertarian culture of self-centered individualism. Communitarians are especially disturbed by the "coarsening" or vulgarization of culture, as reflected in the mass media and popular culture, and by the attendant loss of basic standards of civility and mutual respect in American life.

Communitarian critiques of American culture serve to remind us that ethics is by its very nature a communal endeavor—a discussion *among* human beings about how we ought to live. Ethics is both personal *and* social, for the question "How ought I to live?" is intimately and forever interwoven with the question "How ought we to live together?" Pushed to its extreme, moral individualism is a contradiction in terms, because it fails to comprehend the inherently social and communal character of ethical discourse. We are connected to each other by thousands of invisible strings—linguistic, economic, political, and cultural—and thus virtually every choice we make affects others for better or worse. As we suggested in chapter 2, ethical inquiry is not concerned merely with your individual well-being or mine, but with the conditions that nurture human well-being in general in an ecologically and socially interdependent world. To ask only "What's in it for me?" is to step outside the ethical question altogether.

Communitarians insist that while a healthy measure of tolerance and respect for individual difference is essential to the survival of democratic institutions, it is equally essential that citizens share some core of common commitments that transcend naked self-interest, including the civic-minded democratic commitment to a common good. Communitarians are right, we believe, to insist on the need for a stronger sense of community and mutual concern, both in American society and throughout our increasingly interdependent and electronically woven world.

The building of community begins with a search for common ground, taking stock of the beliefs and values that unite us rather than accentuating those that divide us. If we are to discover common moral ground in a world torn apart by destructive difference, communitarians seem to say, we must be willing to seek the highest (not the lowest) common denominator among divergent views as a step toward their reconciliation.

To its defenders, communitarianism offers an escape from the perils of selfish individualism and the "everyone for himself" society. To its detractors, however, it rests on nostalgic fantasies of a rural or small-town past (Phillips 1993), threatening to suffocate exuberant individuality and homogenize cultural diversity in the name of community. Critics worry that a communitarian "tyranny of the majority" might suppress and coerce those who refuse to march to the beat of the community's drum.

Is There a Higher Law?

Underlying many current philosophical and ideological debates over competing values (such as the values of tradition and order, equality, individual liberty, and community) are deeper disagreements over the ultimate source or basis of morality itself. Postmodernists have tended to regard moralities as largely arbitrary social

constructions that can be shown to vary profoundly from one culture or historical period to another. Recognizing the cultural relativity of moral beliefs leads
them to become ethical or moral relativists as well, skeptical of the existence of
any universal or transcendent standards capable of arbitrating disputes among
the claims of competing moral systems. In short, postmodernists tend to doubt
the existence of a higher law to which ordinary human rules and laws are subject. At the opposite extreme are those (particularly in fundamentalist Christian, Jewish, and Islamic religious traditions) who continue to believe firmly in
the existence of moral absolutes (although they do not always agree among themselves as to what these absolutes are or how they are to be interpreted.) Between
the extremes of moral relativism and moral absolutism lie a variety of intermediate philosophical and religious positions (Bernstein 1983; Stout 1988).

Both moral relativism and moral absolutism, in their extreme forms, have severe
liabilities. On the one hand, moral relativism appears to preclude the very possibility of a universal human ethics. In the absence of ethical standards that transcend any particular culture, we have no compelling moral argument against the
Holocaust or any other atrocity in the human experience, past or future, because
there is no higher law against which to judge the adequacy of the moral beliefs
of the perpetrators. Moral relativism thus gives us no basis for a concept of human rights. In an international and intercultural world it can offer no principle,
beyond the rule of "might makes right," with which to reconcile cultural and
moral disagreements. On the other hand, militant moral absolutisms are also to
be feared, for rivers of blood have flowed in their name, often in holy wars against
other competing absolutisms. If ethics is fundamentally about human well-being
and its attainment, one may argue that moral relativism and moral absolutism
have both contributed to the degradation of human life, and are therefore both
morally suspect.

Is there a middle way that avoids these dangers and yet offers the possibility
of a planetary ethics in a diverse and interdependent world? Arguing on behalf
of the possibility of a universal human ethics, Rushworth M. Kidder (1994) and
others have noted that cultures around the world do tend to share certain core
values in common, such as the values of truth telling, fairness, and responsibility.
We may further note that moral norms such as the golden rule have appeared in
the ethical teachings of diverse societies through history. Moreover, many religious and philosophical traditions, including Taoism, Buddhism, and Aristote-
lian philosophy, have taught that some ways of living are naturally more conducive to human well-being than others, and hence that there is a natural ethics.
(This is a hard claim to deny; for human beings, like rose bushes, undeniably
thrive under some conditions and wither under others.) Jewish and Christian
traditions have also upheld the existence of a natural moral law (e.g., John Paul

II 1993), although honesty compels us to acknowledge that their traditional formulations of natural law doctrine have often been invoked to justify such social practices as slavery and the suppression of women, homosexuals, and other marginalized people on the grounds that such practices are "God's will."

While traditional Jewish and Christian versions of natural law doctrine have emphasized our moral *obligations and responsibilities*, a more modern natural law tradition, with its roots in the Enlightenment philosophy of John Locke and expressed by Thomas Jefferson in the Declaration of Independence, emphasizes our moral *rights* as human beings. This is the natural law tradition that underlies much of the modern civil and human rights movements (Laqueur and Rubin 1989) and is encoded in international law in the articles of the Universal Declaration of Human Rights (United Nations 1948), which states that the "inherent dignity and . . . equal and inalienable rights of all members of the human family is the foundation of freedom, justice and peace in the world." Natural law doctrines, whether they emphasize responsibilities or rights, and whether they are religious or secular in origin, affirm the possibility of a universal human ethics—a "higher law" to which we may appeal when we encounter conflicts among competing moral systems.

Both conservatives and liberals have appealed to natural law doctrines in their political rhetoric. Thus, conservatives have appealed to a higher moral law than human law in their opposition to abortion, while liberals such as Martin Luther King have appealed to a higher moral law in their opposition to racial oppression. Religious and secular thinkers alike have invoked the authority of a higher law in the pursuit of their respective ideals. Still there is far from perfect consensus, even among intelligent and reflective people of good will, regarding precisely what this higher law is, where it comes from, and how it should be applied to contemporary issues. The problems involved in establishing an enduring and universal ethics in a culturally diverse world are painfully difficult. Yet despite our differences we can nearly all agree that we cannot live without ethics; for without moral rules, we are condemned to the social disintegration of Anomia and to the Hobbesian war of all against all.

CHAPTER SIX

~

Society as Market

Through the ages our ancestors have lived by the sweat of their brows (or the brows of others), adapting themselves to their natural environments, gaining sustenance from them and transforming them in the process. Economic activities of this kind are essential to human survival. And because this is so, many social theorists have come to regard economic institutions as the very foundation of social life. From this materialist perspective, every other social institution, from family and religion to politics and education, is fundamentally an economic institution insofar as it produces, distributes, and/or consumes scarce resources. Thus, every social analysis becomes an economic analysis, and economic concepts become the ruling metaphors for understanding and explaining the whole of social life. Pushed to extremes, the attempt to explain every aspect of social life in economic terms is known as economic reductionism.

Economic images of society are not the stuff of romantic poetry or sentimental spirituality. They present us with a rather cold, tough-minded, and hard-edged view of life, immersing the analysis of social relations in the icy language of calculation and control. When we view human society through economic lenses, social life is revealed as a self-interested struggle for survival and competitive advantage—whether a capitalist struggle among competing individuals in the marketplace or a socialist struggle among contending economic classes. Economic theorists are the "worldly philosophers" (Heilbroner 1972) who seek to reveal the deeper dynamics of these struggles. Two worldly philosophers in particular, Adam Smith and Karl Marx, have dominated economic thought during the past two centuries. Let us visit each of them briefly.

Philosophies of the Marketplace

Adam Smith was an eighteenth-century Scotsman whose most influential work, *The Wealth of Nations*, appeared in the memorable year 1776. In its pages, Smith championed the cause of laissez-faire ("let it be") capitalism, advocating free exchange in the marketplace with minimal governmental interference. Smith viewed human nature as essentially selfish. "It is not from the benevolence of the butcher, the brewer or the baker that we expect our dinner," he wrote, "but for their regard to their own interest. We address ourselves, not to their humanity, but to their self-love, and never talk to them of our necessities, but of their advantages" ([1776] 1937, I: 14).

While Smith did not trust the central authority of the state to make competent economic decisions, it may surprise some to know that he was equally mistrustful of the motives of wealthy capitalists as well, whose "natural selfishness and rapacity" caused them to seek the "gratification of their own vain and insatiable desires" ([1759] 1982: 184–85). Smith acknowledged the need for a social mechanism capable of restraining the worst excesses of selfish individualism, and he thought he had found that mechanism in the competition of the marketplace. In the free exchange of goods and services, greedy producers who sold their wares at exorbitant prices would soon be undersold by their competitors, and consumers would benefit from the resulting price competition.

Smith understood that, in a certain ironic sense, capitalists do not desire capitalism. He observed that their desire is not to compete with others in the marketplace, but rather to drive their competitors out of business so as to establish monopolistic control and raise prices through the roof. But Smith had faith that the market mechanism would correct this problem automatically as new competitors entered the marketplace to undersell monopolists. Workers also would benefit from the operation of free markets, Smith believed, because their wages would increase as employers competed for their services, drawing the best workers away from less productive and efficient enterprises. By rewarding efficient production, the market system would create abundant wealth, to be shared equitably by employers and employees alike. Like an "invisible hand," the market system would harness private selfishness toward the creation of general prosperity.

Smith was confident that as the tide of economic prosperity rose, all boats would rise. This, in any case, is what his classical economic theory predicts. But in reality, not everyone has a boat, and some inevitably sink and drown in the whirlpool of economic competition. Competition, by definition, creates both winners and losers, and winners are more apt than losers to celebrate its blessings. Some modern-day disciples of Adam Smith seem at times to invest an almost religious faith in the market as a mechanism for determining prices, wages, and the quantity and quality of goods and services produced, as though it were a kind of infallible god whose outcomes are beyond question or criticism. Some tend to view the law of supply and demand as a veritable law of nature, contending that the free market system, by allowing supply and demand to operate without "unnatural" interference from the state, responds sensitively to consumer demands and creates wealth more efficiently than any possible alternative.

Today, few deny that market systems can serve as useful means of allocating goods and services. The productive powers of the market are indeed impressive by any historical standard. But it is shortsighted, even in an age of triumphal capitalism, to elevate the invisible hand of the marketplace to the status of infallibility. Although market solutions are at times presented as virtual panaceas to social problems, they often bear hidden costs and dangers (e.g., Henig 1994), raising serious concerns for the well-being of those who are left behind. Critics of Smith's classical economics note that the market *is* responsive to the wants and needs of those who have money to spend (whether earned, inherited, or ill-gotten). But the market scarcely registers the human existence, let alone the needs or wants, of those who, for whatever reason, lack significant economic resources. Critics point out that in actual practice, unrestrained market systems tend to produce extreme inequalities of wealth and income, and that these inequalities are reproduced in each successive generation as economic advantages (as well as disadvantages) are passed from one generation to the next. The tendency of competitive systems to reward initial advantage and thereby intensify inequality over time has come to be called the Matthew effect (Merton 1973: 439–59), from the biblical scripture which observes that the rich get richer while the poor get poorer.

Karl Marx was more attentive than Adam Smith to the inherent limitations and defects of market systems. Marx was, however, also enormously respectful of the achievements of modern capitalism, contrary to ideological caricatures of his thought that were widely promulgated during the cold war era. While criticizing its defects, Marx applauded the capitalist system for revolutionizing the technological forces of production, destroying the oppressive institutions of feudalism, and internationalizing the world through trade and commerce (Marx and Engels [1848] 1955: 12–13). But Marx did not regard capitalism as the end-point of human history. He believed that its inherent defects would eventually lead to its own transcendence. Just as capitalism had transcended feudalism, so would socialism and, ultimately, advanced communism transcend capitalism.

Among the defects of the marketplace, Marx noted, was the brute fact that exchanges between capital and labor do not naturally occur on a level playing field. The capitalists of his day brought vast resources to the bargaining table, while unorganized workers had only their labor power to offer in exchange for wages so low that they scarcely sustained life. Marx argued that the worker's labor was the ultimate source of the creation of wealth, but that the capitalist production process separated or "alienated" workers from the fruits of their labor.

In return for their labor, workers received only a fraction of the value their labor had produced. Reduced to mere commodities in the labor market, workers became "appendages of the machine," alienated not only from the fruits of their work but also from each other and, ultimately, from their own humanity.

Marx clearly recognized that in exchange relationships, dominant parties tend to regard subordinates as mere objects or instruments in the attainment of their own interests. Systems of class inequality, he argued, serve the interests of those classes that own and control the means of production, reducing those below to the status of mere pawns in the game of capital accumulation. Marx's solution to this defect of market systems was to strengthen the bargaining power of the pawns by organizing the industrial laboring class (or proletariat) to challenge unfair relations of exchange in the marketplace, and ultimately to transform the rules of the game itself on behalf of its own interests as a working-class majority. Thus, Karl Marx and Friedrich Engels called for an explicitly democratic movement ([1848] 1955: 19, 31, 46) to overturn capitalism and to replace it with an unspecified form of participatory economic democracy that would prohibit the exploitation of the many by the few.

To be sure, Marx seems to have understood democracy in rather crude majoritarian terms as a "dictatorship" of, by, and for the proletariat. He was openly contemptuous of "bourgeois civil liberties" such as freedom of speech and press, observing that in practice such rights are available mainly to the privileged few. (Freedom of the press, Marxists like to say, exists only for those who can afford to own a press.) In retrospect, Marx vastly underestimated the potential abuses of centralized state power exercised in the name of the people, naively imagining that the state might eventually wither away in a future classless society. His writings, interpreted by his disciples in a multitude of conflicting ways, have been invoked to justify harrowing atrocities. Yet it must also be said that whatever economic gains working classes have made in the past century and a half are attributable in large measure to the organized labor movements that his writings helped to inspire.

Nowhere in reality do we find either the "pure" free-market capitalism of Adam Smith or the "pure" socialism of Karl Marx. Both systems are defective in practice. Market systems have generally been far more successful at producing wealth than nonmarket systems, rewarding creativity and efficiency in the competition for economic resources. But market systems have been much less successful in achieving equitable distributions of wealth, instead creating vast and potentially explosive inequalities between rich and poor.

In actual practice, all modern societies have *mixed economies*, blending elements of free-market capitalism and social planning in varying proportions to produce hybrid systems that work, with varying success, to meet the basic needs of their people. If we allow governmental expenditures as a percentage of total gross domestic product to serve as a rough measure of the mix of public and private (or socialist and capitalist) elements in a national economy, we find that public spending accounts for about one-fourth of the total U.S. economy, and between 30 and 60 percent of the economies of Western European social democracies (Kurian 1991: 91). In mixed economies, the worst excesses of cut-throat competition are somewhat blunted by social legislation (such as social security, public health care, aid to the poor, and labor laws), while the worst inefficiencies of socialism are wrung out in the competitive vigor of the marketplace.

With the collapse of Stalinism and the winding down of the cold war, perhaps we can now begin to consider with new honesty the respective strengths and shortcomings of the competing visions of Smith and Marx. Perhaps we can begin to acknowledge that capitalism and socialism, as human inventions, are both deeply flawed but nonetheless partially successful strategies for fulfilling human need, and that some blend of the two, tailored to the unique circumstances of each society and its culture, may offer the best hope of achieving prosperous and humane economies (Kuttner 1997).

Exchange Theory

Social theories tend to reflect the cultural assumptions of the societies from which they emerge. We should not be surprised, then, that in the predominantly capitalist cultural environment of the United States, social theorists should arise to propose that societies resemble economic marketplaces. In sociology, exchange theorists and rational choice theorists candidly employ this economic metaphor in their analyses. They are in many respects the intellectual descendants of the classical economist Adam Smith and his utilitarian economic philosophy (Collins 1994: 133–89).

Exchange and rational choice theorists are by no means the first to recognize the central significance of exchange relationships in social life. Even before Adam Smith, early social contract theorists such as Thomas Hobbes ([1651] 1964), John Locke ([1690a] 1965), and Jean-Jacques Rousseau ([1762] 1973) were already viewing society as a kind of exchange relationship in which we agree among ourselves to trade a measure of unrestrained freedom for a measure of mutual security. A number of classic anthropological studies also have focused on the social uses of exchange, including Bronislaw Malinowski's (1922) analysis of the social functions of the Kula gift-exchange rings of the Western Pacific, Marcel Mauss's ([1925] 1990) essay on the giving and receiving of gifts, and Claude Lévi-Strauss's (1958) studies of social reciprocity in the exchange of women. Each of these studies has explored in its own way the crucial role of exchange in forming social bonds of reciprocal obligation within or among societies.

Sociological exchange theory diverges from these previous anthropological approaches by shifting attention from the collective to the individual level of analysis (Ekeh 1974). In this respect, exchange theory mirrors the individualistic Anglo-American culture from which it has emerged. Like English social contract theory before it, exchange theory tends to paint an "atomistic" picture of society as a loose collection of autonomous individuals held together by relations of reciprocity.

The principal architect of sociological exchange theory, George Homans (1958, 1961, 1974), hoped to demonstrate that societies are built up out of countless exchange transactions among individuals. Homans aspired to establish a rigorous science of society by beginning at the individual level of analysis and working upward, borrowing concepts and assumptions from the most advanced behavioral sciences of his day (or so he believed). Thus he combined elements of neoclassical economics and behaviorist psychology to create a psychoeconomic account of social behavior. As the late Kenneth Boulding (1962: 458) cleverly observed, in Homans's work "economic man is crossed with the psychological pigeon to produce what the unkind might call the Economic Pigeon theory of human interaction."

From neoclassical economics, Homans borrowed the utilitarian assumption that human beings naturally seek to maximize their own happiness. Like capitalists seeking to maximize gains and minimize costs, social actors are essentially rational and calculating in the pursuit of their interests. Unlike many economists, however, Homans did not focus narrowly on financial interests. He criticized this purely mercenary conception of the human being as "antisocial and materialistic, interested only in money and material goods and ready to sacrifice even his old mother to get them" (1961: 79). Homans rightly observed that we seek not only material but also psychological and social gratifications, such as love and the approval of others.

In most other respects, however, Homans accepted the economic image of society as a network of exchange relations among individuals based on rational and self-interested calculations of reward and cost. In particular, he appropriated the economic concept of profit (rewards gained minus costs incurred in a transaction), defining the concept broadly to include nonmonetary gain. Homans argued that "no exchange continues unless both parties are making a profit" (1961: 61). This hypothesis, although suggestive, is difficult to test in practice. While we can conveniently measure economic transactions using units of currency as a generalized medium of exchange, there is no such convenient metric—no commonly accepted standard measure of enjoyment or pain—with which to neatly calculate the psychological "profitability" of nonmonetary transactions.

Economic exchanges, Homans argued, are merely a special instance of social exchange in general. Thus, Homans did not seek to reduce sociology to economics. Rather, he sought to discover the general principles of exchange that govern both economic *and* noneconomic transactions, and he thought he had found these fundamental principles in the behaviorist psychology of B. F. Skinner, his Harvard colleague. Skinner was renowned for his laboratory studies of learned behavior in pigeons and rats, and by the 1960s his name had become a controversial household word (Bjork 1993). Skinner's behaviorism, which dominated experimental psychology during the 1950s, viewed the behaviors of organisms (whether pigeons, rats, or human beings) as responses to external stimuli. Hence, behaviorism is sometimes referred to as "stimulus-response," or S-R, psychology.

In behaviorist terminology, stimuli that increase the frequency of a given response are called reinforcments (or in more popular terms, rewards), while those that diminish the frequency of a response are termed punishments. We may condition the behavior of an organism, Skinner demonstrated, by manipulating external stimuli in order to produce desired results. We may even enlist the organism in its own conditioning by allowing it to increase the frequency of a reward by exhibiting a specific behavior. Thus, in operant conditioning, we may rig up a device that rewards a pigeon with a food pellet each time it pecks a metal bar. The pigeon will continue to peck the bar so long as this behavior is rewarded with more food pellets, or until the pigeon becomes satiated (Skinner 1974; Shaw and Costanzo 1982: 23–40).

Through experimental demonstrations of this kind, Skinner sought to develop an objective science of psychology based purely on observable behavior, without reference to such ghostly concepts as "mind," "cognition," or "consciousness." (This led some critics to describe behaviorism, only half in jest, as a mindless psychology.) Thus, when we apply a stimulus (S) to the organism (O) we may objectively observe a response (R). In this S-O-R model of behavior, the internal operations of the organism are, for Skinner, a mysterious "black box" that we can never observe directly and that therefore have no place in a true science of behavior.

Behaviorism is now rather passé in psychology, having been absorbed or surpassed by rival approaches, and especially by the cognitive revolution that overtook the field in the 1960s (Gardner 1985). Cognitive psychologists, unlike behaviorists, devote themselves to decoding the black box of the mind, which they interpret with the aid of analogies to computers and other cybernetic systems. While behaviorism has by now lost much of its luster, it was still preeminent at the time Homans was developing exchange theory. From behaviorist psychology Homans borrowed such concepts as stimulus, response, reward, and punishment. Joining these with concepts from neo-classical economics, he fashioned a set of simple (some would say obvious) propositions from which he attempted to de-

rive explanations of more complex social phenomena. The following is a sample
of propositions at the foundation of Homans's theory:

- *The Success Proposition:* "For all actions taken by persons, the more often
  a particular action of a person is rewarded, the more likely a person is to
  perform that action" (Homans 1974: 16).
- *The Stimulus Proposition:* "If in the past, the occurrence of a particular
  stimulus, or set of stimuli, has been the occasion on which a person's action
  has been rewarded, then the more similar the present stimuli are to the
  past ones, the more likely the person is to perform the action, or some
  similar action, now" (1974: 23).
- *The Deprivation-Satiation Proposition:* "The more often in the recent past
  a person has received a particular reward, the less valuable any further
  unit of that reward becomes for him" (1974: 29). This proposition, borrowed from behaviorist psychology, is closely akin to the concept of mar-
  ginal utility in economics.

From simple psychological propositions of this sort, Homans derived more complex propositions governing exchange relationships. Thus:

- *The Rationality Proposition:* "In choosing between alternative actions, a
  person will choose that one for which, as perceived by him at the time,
  the value of the result, multiplied by the probability of getting the result,
  is the greater" (1974: 43). This proposition clearly corresponds to the
  assumption of rationality in neoclassical economics. The rational actor
  weighs not only the potential profit to be gained by pursuing a given course
  of action, but also the estimated probability of success. One does not
  normally invest in a new business, for example, if the probability of its
  success seems extremely low.
- *The Rule of Distributive Justice:* "A man [sic] in an exchange relation with
  another will expect that the rewards of each man be proportional to his
  costs . . . and that the net rewards, or profits, of each man be proportional
  to his investments—the greater the investments, the greater the profit.
  . . ." Hence, "the more to a man's disadvantage the rule of distributive
  justice fails of realization, the more likely he is to display the emotional
  behavior we call anger" (Homans 1961: 75). This concept of distributive
  justice is directly pertinent to a body of social-psychological literature
  known as equity theory (Walster 1972). It says, in effect, that we become
  angry when we believe we have received significantly less in return than
  we have contributed to a social relationship.

Criticisms and Elaborations of Exchange Theory

Homans hoped to build a general science of social behavior on the foundation of propositions such as these. But critics have challenged Homans's formulation of exchange theory on several grounds (Turner 1991: 317–22; Scott 1995). His neo-classical economic assumption of rationality presumes that human beings weigh benefits and costs in a coolly calculating manner, and that the rewards and costs they receive are the result of these calculations. Thus, the theory does not take nonrational motives into account, nor does it account for the rewards and costs that people receive inadvertently, through no conscious choice of their own.

Critics further note that the theory's propositions are tautological and there-fore unfalsifiable. Because its key concepts are defined in terms of each other, its core propositions are valid simply by definition. Thus the theory asserts that people make choices based on what they value, and we know what they value by ob-serving the choices they make. Given the circular logic of Homans's propositions, it is difficult to imagine how they could possibly be refuted.

Finally, Homans's theory reduces complex social phenomena to the level of individual psychology (a strategy sometimes called psychological reductionism or methodological individualism), precluding the possibility that social structures might emerge according to higher-order principles of their own that transcend the principles that govern individual behavior. Psychological reductionism fails to acknowledge that the social whole is more than the sum of its parts, because relationships among the parts (i.e., among individuals) are not contained within the parts themselves, considered separately, but emerge only through their inter-action.

Social structures have properties all their own over and above the properties of the individuals who comprise them. Thus, the very same set of individuals might be organized in a variety of different configurations. They might be ar-ranged, for example, in a tall, pyramidal structure with many layers of authority, or alternatively, in a flatter and more egalitarian configuration—same individu-als, different social structure. Homans's exchange theory may tell us a great deal about the motivations and choices of individual actors, but it is less successful in accounting for the larger social structures that limit their choices and constrain their actions. In short, it tells us more about the mice than about the maze.

Among the external constraints that social actors face daily are the structured inequalities of power that exist in virtually all human groups. Some actors, by virtue of the positions they occupy within social structures, have vastly greater access to economic, political, and symbolic resources than do others, and these inequalities of power confer bargaining advantages on the more powerful in their exchanges with those less powerful. Homans had rather little to say about such one-sided power relationships. Peter Blau, in an improved version of exchange theory, was more attentive than Homans to the role that power advantages play in social exchange. In *Exchange and Power in Social Life* (1964), Blau observed that power inequalities create enormous potential for conflict in social groups. It is often in the interest of dominant parties to establish norms of reciprocity that subordinates accept as fair and legitimate. To do otherwise is to invite the mutual exchange of punishments, rather than the exchange of desired rewards, in the form of labor strikes, civil unrest, and even social revolution.

Blau's version of social exchange theory surpassed Homans's in still another respect. While Homans confined his analysis mainly to microlevel interactions among individuals, Blau's analysis rose to the macrolevel, applying the principles of social exchange to large-scale relations among groups, and even to entire societies. Thus, Blau went beyond the limits of individual psychology toward an analysis of the larger social structures, including power structures, that channel and constrain individual choices.

A variety of studies have investigated exchange relations, although not always within the formal context of Homans's and Blau's theories. In *All My Kin*, for example, Carol Stack (1974) examines the reciprocal exchange of material goods and personal assistance as an essential strategy for economic survival in African American communities, while John Scanzoni (1982), in *Sexual Bargaining*, unsentimentally analyzes intimate relationships as products of power politics and negotiated exchange. Many others besides Homans and Blau have employed economic concepts in their sociological analyses. Kingsley Davis's and Wilbert E. Moore's (1945) influential theory of social stratification, for example, implicitly relies on the economic concepts of supply and demand to account for the unequal distribution of rewards among occupations (Grandjean 1975). Robert Merton's ([1948] 1968: 73–138) classic formulation of structural-functionalism resembles a cost-benefit analysis in its postulate that persisting social and cultural forms show a net balance of positive consequences (taking into account hidden or latent costs and benefits) for a given social system. Others have invoked the economic metaphor of "social capital" to describe the noneconomic resources (such as prestige, trust, and communal spirit) that social groups use to their advantage (e.g., Bourdieu 1984; Coleman 1990; Fukuyama 1995; Putnam 1995, 2000). Nonetheless, Homans and Blau were among the first to apply economic concepts explicitly and systematically to the study of social relations.

From Rats to Rational Choice

What was once known as exchange theory is now largely superseded and absorbed by a larger and more powerful theoretical movement known as the theory of rational choice (Heath 1976; Elster 1986; Coleman and Fararo 1992)—or simply "rat choice" to its detractors. Rational choice theory originated in economics, but by the Reagan era of the 1980s it was sweeping across the social sciences. Like exchange theory, rational choice theory borrows key assumptions from neoclassical economics (Green and Shapiro 1994: 13–17; Abell 1996). Common to these approaches is the assumption that human beings make choices based on rational calculations of reward and cost in the pursuit of their self-interests. It is important to realize that *rational*, as the word is used in these circles, is generally a euphemism for "cunningly selfish," as though there were some necessary connection between reason and self-interestedness. Thus, one rational choice theorist (Elster 1989: 28) states that to "act rationally is to do as well for oneself as one can," uncritically equating reason with selfishness. But in fact, one could just as well be rationally altruistic, provided that one pursued the well-being of others in the most intelligent way possible. We will have more to say about economic abuses of the term *rationality* further on.

Rational choice theory first emerged in political science as an attempt to explain political behavior in economic terms (e.g., Arrow 1951; Downs 1957; Buchanan and Tullock 1962; Olson 1965). From this perspective, voters are viewed as "consumers" in the political marketplace (Green and Shapiro 1994: 1), and campaign contributions and other political behaviors are seen as "investments" in future political outcomes (Snyder 1990). Rational choice approaches sometimes go by other names, such as public choice, social choice, or simply the economic approach to politics and human behavior (Becker 1976; Elster and Hylland 1986; Bonner 1986; Hindness, 1988; Monroe 1991).

Rational choice theory surpasses exchange theory in the technical sophistication of its arguments, now often expressed in elegant mathematical equations and diagrams. James Coleman's monumental *Foundations of Social Theory* (1990), for example, carries over into sociology much of the analytical apparatus that modern economists rely on to build logical and mathematical models of economic phenomena. Critics of neo-classical economics often note a lack of correspondence between its abstract models and the gritty, messy realities of actual economies. But defenders of economic theory counter that such formal, idealized models are as essential to economics as they are to any other science, and that the models do predict, at least to some degree, the actual behavior of economic systems. Coleman, by importing formal economic analysis into sociology, has hoped to raise social analysis to a higher level of scientific rigor and respectability.

Rational choice theory begins with the assumption, previously articulated by Homans, that the probability of a choice is a function of two factors: (1) the actor's calculations of the potential rewards and costs of a given choice, multiplied by (2) the probability of achieving the desired result. Thus, if I am deciding whether to buy a lottery ticket, I consider not only the potential payoff (let us say $1 million) and the cost of the ticket ($1), but also the probability of winning the jackpot (one in two million).

Rational choice theory incorporates elements of mathematical game theory (which we will consider in the next chapter) into its analyses (Abell 1996). When we play strategic games, we make choices with an eye toward the choices we think others will make, and other players do likewise. Thus, if my chances of winning a lottery jackpot depend on how many others are competing for the same pot, I am more likely to buy a ticket if I believe that few others are buying tickets in the same lottery, for then my investment has a greater probability of paying off.

We make investment decisions of this kind every day. Indeed, from a rational choice perspective, every aspect of our lives (including even our spiritual lives) may be viewed as a kind of investment portfolio (Iannaccone 1995; Spickard 1998). We are each in the business of deciding where to invest our limited time, energy, money, and other resources in order to realize the maximum possible gain. Should we spend more time advancing our careers or enjoying friends and family? Should we commit ourselves to a religious organization, or would our limited resources be better spent in recreational pursuits? Our choices are influenced by numerous considerations, including our initial preferences, the amount of resources we have to invest, our knowledge of the probable returns on alternative investments, and our willingness to take risks. Rational choice theory also employs the economic concept of *opportunity costs* in its analyses. In deciding where to invest, I must consider not only the potential payoff of investing in A, but also the opportunities I would lose by not investing in B instead. Every resource (time, energy, money, etc.) not invested in A is a resource I might have invested elsewhere at a higher rate of return.

If each of us is an investor, society is the marketplace in which we meet to make our deals. Pursuing this analogy, the economic sociologist Gary Becker (1976, 1991) has received the Nobel Prize for his ingenious applications of economic principles to seemingly noneconomic social phenomena. Becker interprets mate selection, for example, as a rational calculation of rewards and costs among prospective partners in "marriage markets" governed by supply and demand. (A similar analysis could be applied to the study of singles bars as "meat markets.") Who marries whom depends on the quality and availability of prospective commodities in the marriage market and the resources that each prospective partner has to offer. Romance, political participation, religious involvement, and other social phenomena are thus largely reduced to the laws of economics—laws that are thought to govern the social world in much the same way that physical laws govern the world of matter.

Like exchange theory, rational choice theory suggests a commercial or capitalist image of human nature. Social life is a series of transactions in which each of us is at once both consumer and commodity. The theory generally "expects" human beings to engage in self-seeking behavior, and thus altruistic or self-sacrificing behavior is apt to be interpreted as "irrational." In the theory world of rational choice, the association of rationality with self-interest sends the subtle message that people are not supposed to act selflessly, a message clearly contrary to the teachings of many ethical and religious traditions. If it is true, as Willer (1992: 72) remarks, that no theory is value free and no values are theory free, then what are the hidden value commitments of rational choice theory? Implicitly, the theory would seem to endorse the virtue of selfishness (Rand 1964), rationalized by Adam Smith's faith that the efficient pursuit of private self-interest contributes ultimately to the common good.

Although their point of departure is the self-interested individual, some theorists have attempted to explain seemingly altruistic social commitments in rational choice terms. Michael Hechter (1987), for example, in *Principles of Group Solidarity*, has employed the tools of rational choice theory to explore the conditions under which individuals form social commitments that extend beyond themselves. Hechter finds that a strong sense of social commitment is most likely to occur in groups whose members depend on each other for the production and consumption of goods and who can effectively monitor and sanction each other's contributions to the common good. Conversely, social solidarity is weaker in groups whose members are less dependent on one another for goods, less able to monitor and sanction each other's behavior, and freer to exit the group in search of alternative opportunities. The conditions that foster group solidarity are, in general, more likely to be met in small than in large groups (Turner 1991: 364), in culturally homogeneous than in heterogeneous groups, and in groups whose membership is obligatory rather than voluntary. Insofar as some societies (such as Japan) meet the conditions for group solidarity more fully than do others (such as the United States), we would expect the former to be more communal and socially cohesive.

When rational choice theorists analyze large-scale, macrolevel phenomena, they typically treat social groups as "corporate actors" who behave much like individual actors in the rational pursuit of their collective interests (Coleman 1990). Thus, business corporations, state bureaucracies, and other large organizations, much like individual actors, pursue their goals with an eye toward the potential rewards, costs, and probabilities of success that will likely result from the pursuit of a given course of action. But whether at the microlevel of the individual actor or the macrolevel of the corporate actor, rational choice theory tends to view social life as a quest to maximize one's own advantage.

Of Mice and Mazes

When rational choice theorists turn their attention to the design of public policy, they focus particularly on the structure of incentives and disincentives that individual and corporate actors encounter when they make choices. To put the matter metaphorically, their attention shifts from the self-interested psychology of individual mice to the structure of the maze in which the mice happen to be running, and to the location of the cheese. That mice like cheese is simply a given in this theory, although rational theorists readily acknowledge that different mice may like different kinds of cheese, and likewise that human beings may pursue many different kinds of rewards. The key to policy making, from a rational choice perspective, is to structure the maze and locate the cheese in such a way as to produce some desired behavior, inducing individual or corporate actors to act in socially beneficial ways. Through the strategic use of selective incentives (Olson 1965), policy makers thus hope to shape public outcomes.

One controversial policy analysis in the rational choice vein is Charles Murray's (1984) critique of the welfare system in the United States as it developed during and after the 1960s. Murray argues that welfare programs unintentionally created a structure of incentives that rewarded overdependence on governmental programs, discouraged welfare recipients from seeking gainful employment, and undermined individual responsibility (especially among husbands and fathers) for the well-being of families. Murray does not argue that welfare recipients were inherently lazy or shiftless, but rather that they were acting rationally within the prevailing rules of the welfare game (a practice sometimes known as "gaming the system"). Murray's proposed solution to this problem was to radically restructure the rules of the game by eliminating virtually all forms of public assistance to the poor, forcing them to rely instead on their own individual, family, and community resources.

Murray's proposal, blending elements of libertarianism and conservatism, reminded many readers of the social Darwinist ideology of the late nineteenth century, which opposed "unnatural" governmental interference in nature's competition to ensure the "survival of the fittest" (Spencer [1864–67] 1966: 630). This is not say, however, that all rational choice approaches to public policy share this ideology. Other policy applications of rational choice theory might include the strategic use of tax breaks and penalties to shape the environmental behavior of polluting corporations, or the use of strategic incentives to reward efficient and responsive performance in public bureacracies (Osborne and Gaebler 1992).

Whether or not one agrees with Murray's draconian proposals, his analysis illustrates one possible rational choice approach to public policy. Murray proposes to shape social behavior by manipulating the structure of incentives and disincentives that rational actors confront (in this instance, by removing governmental incentives to remain dependent). One shapes the behavior of the mouse not by attempting to change the mouse directly, but by altering the shape of the maze or by relocating the cheese. In certain respects this approach resembles Skinnerian behavior modification elevated to the level of public policy, with the rational choice policy maker in the role of experimenter and the rational actor in the role of experimental subject (i.e., the mouse).

There is no question that rational choice theory has opened up new lines of social inquiry by articulating a set of basic assumptions about human nature and exploring their implications with logical and mathematical rigor. In the metaphorical marketplace of ideas, rational choice theory has enjoyed considerable success in recent years, particularly since the Reagan–Thatcher era of the 1980s. It is no accident that variants of this theory flourished at the University of Chicago, the mecca of neoclassical market economics, whose faculty has included Milton Friedman, Gary Becker, James Coleman, and many other prominent intellectual descendants of Adam Smith.

The future of rational choice theory is, however, by no means certain. Donald Green and Ian Shapiro (1994), in a far-ranging critique of its applications in political science research, document that rational choice theory has become a dominant force in political science, accounting for nearly 40 percent of articles in the *American Political Science Review* by the early 1990s. Yet they contend that even if we accept its dubious assumptions, rational choice theory has done a rather poor job of explaining political behavior. For all of its theoretical sophistication, its empirical successes have thus far been meager. Peter Abell (1992) asks: "Is rational choice theory a rational choice of theory?" While Abell thinks it is a sound choice relative to other products available on the shelves of the theory market, many others are not yet sold on it.

Homo Economicus Criticized

Insofar as social exchange and rational choice theories accept and build upon the basic assumptions of neoclassical economics, they are open to many of the same criticisms that have been leveled against *homo economicus*, the economist's model or simplified representation of the rationally self-interested human being. Neoclassical economic analyses typically make certain simplifying assumptions regarding human behavior (e.g., Arrow 1951; Friedman 1953; Green and Shapiro 1994: 13–17). Although these assumptions may vary somewhat from one analysis to another, they typically include the following:

1. *Self-interest.* The neoclassical economic model, as we have previously noted, assumes that we as human beings naturally pursue our own individual self-interests, seeking gratifications and pleasures (or "maximizing our utilities"—hence the term *utilitarian*) without regard for the interests of others except insofar as their interests are compatible with our own. Pushed to its limit, this assumption calls into question the possibility of true altruism, the sacrifice of one's own interests for the sake of others. Classical economists acknowledge that helping others may sometimes be in our "enlightened" self-interest, benefiting us overall and in the long run. But enlightened self-interest is actually quite distinct from true altruism (although the two are often confused), for it involves no long-term net sacrifice of self-interest. Altruistic self-sacrifice is "irrational" in the narrow economic sense of the term (see assumption 4), and therefore has no place in this rationalist model of social reality.

2. *Clear preferences.* The model commonly assumes that each economic actor, at any given moment, has a clearly defined and stable hierarchy of preferences or interests.

3. *Knowledge of alternatives.* The model commonly assumes that each actor has full knowledge of alternative choices available in the marketplace, and of the probable rewards and costs that would result from pursuing one or another alternative choice. This is sometimes known as the assumption of perfect information.

4. *"Rationality."* The model further assumes that each actor pursues his or her preferences "rationally," coolly calculating the balance of rewards and costs that are expected to result from pursuing one or another alternative, and choosing that alternative which maximizes the ratio of expected rewards to costs. Rationality is thus equated uncritically with individual self-interest (e.g., Elster 1989: 28).

5. *Free exchange.* Finally, the model commonly assumes the existence of a free marketplace of exchange in which economic actors make choices without coercion or the threat of coercion.

In reality, each of these assumptions is demonstrably false in at least some circumstances. First, human beings do sometimes sacrifice their own interests for the sake of others. The firefighter who dies to save a child from a burning house, for example, appears to be making a genuine sacrifice. A cynic may try to explain away such sacrifices by claiming that altruistic acts are really acts of self-interest in disguise. Maybe the firefighter was seeking a reputation for heroism. Maybe Mother Teresa was really a self-serving publicity hound or (given her religious beliefs) a shrewd investment strategist with an eye toward her eternal future. In this manner the clever cynic can claim to find a selfish motive in even the most seemingly unselfish act. The cynic's reasoning is unfalsifiable in the final analysis—i.e., stated in such a way that it could not be shown false even if it were so (Popper 1963). Such reasoning may tell us more about the interpreter of the act than about the act itself, and more about the pervasive cynicism of our culture than about human nature in all of its dimensions.

The second neoclassical assumption, that human beings possess clearly defined hierarchies of preference, flies in the face of experience. Many of us, much of the time, are not entirely sure *what* we want. We vacillate, we waver, we are ambivalent and uncertain. To the extent that we do have clear preferences, neoclassical economics takes these preferences as a given and offers no theory to explain how they came into existence, or why we prefer one thing rather than another. Individuals simply prefer what they prefer. Thus neoclassical economics has little to say about the manipulation of preferences through advertising and other forms of rhetoric and propaganda that operate beneath the level of our conscious awareness and control.

Third, the neoclassical model assumes that human beings pursue their preferences rationally. Real human decisions, however, are driven not only by rational cost-benefit analysis, but also by impulses, habits (including addictions), false beliefs, and unconscious motives that may be nonrational, if not plainly irrational, from the standpoint of self-interest.

The economic usage of the term *rationality* is itself problematic. Economists apply the term narrowly to the selection of those means that most efficiently maximize rewards relative to costs in the pursuit of some preferred end. But as Habermas (1970) and others have argued, this purely instrumental conception of reason suppresses critical reflection on the ends toward which means are directed. Thus, if a man finds rape deeply gratifying, his "rational" course of action (in the narrow, instrumental sense) is to assault as many women as efficiently as possible without being caught and punished. Is this really what we want to call rational? Because the words *rationality* and *efficiency* have positive connotations in our culture, their uncritical use in economic analysis camouflages the potentially destructive consequences of purely instrumental behavior. As economists misuse the term, any choice at all—including suicide or mass murder—could hypothetically be construed as "rational" from one self-interested perspective or another (Riker 1990: 173; Green and Shapiro 1994: 18).

A fourth assumption of neoclassical economics, that actors make rational choices based on a complete knowledge of available alternatives and their consequences, is clearly false. Neoclassical economists readily admit that the theoretical assumption of perfect knowledge is rarely met in reality. As finite beings, we make choices based on limited knowledge of alternatives and of the eventual rewards and costs of pursuing one or another course of action. Ours is a "bounded rationality" (Simon 1983), and the boundaries of our knowledge are often painfully limiting.

The fifth assumption of the neoclassical model—perfect competition in a free marketplace—exists nowhere in its pure form. Defenders of neoclassical economics readily concede that this and other assumptions are not fully warranted in real life. But they insist that without some set of simplifying assumptions or basic axioms, no science of human behavior is possible. Borrowing an analogy from physics, they point out that a perfect vacuum exists nowhere in nature, and yet physicists must *assume* a perfect vacuum for the purpose of making predictions about the behavior of matter under hypothetical or idealized conditions. Likewise, neoclassical economists make predictions about human choice based on an idealized set of assumptions, and they contend that these predictions are roughly approximated in the actual behavior of real human beings. Judge us not, they say, by the ultimate validity of our assumptions but by the accuracy of our predictions. On this score, economic science has a mixed record. The old joke is that economists have predicted eight of the past three recessions.

Smith's followers, as we have noted, seem at times to have elevated the laws of the marketplace to the status of laws of nature. The global ascendance of market economies in recent years has no doubt lent considerable prestige to their efforts. But critics of market economics continue to challenge some of the central assumptions of this worldview. They contend that the laws of the marketplace are not universal laws of history, but rather historically specific human inventions—and like all human inventions, limited in their applicability. The market is not an omniscient or infallible god, and its outcomes are not always fair and just. Those who come to the bargaining table with initial advantages tend to multiply these advantages in their exchanges with the less advantaged. Imagine, for example, a rigged game of Monopoly in which some players begin with $5,000 and substantial property while others start with only $100 and no property (Beeghley 1989: 71–72). Those who begin with more resources can afford to buy up everything in their paths, while the unfortunates who follow must spend their meager resources in rent payments, further enriching the rich—hence the old business adage that it takes money to make money. The almost inevitable result of the game (a far more realistic simulation of American society than the original Parker Brothers game) is the familiar Matthew effect (Merton 1973: 439–59): the rich get richer and the poor get poorer owing to the ruthless arithmetic of initial advantage. Not only economic advantages, but educational and cultural advantages as well, are reproduced through time as each new generation inherits the cultural capital (or deficits) of the previous generation (Bourdieu 1984). To vary the game metaphor, some are born with two strikes against them, while others are born on third base and think they have hit a triple. And while it is true that everyone in the game has *some* opportunity to succeed (however miniscule), the game clearly fails to provide anything even remotely approaching equal opportunity. These are hard truths to acknowledge for those of us, like myself, who have enjoyed more than our share of initial advantages. In rational choice terms, honest insights are not always personally profitable.

In market systems, severe inequalities exist not only within but also among societies. World system theorists (e.g., Wallerstein 1974/1980; Chase-Dunn 1989; Frank 1993) note that historically, the emergence of international markets has tended to produce relationships of dominance and dependence among societies, with great powers occupying privileged positions at the center of the world system and dependent societies orbiting their peripheries like planets around a sun. World systems theorists observe that in the relationship between center and periphery, dominant societies have enjoyed exploitive advantages, and have perpetuated and enlarged these advantages through the exercise of inequitable bargaining power, more advanced technologies, superior military force, and the propagation of sophisticated and self-serving ideologies.

From the international to the interpersonal level, critics argue that market systems tend to reduce humanity to the status of a commodity, promoting the instrumental view that others are to be used and even consumed in the pursuit of one's own interests, thereby undermining their moral value as human subjects. In this process we all become "marketable selves" (Swanson 1977), and those who lack the resources currently in demand—whether financial, educational, or personal—are condemned to the status of losers in the social stock market.

No sphere of culture is immune to the values of the marketplace. From a pure market perspective, personal relationships come to resemble business deals. Marriage, negotiated in the mate market, is essentially a contractual arrangement. In the political sphere, voters become purely self-interested "consumers" of political decisions, and politicians become commercially advertised commodities. In the religious sphere, spiritual commitments likewise become consumer choices, made according to taste and preference among competing prepackaged products on the shelves of the religious supermarket (Berger 1967; Spickard 1998). In such a society, everything is for sale (Kuttner 1997), and it is everyone for himself.

Whether or not this social caricature is entirely on the mark, there is no denying that the image of society as marketplace is currently a powerful cultural metaphor in the United States, the world capital of capitalism. With the ascendancy of global corporations, Marxist alternatives to the market system are in retreat. Yet ironically, orthodox Marxism and capitalism share many assumptions in common, including the assumption that human behavior is motivated primarily by material gain and that scientifically discoverable laws (whether Marx's law of historical stages or Smith's law of supply and demand) govern human destiny. If there is to be a compelling alternative to the image of human society as a marketplace, the critique will have to challenge the tendencies toward materialism and economic reductionism that capitalism and Marxism have often shared in common. From what unexpected direction might such a challenge come?

CHAPTER SEVEN

~

Society as Game

There are at least two kinds of games. One could be called finite, the other infinite. A finite game is played for the purpose of winning, an infinite game for the purpose of continuing the play.

—James P. Carse (1986: 3)

Play is the wellspring of human civilization, or so argued Dutch social philosopher Johan Huizinga in his provocative work, *Homo Ludens* ("The Playful Human"). Huizinga traced the origins of such diverse cultural phenomena as theater and religious ritual, law, philosophy, and even war to the universal human impulse to indulge in serious play. For Huizinga, play is no mere frivolous pastime. When animals, children, or adults play, they often do so in earnest. Huizinga noted that free play is paradoxically pointless, yet nonetheless meaningful ([1938] 1950: 16). There is something enchanting and captivating about playing games—something that draws us into their imaginary worlds and seals us off from the world outside. Anyone whose attention has been completely captured by an athletic, chess, or computer game knows the experience of losing oneself in serious play. Games are at once both imaginary and vividly real to those who fall under their spell.

Work also can be a kind of serious play. The work/play distinction seems to dissolve when we lose ourselves in the fascinations of a complex task. Intellectual work in particular can be an intense and intricate game, not unlike the mysterious and infinitely complex "glass bead game" envisioned by Hermann Hesse (1949) in his celebrated novel *Magister Ludi*. Immanuel Kant, the most serious of German philosophers, invoked the gaming metaphor when he referred repeatedly in his writings to "the play of imagination" and the "play of ideas" (Huizinga [1938] 1950: 38), while linguistic philosopher Ludwig Wittgenstein (1953) spent the latter part of his career analyzing cultural performances as "language games."

In the business world, corporate competition is frequently described as a game, a ferocious contest for financial supremacy and market domination in pursuit of the prizes of wealth, power, and glory. In a psychological study of corporate executives, Michael Maccoby (1976) found, perhaps not surprisingly, that the most successful business people tend to be "corporate gamesmen" who regard their work as a form of intensely competitive play.

Play is a kind of pretending, and pretending is essential to the creation of culture. The money we exchange for goods, the borders we draw on political maps, and the stories we watch on stage and screen are credible only because we agree to pretend they are. It is this capacity to pretend, and to invest our pretendings with high seriousness, that make the game—and society itself—possible. The anthropologist Clifford Geertz (1973) found that in the "deep play" of the Balinese cockfight, competitors and spectators earnestly enacted not just the game, but Balinese society itself. The game was no mere diversion from the "real" life of the society; it *was* that reality, expressed in a highly stylized and ritualized form.

Learning the Social Game

Play and games are crucial elements in the process of socializing the young. When children play "mommy," "daddy," "dress-up," "lemonade stand," or "war," they are practicing at positions they may be called upon to occupy in later life. Perhaps more importantly, they are internalizing the cultural assumptions on which such games are based. What better preparation is there for life in a competitive and individualistic market society than to learn the game of Monopoly, in which players are asked to assume uncritically, at least while they are playing, that life is a game whose principal object is the private accumulation of material advantage at the expense of others? The games of youth are subtle indoctrinations into the social games and systems of adult life.

The pioneering social psychologist and philosopher George Herbert Mead (1934) was particularly intrigued by the role that games play in socializing the young. Small children, he noted, begin by playing make-believe games with imaginary playmates and eventually graduate to organized games such as checkers or baseball. In a complex game such as baseball, children must learn not only their own positions but also the positions of others in relation to their own. By analogy, society is a game that requires the capacity to internalize the perspectives of others. Through the mastery of games, Mead argued, children develop the ability to "take the role of the other," learning to view their own positions from within the more general context of the game as a whole, and cultivating their talents for mutual coordination and team play. The mastery of team games in childhood is playful preparation for the serious play of adult life.

Paradoxically, preparing children for life in a competitive market economy demands training in both competition and cooperation. Corporate life, not un-like youth league baseball or soccer, demands high levels of cooperation with one's own corporate teammates even as it demands strenuous competition against the players of rival teams. Corporate rhetoric is rife with sports metaphors. A major corporation styles itself as Team Xerox, and a best-selling book touts the corpo-rate manager as coach (Miller 1994). Sporting imagery is no less evident on the field of political competition, as rival parties and interest groups play "hardball," devise electoral game plans, lobby for level playing fields, and strive to score major legislative victories. For Americans, no less than for the ancient Greeks, athletic competitions are powerful metaphors for the struggle to achieve mastery over oneself and others. Every game seems to offer its own distinctive metaphorical idiom. Football and baseball, for example, present very different poetic opportu-nities; for while football conjures images of helmeted warriors in pitched battle, baseball finds the runner safe at home (Carlin 1997).

We can learn much about a culture from an examination of its favored meta-phors. That newspapers typically devote more space to athletics than to all other cultural endeavors (e.g., education, religion, science and the arts) combined is a revealing commentary on the ordering of our cultural priorities. In North Ameri-can culture today, the popular notion that life is a game, to be played hard and played to win, reflects the positive values we assign to working hard, having fun, and beating the competition. A wearier and more cynical version of the game metaphor depicts work and life as "*just* a game"—i.e., artificial, perhaps duplici-tous, and not to be taken too earnestly. The world-wise among us thus speak sardonically of "the political game," "the dating game" or "the academic game," implying that these tired and jaded routines are existentially empty. These vari-ous usages suggest that the metaphor of the game, like metaphors generally, can mean different things to different people in different contexts.

Gaming and Simulation

Games like Monopoly and football are *simulations* or simplified models of social systems. They selectively represent certain salient features of the social phenom-ena, such as commerce or warfare, on which they are based. Military organiza-tions have long understood the value of simulations in their use of war games as strategic training devices. Social scientists, recognizing the potential of games to model social relations, have devised games of their own which attempt to cap-ture the essential features of social life. Political scientist Bertell Ollman (1978), for instance, has sought to model a Marxist analysis of society in a board game called Class Struggle, a democratic–socialist alternative to Monopoly. A more popular simulation of society is SIMSOC, developed as a teaching tool at the University of Michigan by political sociologist William Gamson (1972). SIMSOC features seven groups (two industries, two political parties, an employee interest group, a mass media group, and a rule-interpreting judiciary) which compete or cooperate with each other in the pursuit of their respective goals. The object of the game is not merely to achieve one's own group goals, but also to achieve societal "success," however players may choose to define this (1972: 4). SIMSOC and other social simulations attempt to reduce social systems to their most essential properties in order to clarify and analyze their underlying dynamics (Raser 1969).

With the advent of computer games, simulations of society (or "virtual societies") will no doubt proliferate and evolve to new levels of sophistication in the years to come. Among the first such computer simulations was the pathbreaking "Limits to Growth" computer model of world system dynamics developed by MIT demographers (Meadows et al. 1972), which forecasted global economic and ecological collapse in the twenty-first century if past trends in population growth, resource depletion, and pollution continued unabated. While the MIT model's assumptions and conclusions have been severely criticized (Meadows et al. 1992), the model will be well remembered for its ambitious scope and innovative methods, if not for the accuracy of its forecasts.

More recently the SIM series of computer simulations games, which debuted in 1989 with the urban design game SIMCity (Wright 1989), has attracted a wide and avid following among the young. Simulations of this kind can be extremely useful in clarifying the basic elements and dynamics of complex social systems. The best simulations are not merely vehicles for amusement and escape from real problems. They also can help to prepare players for active and responsible participation in real communities and societies facing real challenges.

Information Games

Game metaphors seem clearly on the rise in contemporary social theory. Clifford Geertz (1983) has noted that many social theorists today, disillusioned with the nineteenth-century dream of a social physics, have looked to the humanities for fresh metaphors, turning for inspiration to such cultural phenomena as games, theater, and language. Some have dropped the term "social science" altogether in favor of terms such as "cultural studies" to describe the kinds of work they do. Alluding to the promise of gaming analogies, Geertz (1983: 23) remarks that "what the lever did for physics, the chess move promises to do for sociology."

This turn toward cultural metaphors is nowhere more evident than in the intellectual career of the late Erving Goffman (Manning 1992). In his earlier work, Goffman envisioned social life in Shakespearian terms as a kind of theatrical production. In his middle years he explored the image of social life as a strategic game. In his later years, Goffman turned his attention increasingly toward the linguistic aspects of social life. We will return to Goffman's dramaturgical and linguistic periods in later chapters. Here we will consider his fascination with games—and con games in particular—as metaphors for social life, revealed in such works as *Encounters* (1961b), *Interaction Ritual* (1967), and *Strategic Interaction* (1970).

Goffman suggests that we are all like con (short for *confidence*) artists when we scheme to win the confidence of others in our fabricated and self-serving presentations. Goffman was particularly fascinated with the cultural worlds of the spy and the gambler. Spies and other secret agents are constantly engaged in "information games" with their adversaries, conniving to gain as much information as possible from others while disclosing as little as possible about themselves. Perhaps there is a sense in which we are all secret agents enmeshed in the social intrigues of everyday life, concealing those aspects of our lives that threaten to damage the carefully cultivated impressions we seek to convey while at the same time maneuvering to uncover the weaknesses and concealments of others.

At times Goffman implies that we are like casino gamblers, looking to maximize our payoffs through cunning and strategic deception, and following the action wherever it leads without much concern for the well-being of others. In this view we are all hustlers, employing "gambits, ploys, bluffs, disguises, conspiracies and outright impostures" (Geertz 1983: 24–25) in pursuit of our private ends.

In fairness, it must be said that Goffman balanced this cynical view with a recognition that a healthy measure of mutual trust is necessary to sustain social life. If each of us, at every waking moment, had to be on constant guard against the possibility of manipulation and deceit, our lives together would be, as Thomas Hobbes ([1651] 1964) imagined, a hellish war of all against all. Civility demands that we expect a decent level of trustworthiness from others, and that we in turn act in ways that inspire their trust in us.

While one side of Goffman's analysis is Machiavellian, the other side evokes the memory of Emile Durkheim, the early French sociologist who spent much of his life exploring the bonds of solidarity that bind us together as members of society. The Machiavellian Goffman is attentive to our deceptions, but the Durkheimian Goffman is equally interested in the ritualized expressions of mutual trust and respect that are encoded in the norms and customs of everyday life, such as rules of etiquette and ritualized exchanges of common courtesy. Actual human societies exist at some constantly fluctuating point between these polar extremes of total cynicism and total trust. If there were "two Goffmans"—one cynical, the other more hopeful—perhaps it is because he was profoundly aware of the power of both poles, and of the competing forces that each exerts upon us. In our daily lives we are by turns both Machiavellian *and* regardful of the needs of others, both calculating *and* courteous (Manning 1992: 60). Goffman captured both of these moments in his analysis of the games and rituals of everyday life.

Although Goffman devoted most of his attention to face-to-face encounters among social actors, his strategic view of life has implications that far transcend interpersonal interaction. In the late 1950s, near the height of the cold war, Goffman spent a year at Harvard University collaborating with the economist and military strategist Thomas Schelling. Goffman's influence left a deep imprint on Schelling's major work, *The Strategy of Conflict* (1960; Manning 1992: 60–64). In the book's preface Schelling wrote that the "philosophy of this book is that in the study of conflict there are enlightening similarities between, say, maneuvering in limited war and jockeying in a traffic jam, between deterring the Russians and deterring one's own children" (1960: v). International nuclear strategy, no less than interpersonal strategy, involves elements of "saving face" and guessing what the other party is likely to do, leading to chains of reasoning such as the following: "He, thinking that I was about to kill him in self-defense, was about to kill me in self-defense, so I had to kill him in self-defense" (Schelling, quoted in Schell 1982: 200).

The disturbing upshot of this chain of strategic reasoning is that in life-and-death games such as Nuclear Showdown, we must be prepared, on seemingly "rational" grounds, to act irrationally, risking mutual annihilation by threatening to annihilate others if they threaten to annihilate us. In a nuclear age in which the destruction of one side is likely to trigger a last-minute retaliatory strike against the other, there can be no real winners. Yet each side, according to the strategically "rational" logic of deterrence, must "coolly resolve to be crazy" (Schell 1982: 204), even to the point of devising a doomsday machine to guarantee the destruction of all others in the event of one's own destruction. In interpersonal relations, the doomsday strategy is implied in such desperate ultimatums as "If I go down, I'm taking you with me." At the international level, the doomsday strategy could result in a nuclear game with a final score of "Reason: 1, Humanity: 0."

Real-life games, whether played at Goffman's interpersonal level or Schelling's international level, are often played in dead earnest and can be lethal in their consequences. Those who believe that social theory has no "practical" implications for the "real" world simply have no idea of the extent to which such theories, and particularly theories based on the metaphor of the game, have come to permeate strategic policy in the nuclear age. Indeed, the mathematical theory of games to which we now turn was born on the eve of the cold war and has profoundly influenced strategic thinking at the highest corporate, political, and military levels.

Mathematical Game Theory

Nuclear strategy is only one application of a powerful form of game theory that explores the quantitative aspects of games in an analytically rigorous way. Mathematical game theory came to rather sudden prominence in 1944, when the Hungarian mathematician John von Neumann and the Austrian economist Oskar Morgenstern, both émigrés to the United States, created a burst of intellectual excitement with the publication of *The Theory of Games and Economic Behavior*. Von Neumann and Morgenstern built their theory of games on mathematical analogies to ordinary games of strategy such as poker and chess. In recent years their approach has taken hold in fields as diverse as economics, political science, and evolutionary biology. This version of game theory converges at many points with neoclassical economics and rational choice theory discussed in the previous chapter, sharing many of the same strengths and limitations. Whatever criticisms we may make of the assumptions on which it rests (and the criticisms are many), one must acknowledge that mathematical game theory has had a formidable impact across a wide spectrum of social and life sciences in recent decades.

Any form of social interaction that involves strategic play (and there are few that do not) may be interpreted in game-theoretical terms. We are "gaming" in this strategic sense each time we drive in traffic, set prices, negotiate a contract, argue a case in court, or fight a war (Binmore 1992: 3). Anyone who has played games such as poker and chess is already familiar with many of the key concepts of game theory: player, strategy, move, outcome, payoff (i.e., winnings), and the like. Strategic interaction occurs whenever players, in choosing their own moves, take into account the moves they believe other players have made or are likely to make in the future. Strategic interaction thus involves not only induction, or reasoning about the present based on past experience, but also "backward induction" (Poundstone 1992: 228–30), reasoning from hypothetical futures to the present. Players may have less-than-perfect knowledge of the moves that others have made in the past, and they certainly have less than perfect knowledge of what others will do in the future. Therefore, strategic interaction always involves some element of uncertainty.

In strategic games, players continually readjust their own behavior in response to the behavior of others. An old joke may serve to illustrate the dynamic character of strategic play. Imagine a population of restaurant-goers who love the food at the Happy Diner but hate large crowds and long waiting lines. As the joke has it, "No one goes to the Happy Diner any more. It's too crowded." We immediately see the comic absurdity of this claim. If no one goes to the diner, it cannot be crowded. This would be a good time, then, for a hungry diner to visit the restaurant again. But the game theorist is quick to note the paradox that if everyone simultaneously reasons in this way, the restaurant *will* be crowded again, and the diner would have done better to stay away. Restaurant-goers in this example are playing a strategic game, seeking to maximize their payoffs (good food) while minimizing their social costs (crowded conditions). As in most versions of exchange and rational choice theory discussed previously, game theory generally assumes that each player is rationally self-interested—or to put it less attractively, cunningly selfish.

Strategic play often involves elements of deception or bluffing. Thus, in the restaurant game, a cunningly selfish player may strive to improve his or her payoffs by spreading the word that the diner is crowded (a move analogous to bluffing in poker), and then sneaking over to enjoy an uncrowded meal. But woe be unto the player who acquires a consistent reputation for bluffing, for the strategic value of the deception will soon decline and the player's payoffs will diminish accordingly.

The stock market offers another example of strategic play. The stock market may be viewed as a form of legalized gambling, as even the head of the Federal Reserve Board acknowledges (Cassidy 2000: 174), in which players attempt to buy promising stocks at low prices and sell them at high prices. It is in the financial interest of individual investors to "visit" the stock market when it is not crowded with other buyers, and to depart after large numbers of buyers have arrived to drive stock prices higher. The problem is complicated, of course, by the fact that everyone else is also pursuing a "buy low, sell high" strategy, each trying to outsmart the others investors. Inside knowledge of the martketplace (including illegal practices such as insider trading) works to the benefit of sharp investors, signaling the best timing strategies for buying and selling stocks. Game theorists and market analysts have devised sophisticated mathematical models to describe the inner workings of the stock market game, although none of these models has thus far succeeded in predicting the behavior of the market with consistent accuracy.

Real-life games such as those played on Wall Street are messy, complex, capricious, and therefore difficult to analyze. Thus, game theorists have resorted to inventing a multitude of hypothetical "toy games" that simulate the salient features of real-life phenomena, stated in highly abstract and simplified terms that lend themselves more readily to rigorous analysis. By far the most famous such game is *prisoner's dilemma*, invented in 1950 by Merrill Floyd and Melvin Dresher, two scientists working at the RAND Corporation, a military think tank in California (Poundstone 1992: 8). Prisoner's dilemma is a deceptively simple game that has subsequently generated countless volumes of research and analysis.

In prisoner's dilemma, we are asked to imagine that two suspects are arrested for committing a crime. The police lack sufficient evidence to convict either suspect unless they can persuade at least one of them to testify against the other. The police put the suspects in separate cells to prevent them from communicating with each other. They then instruct each suspect as follows:

1. If both confess, both will be sentenced to (let us say) three years in prison.
2. If just one confesses, he or she will go free, but the other will be sentenced to ten years.
3. If neither confesses, they will both be sentenced to one year in prison on some lesser charge.

If you were a suspect under these circumstances, what would you do?

The dilemma can be summarized in a simple payoff matrix as shown below. The "cooperative" strategy means that the prisoners cooperate *with each other* (not with the police) by keeping their mouths shut. The "defect" strategy means that one prisoner refuses to cooperate and instead chooses to testify against the other. The numbers in the matrix indicate the years in prison that each suspect will serve under each joint outcome. Thus:

		Suspect X	
		Cooperates (Remains Silent)	Defects (Testifies)
Suspect Y	Cooperates	$1 \backslash 1$	$10 \backslash 0$
	Defects	$0 \backslash 10$	$3 \backslash 3$

This basic version of prisoner's dilemma can be modified in a variety of ways. For example, we may vary the size of the rewards (or in this instance, punishments) in the payoff matrix, which may accordingly alter the players' choices. We may allow suspects to communicate in advance, engaging in "cheap talk" about whether or not to cooperate with each other. We may increase the number of players beyond two, creating the possibility of coalitions. We may specify a "one-shot" game, or we may allow for repeated iterations of the game over time, so that players have the opportunity to adjust their strategies in response to the strategies of the other. But in every case, the essential logic of the game remains the same. Each player must decide whether to risk cooperation or to defect based on uncertain knowledge of what the other player will do.

Prisoner's dilemma has many analogues in everyday life. Each time we confront a situation in which we must decide whether or not to cooperate with others (e.g., to sign a business contract, to take a marriage vow, or to form a political coalition), we are playing a game that resembles prisoner's dilemma. We must make choices based on judgments about what our partners are likely to do in the future, because their future choices will influence our future outcomes or payoffs, just as ours will influence theirs.

Prisoner's dilemma, like every abstract model of human behavior, is based on certain simplifying assumptions. Just as the quality of a computer's output depends on the quality of its input (the famous "GIGO" principle, or "garbage in/ garbage out"), so does the validity of a model's conclusions depend on the validity of its initial assumptions (the "AICO" principle, or "assumptions in/conclusions out"). The prisoner's dilemma model is no exception. The game makes numerous simplifying assumptions that are often unmet in reality (Axelrod 1984: 11–12). Among these is the assumption that a player will have no moral qualms about choosing a strategy that harms the other player (Axelrod 1984: 125). Game theorists acknowledge that players who care about the welfare of their opponents, who seek to keep moral commitments, or who feel guilty about their choices are not really playing prisoner's dilemma at all, but some other game with different payoffs (Binmore 1992: 313). In other words (although game theorists would surely prefer not to put it this way), prisoner's dilemma and many other toy games assume that players are what psychiatrists call *sociopaths*, persons utterly without conscience or moral scruple. This is the model of human nature that game theorists assume, and perhaps unwittingly promote, when they apply the logic of the prisoner's dilemma to real-life human situations. The sociopathic assumptions of games like prisoner's dilemma are not widely advertised by game theorists, perhaps for strategic reasons.

To those who charge that game theory is amoral, if not outright immoral, in its assumptions, Ken Binmore responds that game theorists "are just as fond of apple pie and their mothers as anyone else" (1992: 382–83). Some would see in this trite response a confirming symptom of the moral vacuity of game theory. Binmore does offer examples of hypothetical games whose payoff matrices reward cooperative "dove" strategies, and thus seem less selfish. But these examples only succeed in demonstrating that in some circumstances it may be in the respective interests of two absolutely selfish and amoral players to cooperate with each other for their mutual benefit (Fudenberg and Tirole 1991: xiii).

Game theorists, like the neoclassical economists discussed in the previous chapter, specialize in the calculation of self-interest, including long-term "enlightened" self-interest. They seem generally less interested in understanding altruism, tending to regard unselfish behavior as "irrational." To be genuinely altruistic is to be willing to act *against* one's own interests (whether crude or enlightened), sacrificing some or all of these interests for the sake of the well-being of others.

Game theorists rightly note that altruistic behavior is severely vulnerable to exploitation and abuse. A person who consistently strives to live according to the golden rule, for example, will be exploited and overrun by hawkish predators in games such as prisoner's dilemma. Thus, game theorists have the numbers to prove that altruism (not to be confused with enlightened self-interest) is a fool's strategy. In this respect, the teachings of game theory and of neoclassical capitalist economics appear to be in direct conflict with those ethical or religious systems, such as Judaism and Christianity, which teach the moral value of genuine self-sacrifice wherein love gives and does not count the cost. This glaring cultural contradiction between economic and religious teachings is rarely acknowledged or discussed openly in the United States. Perhaps it is unprofitable to think about such things.

In the face of moral criticism, game theorists might take up an alternative strategy of defense. They might respond that game theory is not really about human beings per se. The players that populate theoretical games, although they may have fictitious names such as John and Mary, are really only imaginary constructs rather than flesh-and-blood people, and the strategies they employ are only mathematical abstractions, valid under strictly defined conditions that are never fully realized in actual life. Yet the farther game theorists travel down this road of moral escape, the more game theory comes to resemble a purely mathematical game without real-world applications, and hence the more remote and irrelevant it becomes to the lives of real people in real situations.

If we keep the limitations of game theory clearly in mind, we may still derive many valuable insights from it. To the degree that human nature really is fundamentally self-serving, and cannot possibly be otherwise, and to the extent that human beings pursue their interests in a "rational" (understood to mean "cunningly selfish") way, game theory does indeed offer a powerful set of tools for analyzing human behavior.

Many Games, Many Strategies

In the mansion of game theory there are many rooms, each corresponding to a different set of gaming conditions. Standard typologies (e.g., Morgenstern 1968; Davis 1970; Michener 1992) distinguish games according to a variety of criteria, such as the number of players. There are one-person games (such as solitaire) in which a single player competes against chance; two-person games (such as chess); and games that may involve more than two players, or n-person games (such as poker). Games with three players or more, where the rules permit, allow for the possibility of coalitions.

There are games of pure strategy (such as chess), games of pure chance (such as random lotteries, in which the most successful strategy is usually to refuse to play in the first place), and mixed games such as poker, which involve elements of both strategy and chance. Lying somewhere between pure strategy and pure chance are most of the games that we play in our everyday lives.

Games also may be classified according to the structure of their payoffs. In zero-sum or constant-sum games, such as poker and chess, the payoffs are fixed, such that the total amount that winners win is exactly equal to the amount that losers lose. Thus, in chess the winner wins the whole game and the loser loses the whole game. In a hand of poker, each chip a winner takes is a chip that someone else has lost. Positive winnings plus negative losses equal zero—hence the term *zero-sum*.

While zero-sum games are always win-lose, variable-sum games allow for the possibility of win-win outcomes. Thus, economist Lester Thurow (1980) has argued that a stagnant economy is a kind of zero-sum game, while a growing economy is a variable-sum game. In a zero-sum economy, all segments of society must fight over a fixed quantity of economic pie, with nasty results, since one segment's gain must necessarily be another's loss. The "win-win" alternative, Thurow points out, is to stimulate economic growth so that the total payoff (the size of the economic pie) expands, hypothetically allowing every segment of society to enjoy a larger slice of prosperity.

Zero-sum games are like all-out war—competitive by the very nature of their payoff structure. They leave little room for cooperation, let alone altruism. Again, consider chess—a game modeled after a zero-sum war between two kingdoms. My object in chess is simply to win, and thereby to make my opponent a loser. If I play chess with my young children, altruistically letting them win, a game theorist will say that I am not *really* playing chess at all, but rather some other game (perhaps a variable-sum, win-win game called "parent's love") with an entirely different set of payoffs.

While some types of games (including zero-sum games) are clearly competitive, others, which Thomas Schelling (1960) calls "coordination games," are structured to reward cooperation. Driving in traffic is a clear example. The object of this game is for each driver to arrive at his or her destination without colliding with other motorists. It is in the enlightened self-interest of all motorists to coordinate their actions for the sake of a common good from which all benefit. Here is an example of a variable-sum coordination game that allows everyone the possibility of winning. Most games in human society are "mixed-motive" games, involving elements of both competition and coordination (Schelling 1960; Manning 1992: 62). In a certain sense, all rule-governed games are simultaneously competitive and cooperative, because in any rule-governed competition, players must simultaneously cooperate to uphold the rules that undergird their competition. Otherwise the game collapses.

Just as there are many kinds of games, so are there many kinds of strategies. In zero-sum games, for example, a "minimax" strategy is generally recommended—a conservative strategy in which each player chooses the option that minimizes his or her maximum possible loss. Psychologists find, however, that strategies may vary depending on the personalities of the players. While some players tend to choose strategies that minimize risk (such as "minimax"), others are inclined toward riskier strategies that offer the possibility of larger payoffs. Some players may play a single strategy consistently, while others may vary or mix their strategies, like baseball pitchers who vary their pitches to confuse the batter (Poundstone 1992: 59), or like poker players who usually play a hand straight but sometimes bluff to avoid becoming too predictable.

Real-life games are considerably more complicated than toy games like prisoner's dilemma. In real life, players may value many different kinds of payoffs (e.g., money, social approval, self-respect, or the well-being of others) and may be involved in a multitude of different games (e.g., occupational and professional games, family games, political games, religious games) simultaneously. This often creates problems as players seek to juggle the conflicting demands of their respective games all at once, as any working parent well knows.

In real life, no game is played in an artificial vacuum. Games are often interconnected or nested (i.e., games-within-games). It is not always clear where one game ends and another begins, which complicates the analysis of a player's actions (Tsebelis 1990). A player's behavior may appear to be irrational within the context of one game, but rational within the context of another. Thus, the medical missionary who chooses to care for the sick in a developing country plagued by epidemics is acting irrationally in the "protect your own health" game, but more intelligibly within the context of a "religious devotion" game, especially if the missionary believes that the ultimate reward for such devotion, in some divine payoff matrix, is eternal life. Note that it is players' perceptions of available payoffs that motivate their choices, whether these payoffs are realized or not.

Tragic Games

Perhaps the most important theoretical insight that emerges from game theory is the paradoxical realization that strategies which appear to be rational from the standpoint of individual self-interest may have tragic consequences for the group as a whole, and ultimately for its individual members. Thus, in the classic one-shot prisoner's dilemma game, the attempt by each player to avoid punishment by testifying against the other will, paradoxically, result in maximum losses for both players if each pursues what appears to be the rationally self-interested strategy (Poundstone 1992: 277).

Garrett Hardin (1968) teaches the same lesson in his famous parable of the "tragedy of the commons." Suppose that a group of herdsmen, each with his own cattle, is allowed unrestricted use of a common pastureland. It is in the individual, short-term interest of each herdsman to allow as many cattle as possible to graze the common lands. But if each herdsman pursues his own individual self-interest in this manner, the pasture is soon exhausted and the herdsmen come to a common ruin. Once again the common good is subverted by the pursuit of individual self-interest. (One wonders whether the outcome of Hardin's thought experiment might have been different if the herdsmen had instead been a group of more cooperative and communally minded herdswomen!)

A similar problem arises in the well-known "free rider" dilemma (Poundstone 1992: 125–29). Suppose that you are a user of a mass transit subway system. When no one is looking, you like to hop over the turnstile and ride without paying. From a narrow economic standpoint, such a move is in your individual self-interest. But if everyone pursued the same self-interested strategy, the subway system would soon be bankrupt, and neither you nor anyone else would enjoy its benefits. The problem of tax evasion poses a comparable dilemma. Everyone wants public services of various sorts, such as streets and highways, police and fire protection, and the like, but few enjoy paying for them—hence the temptation to evade taxes and ride for free. But if everyone rides free, the system soon goes bankrupt and services cease. Problems of free-ridership such as these come up continually in the real world of public policy making.

Game theory can be useful in analyzing voting behavior in democratic systems. From a purely self-interested standpoint it is not "rational" (i.e., shrewdly selfish) to vote unless one expects an election to be extremely close, for otherwise one's vote is unlikely to affect the outcome, and one will have wasted valuable time and energy in the process. (For this reason, one prominent political scientist is reputed to pride himself on going to the polls only when he expects a close vote.) Yet paradoxically, if most voters were to follow this rationale and stay away from the election booth, each remaining vote would have an increased likelihood of affecting the outcome, thus increasing the potential payoff for voting.

The foregoing analysis presupposes that there is no other reason to go to the polls than to determine an election's outcome. But in fact, every act of voting is really two votes: one for the candidates and the other for the democratic process itself. One could perhaps argue that choosing not to vote amounts to a vote against the democratic process, constituting a "free ride" on the democratic system at the expense of those who take their civic responsibilities more seriously.

One of game theory's most tragic scenarios is the game of "chicken." Two drivers speed toward each other in a straight line, each hoping the other will swerve at the last possible moment. If one swerves, the other "wins." If both swerve in opposite directions, they tie. But if neither swerves, they both lose not only the game but their lives. By analogy, two international powers that threaten each other with mutual annihilation in a game of nuclear chicken risk destroying themselves, each other, and countless millions of innocent bystanders by striving to win a game that threatens to destroy them both. In the nuclear era, the traditional notion that large-scale wars can be "won" is increasingly obsolete (Schell 1982). The truly rational solution to the chicken dilemma is not to play the game more skillfully, but rather to avoid playing the game altogether.

Some games can result in vicious cycles. Consider, for example, Martin Shubik's (1971) dollar auction. Imagine a game in which a dollar is auctioned off to the highest bidder. Furthermore, suppose that the second bidder is expected to pay off as well, but receives nothing in return. Two bidders thus enter a vicious cycle in which each continues to outbid the other in an effort to avoid coming in second and thus sustaining a total loss of investment. Game theorists find that in actual practice, competitors continue to bid against each other long after their bids have exceeded one dollar. Each bidder continues to throw good money after bad "so that all won't have been in vain," because both have too much invested to quit and thus cut their losses. Real-world analogies to the dollar auction have been observed to include U.S. involvement in the war in Vietnam and the nuclear arms race (Poundstone 1992: 270–72), both of which threatened to spiral out of control as each side in the conflict continued to escalate its sunk investments. As in the prisoner's dilemma and the tragedy of the commons, the wisest strategy, one can well argue, would have been to avoid the game in the first place.

Cynicism and Hope

By now it should be obvious that game theory is more than a mere intellectual amusement. Game theory is not just a game. The fate of the earth may depend upon our grasp of its basic principles and appropriate applications. And the deeper tragedy of tragic games such as prisoner's dilemma, tragedy of the commons, chicken, and dollar auction is that we cannot always avoid them, try though we may. Once one is in a payoff matrix, there may be no avoiding difficult and painful choices. And all of us are always in payoff matrices of one sort or another, whether we want to be or not.

Early game theorists such as John von Neumann and John Nash were well aware that game theory has serious implications for real life. Their cynical and pessimistic view of human nature, combined with their mathematical analyses, led them to some rather grotesque conclusions. Von Neumann's deep cynicism is

apparent in his remark that real life "consists of bluffing, of little tactics of deception, of asking yourself what is the other man going to think I mean to do. And
that is what games are about in my theory." Elsewhere he observed that it is "just
as foolish to complain that people are selfish" as it is to complain about the behavior of magnetic or electrical fields (in Poundstone 1992: 6, 235). Von
Neumann's cold vision of the world in the early years of the cold war led him to
recommend that the United States launch a preemptive nuclear strike against
the Soviet Union, at an incalculable cost to human life, to prevent the prospect
of a future Soviet nuclear threat. It was Machiavellian defense intellectuals such
as von Neumann whom C. Wright Mills (1958) had in mind when he warned of
the presence of "crackpot realists" among the American power elite. Von
Neumann is reputed to have been one of the models (Henry Kissinger was another) for the title character in Stanley Kubrick's film *Dr. Strangelove*, which
wickedly satirized the belligerent paranoia of the period. Another prominent game
theorist of the period, John Nash, was in fact committed to a psychiatric hospital
for paranoia (Poundstone 1992: 167) while his colleagues at the RAND Corporation continued to shape defense strategy following World War II, basing their
recommendations, at least in part, on the assumptions and conclusions of game
theory.

Von Neumann and his colleagues represented what we might call the "hawkish" wing of game theory during the postwar period. In general, theoretical hawks
favor "defect" strategies over more dovish "cooperate" strategies in games that
resemble prisoner's dilemma (Poundstone 1992: 128). To risk cooperation, they
argue, is to invite having one's generosity exploited by free riders (such as welfare
cheats) or external adversaries (such as the former Soviet Union). Doves, on the
other hand, are more inclined toward conciliatory and forgiving strategies and
more willing to risk cooperating in the optimistic hope that such cooperation
will be reciprocated. Poundstone (1992: 128) suggests that among game theorists, hawks tend toward political conservatism, while doves tend toward liberalism.

The dovish wing of game theory is represented by theorists who actively explore the possibility of cooperation in the resolution of conflict (hence the title
of a leading game theory periodical, *The Journal of Conflict Resolution*). Anatol
Rapoport has been a leading figure in this movement. In *Fights, Games and Debates* (1960), Rapoport argues for the wisdom of risking cooperative strategies,
even when these might result in short-term losses, for the sake of establishing
long-term trust and mutual benefits.

More recently, the political scientist Robert Axelrod has developed Rapaport's
line of argument further. In *The Evolution of Cooperation* (1984), Axelrod notes
that while a one-shot prisoner's dilemma game rewards defection, an iterated game

in which players meet each other in repeated rounds may well reward mutual cooperation. To test this possibility, Axelrod organized a round-robin tournament, inviting game theorists from far and wide to submit prisoner's dilemma strategies to be run in competition against each other with the aid of a computer. The competition would comprise 200 rounds per game, with a maximum payoff of five points per round or 1,000 points per game. Among the fourteen strategies submitted, the tournament winner turned out to be the simplest one of all, a strategy called "tit for tat" submitted by none other than Rapoport himself.

"Tit for tat" instructs a player to cooperate in the first round of prisoner's dilemma (by remaining quiet and refusing to testify against the other player) and then to imitate whatever the other player did in the previous round. In short, the strategy calls for a "nice" first move, and thereafter mirrors the behavior of the other player. After the first move, the other player is unwittingly playing a mirror-image of himself. Thus, whatever "personality" the other player's strategy has, whether generous or vicious, will soon come back to help or haunt the player.

"Tit for tat" is not the golden rule (a consistently cooperative strategy that would be easily exploited by a vicious adversary), but it is the next best thing: Do unto others as others would do unto you, or *suffer the consequences* (Poundstone 1992: 240). In this regard it resembles the Old Testament maxim, "an eye for an eye and a tooth for a tooth," which was in any case an improvement over the previous rule, "a thousand eyes for an eye and a thousand teeth for a tooth." "Tit for tat" punishes defection immediately, but it is also a "forgiving" strategy inasmuch as it "forgets" past defections as soon as the opponent chooses to follow the path of cooperation.

In a follow-up tournament, Axelrod challenged game theorists to submit strategies that could beat "tit for tat." Despite the best efforts of sixty-two entrants from six countries, "tit for tat" won again. This is not to say that "tit for tat" is the perfect strategy for every occasion. It does better against some strategies than against others (Poundstone 1992: 244–46). One problem in real-world applications of "tit for tat" is that while one party may regard its response as proportionate to the previous move of an opponent (i.e., as tit for tat), the opponent may interpret the same response as disproportionate (three tits for a tat) owing to psychological or cultural differences in the meanings that the respective players assign to given actions. I may *think* I'm playing "an eye for an eye," but from the other player's point of view I may be playing "three eyes for an eye." The logical result of this miscommunication is a vicious cycle of escalated violence. Yet despite limitations of this sort, "tit for tat" remains the leading contender among competing strategies, offering hope that mutual cooperation might win out in the long run against hawkish cynicism and short-term selfishness.

Civilization itself is built upon mutual cooperation, and so it is in the interest of civilized people everywhere to seek cooperative strategies for the resolution of conflict. Axelrod offers a series of practical suggestions for promoting cooperation (1984: 124–41). Prospects for cooperation increase, he observes, when players know that they are likely to meet each other again in the future. Under the "shadow of the future," players are less likely to exploit each other for present gain for fear of future retaliation. (It has been suggested, for example, that one reason for increasing crime rates in past decades is that people have lived increasingly in the anonymous environments of large metropolitan areas, where criminals are unlikely to face future encounters with potential victims). Policies that increase the likelihood of future encounters accordingly increase the likelihood of cooperative behavior.

Axelrod observes that the probability of cooperation also increases when we alter the payoff matrix by raising the payoffs for cooperation and the penalties for defection. Government policy can play an important role in promoting cooperation by establishing higher incentives for prosocial behavior (such as energy conservation) and higher penalties for antisocial behavior (such as crime or environmental irresponsibility). The chances of cooperation further increase when citizens are taught, preferably from an early age, to care about the well-being of others. Human preferences are, to a considerable degree, learned rather than purely innate. When we are taught, and teach our children in turn, to prefer arrangements that serve others as well as ourselves (whether from genuinely altruistic motives or from our own enlightened self-interest based on the principle of reciprocity), we increase the likelihood of cooperative behavior. Finally, Axelrod concludes, we increase the likelihood of cooperation when we recognize and respond to the past behaviors of others, or in other words, when we make choices with as much information as possible about how others have acted in the past and their prospects for cooperative interaction in the future.

Biological Games

Axelrod's research converges at many points with recent applications of game theory to problems in evolutionary biology. Contrary to the popular image of Darwinian evolution as a relentlessly vicious and violent struggle for survival—"nature red in tooth and claw"—we actually find in nature innumerable instances in which organisms and species survive and prosper by cooperating with each other to their mutual advantage, as well as instances of competition and conflict. How are such patterns of cooperation and conflict amenable to game theoretical analysis?

Several prominent evolutionary biologists, including John Maynard Smith

(1982) and Richard Dawkins (1989), have discovered ingenious applications of game theory to "strategies" in nature. At the core of their analysis is the concept of the evolutionarily stable strategy, or ESS, analogous to the concept of equilibrium in game theory. A population of organisms is said to be playing an ESS if a strategy adopted by most of the population's members is not surpassed by any alternative strategy, as measured by genetic survival and reproductive success (Dawkins 1989: 69–70).

Suppose, for example, that within a population of a given species there are two available strategies for resolving conflict. The hawk strategy instructs the organism always to fight in a conflict situation, and to retreat only when seriously injured. The dove strategy instructs the organism to threaten, but never to harm, an opponent, and to retreat if a fight starts. Thus, when a hawk strategist plays against another hawk strategist, one hawk wins but the other is seriously injured. When hawk plays dove, dove runs away and hawk wins by default. And when dove plays dove, they split the payoff evenly between them (minus the loss of time and energy spent exchanging false threats—time and energy that might have been spent more profitably elsewhere). Which of these two strategies, hawk or dove, is superior from an evolutionary standpoint?

Game theory suggests that the answer depends on the relative proportion of hawks and doves in the population. In a population consisting almost entirely of doves, a few hawks will have a field day (because they always defeat doves), and their numbers will soon increase dramatically as their survival advantage is reproduced genetically in subsequent generations. But as the hawk population grows, hawks increasingly find themselves in costly combat with each other, and the injuries they inflict on each other soon drive down the payoff of the hawk strategy relative to the dove strategy. The proportion of doves increases accordingly, until the payoff of the dove strategy equals the payoff of the hawk strategy. At this point, the proportion of hawks and doves has reached a stable equilibrium, such that any further increase in the population of doves will trigger an increase in the proportion of hawks, and vice versa.

Now suppose that a third strategist, the "retaliator," enters the picture. The retaliator plays a conditional strategy, acting like a hawk when attacked by another hawk, but acting like a dove when it meets a dove. The retaliator never initiates violence, but simply mirrors the moves of the other player, as in Rapoport's "tit for tat" strategy. The retaliator strategy has been shown to equal the performance of the dove strategy and to do better than the hawk strategy, although other mixed strategies may outperform the retaliator (Dawkins 1989: 283).

One major criticism of game theory has been that it assumes perfect rationality on the part of players (Peterson 1994). Interestingly, biological applications of game theory cast serious doubt on the need for a rationality assumption in game theory. As currently applied by evolutionary biologists, game theory can account for the behavior of species (even plant species) which have little or no capacity for conscious reason. Biologists have amply demonstrated that natural selection, operating on genetic variation, frequently produces results that mimic rational design without being the products of conscious rationality. Thus, Dawkins (1986) has described natural selection as a kind of "blind watchmaker" capable of producing elegant designs in nature that do not presuppose any sort of conscious purpose or rational plan, whether divine or human.

When evolutionary biologists say that organisms and species play "games," execute "strategies," and exhibit elegant "designs," they are usually speaking figuratively, invoking the language of planning and purpose as a clever metaphorical shorthand for explanations that are ultimately nonteleological. The living world behaves *as if* it were the product of conscious design, they would say, and no harm is done in talking about nature's "purposes" so long as we understand that what is being spoken is a kind of scientific poetry. One prominent evolutionist (Wright 2000), however, has recently speculated that evolution, insofar as it creates non–zero-sum or cooperative (i.e., potentially win-win) games, may be said to have the ultimate direction or "purpose" of producing ever more complex and interdependent forms of life, both biological and cultural. Furthermore, we would argue that some forms of life created by evolution, such as human beings, do in fact create purposes and goals for themselves, and are therefore special examples of teleology in nature. Human beings, as purposeful creatures, are capable of consciously altering the course of evolution itself to some small degree. It follows, therefore, that nature is not entirely without purpose.

Life as Game

While game theory may not require the assumption that players are consciously rational, it does assume that they are, in some sense, "selfish"—whether the blind "selfishness" of genes that behave as if they are trying to maximize their reproductive success (Dawkins 1989) or the more sighted selfishness of human actors. Game theory suffers from some of the same limitations as neo-classical economics, discussed in chapter 6. Game theorists can talk about *enlightened* self-interest when one player's interests happen to coincide with the interests of others. But they have little to say about the possibility of moral sacrifice for the sake of others, except to say that such altruistic behavior is a fool's strategy from the standpoint of rational self-interest.

Game theory is itself a seductive intellectual game, and its insights are many. But it is perverse when it entices its players to accept uncritically the necessity or inevitablity of selfish rationality, not merely as a description of human nature but (more subtly) as a normative expectation and standard of judgment. In the world of competitive games, smart people are *supposed* to behave selfishly. Those who enter this intellectual labyrinth may win the game but lose their ethical sensibilities.

The Nobel Prize–winning physicist Richard Feynman unwittingly made this point when he confessed a great personal debt to John von Neumann, patriarch of mathematical game theory:

> Von Neumann gave me an interesting idea: that you don't have to be responsible for the world that you're in. So I have developed a very powerful sense of social irresponsibility as a result of von Neumann's advice. It's made me a very happy man ever since. But it was von Neumann who put the seed in that grew into my *active* irresponsibility. (quoted in Poundstone 1992: 26)

It is hard to imagine a more revealing tribute to the moral depth of the theory of competitive games.

The philosopher Ludwig Wittgenstein (1953) observed that all of us, all of the time, are caught up in the "language games" that we have learned as members of society. Game theory is itself a kind of language game—a game about games, the object of which is to say insightful things about the games people play. Binmore (1992: 3) goes so far as to suggest the imperial possibility that "all of the social sciences are nothing more than subdisciplines of game theory."

What is it about our time in history that inclines us to view all of life as one great elaborate game—or perhaps more aptly, a loose and fragmented collection of mutually unintelligible games, as postmodern philosophers (e.g., Lyotard and Thebaud 1985) sometimes suggest? References to life-as-game permeate our popular culture, from popular psychology (e.g., Berne 1964) to popular movies such as *The Game*. Athletic, video, and computer games are national obsessions. Business is a game ("I'm in the insurance game. What game are you in?"). Manipulating bureaucratic rules to one's own advantage is a game (hence the term *gaming the system*). Personal relationships are a game among "players" ("Did you score?"). Politics, education, and even war are now described in the metaphorical language of gaming, with "war games" preparing high-tech militaries for conflicts that increasingly resemble video games. Do we control this metaphor, or does it control us? Are we playing the social game, or is the social game playing us?

Whether Huizinga was right to claim that play is the wellspring of civilizations, the game is certainly a central theme in contemporary North American civilization, readily apparent in virtually every sphere of our lives. Perhaps no metaphor in social theory more aptly captures the fast-paced, exciting, competitive, aggressive, ego-driven, goal-oriented, and amoral character of life in a postmodern consumerist society than does the metaphor of the social game.

CHAPTER EIGHT

∼

Society as Theater

All the world's a stage,
And all the men and women merely players.
They have their exits and their entrances;
And one man in his time plays many parts. . . .
— William Shakespeare, *As You Like It* (II, vii)

William Shakespeare played many parts in his time. Not least among these was the role of social theorist, for as Stanford Lyman and Marvin Scott (1975) observe, Shakespeare's plays were theoretical as well as theatrical productions. Shakespeare's *Macbeth*, for instance, may be read as a theoretical reflection on the emptiness of social titles gained by cynical and duplicitous means. King Macbeth, ascending to the throne of Scotland by an act of murder, and realizing the absurdity of his life in "borrow'd robes," comes to this rueful view of our social condition:

Life's but a walking shadow, a poor player
That struts and frets his hour upon the stage
And then is heard no more: It is a tale
Told by an idiot, full of sound and fury,
Signifying nothing.
—*Macbeth* (V, ii)

In this memorable reflection on the disparity between social appearance and reality, Shakespeare speaks to the existential despair, cynicism, and moral uncertainty of our own time. Throughout his works we find Shakespeare investigating sociological themes long before sociology existed as a distinct field of study, viewing human action sometimes as comedy, sometimes as tragedy, sometimes as history, but always as social drama.

In light of Shakespeare's role as a theatrical theorist, it is interesting to note that the words *theater* and *theory* share a common origin. In ancient Greece, *theoria* were ambassadors sent out to witness various significant events—foreign games, public spectacles, and religious ceremonies—and to return with reports and interpretations of their meaning (Lyman and Scott 1975: 1–2). Modern-day social theorists, like their ancient predecessors, seek to observe and interpret the puzzling phenomena of social life and to insert these interpretations back into the social world they have observed. Theorists are not mere passive spectators of passing scenes, but rather active participants in the unfolding drama of social reality.

Shakespeare was neither the first nor the last to notice that theater mimics social life, and that social life in its turn mimics theater. The theatrical metaphor was already familiar to the ancient Greeks, and by Shakespeare's time it was commonplace (Burns 1992: 107–8). But Shakespeare breathed new life into the metaphor, developing its implications with a depth and subtlety rarely seen before or since. More recently, twentieth-century social theorists have revisited the theatrical metaphor and have developed it in distinctive ways. Two theorists in particular, the sociologist Erving Goffman and the anthropologist Victor Turner, are especially well noted for their dramaturgical analyses of social life. We will consider their contributions shortly. But first let us take a few moments to explore the metaphor on our own, drawing out some of its hidden implications.

Theatrical Analogies and Disanalogies

Before we can ask how social life is like theater, we must first consider the nature of theater itself. A conventional theatrical production typically (though not invariably) displays the following elements: (1) An actor or actors (2) assume the roles of imaginary characters and, (3) with the support and guidance of various confederates behind the scenes (producers, directors, stage crew, benefactors, etc.), (4) rehearse and perform a scripted story (5) authored by a playwright (6) and performed onstage with the aid of props, costumes, and the like (7) in the presence of an audience (including critics), which (8) evaluates the performance and (9) communicates these evaluations through applause, critical reviews, and the like. A feedback loop is closed when (10) audience evaluations reach those who staged the performance, causing them to replicate, alter, or close down the performance. Theater is thus a circular process in which performer and audience exert mutual influence upon each other. As such, it is prototypical of all social interaction. In theater we witness society in microcosm.

Some of these features of conventional theater are more crucial than others.

As the Polish experimentalist Jerzy Grotowski (1968: 19) observes, theater "can exist without make-up, without autonomic costume and scenography, without a separate performance area (stage), without lighting and sound effects, etc." But Grotowski insists that theater absolutely cannot exist in the absence of the actor–audience relationship. Where there is no audience, there is no one to show, and so the show cannot go on.

Also essential to theater is the element of imagination. Actors strive to convey characters that are not strictly or literally real but are, at least in part, creative fictions. In theater there is always some element of contrivance or illusion, driving a wedge between reality and its mere appearance. Theater is "make believe," as performers labor to make audiences believe their performances. Audiences are in turn asked to "play along" with the illusion and share the pretense, temporarily suspending their disbelief that what the actors are pretending is real.

Yet audiences must not be *too* fully taken in by the pretense, lest they mistake appearance for reality, like the naïve spectators in Jane Campion's film *The Piano*, who mistake a stage production for a literal event and storm the stage to save an imaginary victim from an imaginary murderer. The successful theatrical performance is suspended somewhere between the extremes of too much belief on the part of the audience (as in this instance) and too little belief (as when bad actors give painfully unconvincing performances).

Let us consider in more detail some parallels between theater and ordinary social life.

Social Roles

The world of make-believe does not end at the stage's edge. Role theorists have long noted that social actors, like actors on the stage, assume made-up characters and play imagined roles—convincingly or not—in concert with others. A social role is the set of behaviors that an audience expects of a person occupying a given social position. And because each of us occupies multiple positions in the social order (e.g., in the economy, the polity, the family, and so on), each of us in our time plays many parts.

Our multiple social roles may at times pull us in opposing directions, a circumstance that role theorists term *role strain* (when a single role makes competing demands on the social actor) or *role conflict* (when two or more different roles pull the actor in competing directions). Thus, parents often complain that they are painfully torn among the competing expectations of work, family, and other demands, making it difficult for them to play any role well. Like circus jugglers, we are sometimes called upon to keep several balls in the air at once, and we may experience performance anxiety (or stage fright) when we fear that these expectations exceed our limited abilities as social actors.

Some roles are socially inherited or *ascribed* (such as the role of son or daughter), while others are to some degree chosen or *achieved* (such as marital and occupational roles in modern societies). In traditional societies, the roles that one plays are largely beyond one's personal control. Thus, in traditional Indian society one's marriage is commonly prearranged and one's occupation preordained by gender and caste. In modern societies, by contrast, we exercise somewhat more choice in the parts we play and more artistic freedom in how we play them, whether in marriage or in work. Yet even in modern societies these apparently free role choices are often severely constrained by such factors as sex, economic class, and race, which may constrict or expand the access of particular actors to particular roles.

Most social roles existed long before we were born and will continue long after we die. Consider the presidency of the United States. The basic features of the presidential role are inscribed in a constitutional script. More than forty incumbents (including one Hollywood actor) have played the president. And while each incumbent has brought a distinctive interpretation to the performance of the role, the role has thus far survived the actors. Actors come and actors go, but roles may endure (though not unchanged) through many generations.

Sometimes it happens that roles themselves, and the social scripts that link these roles together, undergo fundamental change—particularly in periods of social revolution. Thus, the French revolution destroyed the role of monarch and created the role of democratic citizen in French society. Revolutions in technology have destroyed the role of buggy maker but created the role of beta tester. Even in nonrevolutionary times we are constantly revising our social roles and scripts in collaboration with others, inventing new parts and playing old parts in new ways. It is as though our social scripts were being continually rewritten even as we perform them, with different actors reciting from different versions at any given moment. In the theater of life, we are not all on the same page, or perhaps even in the same play.

Rehearsals

Like stage actors, we rehearse our roles before taking them on the road. Who among us has not had the experience of talking to the mirror, or to ourselves, as we prepare mentally for some coming performance? This ability to rehearse or practice the future, mentally if not physically, is essential to our competence as social actors. Social rehearsals begin in the earliest years of life, in the child's mimicry of adult roles. The social philosopher George Herbert Mead (1934) long ago noted that juvenile role-playing is a critical stage in social development. Through imaginary play, children learn to "take the role of the other"—to imagine social interaction from several points of view—thus gaining a rounded understanding of the interrelationships among roles in the social scripts they will enact later in life. In hunting and gathering societies, for example, small children are observed to "play the hunt," some dressing in animal skins as others chase them down with sticks (Lenski and Lenski 1982: 125). Meanwhile, in advanced industrial societies, privileged children "play office" on their personal computers in preparation for careers in a competitive information economy. In either case, play is children's work, and play-acting is preparation for life's later roles.

Stage Directions

In ordinary life, as in theater, some are positioned to direct performances while others receive direction, or resist direction at the risk of being cut from the cast. Most of us have been both director and directed at one time or another. In corporate settings, for example, middle managers are at once both directors of those below and actors under the direction of those above.

To be directed, whether by choice or circumstance, is to be under remote control. The docile employee, the telemarketer who works from a prepared script, the military recruit in basic training, and the fanatically devoted follower of a charismatic leader may all be viewed, from a certain jaundiced angle, as externally controlled marionettes in life's puppet show. Even directors themselves are externally controlled to the degree that rules and cultural traditions constrain their options. Thus, the theatrical metaphor poses the unsettling thought that we are all, more than we care to acknowledge, animated by directive forces that lie largely beyond our conscious awareness or control.

Casting

In ordinary life, as in theater, we cast others for parts in our personal and public dramas, and they in turn cast us. The job interview, the mate search, and the process of adopting a child all resemble theatrical casting calls, conducted for the purpose of achieving a good fit between actors and their prospective roles. Most of us have had the experience of being "miscast" in roles that others have expected us to play, as well as the experience of being "typecast"—locked into roles we have played in the past—when we would really rather be expanding our repertoires and developing our characters in new directions. Social transitions, such as the transition from high school to college, or from one job or locale to another are, for many, an opportunity to recast or rewrite their social identities, shedding old personas and growing new ones. Interestingly, the English words *person*, *personality*, and *persona* all derive from the same Greek root meaning "actor's mask," implying that in the social masquerade we alter our identities through time and across situations, taking off and putting on personas to suit the occasion.

Costumes and Props

In ordinary life, as in theater, we display costumes and props as accoutrements in the performance of our roles. The officer's uniform, the executive's suit and suite, the judge's robes, the professor's briefcase, and the athlete's gear are all standard stage devices in the fabrication of believable social performances. Standard props, even when they are not technically necessary, serve to prop up performances that might otherwise fall flat, lacking credibility in the eyes of an audience trained to expect them. There is a certain sociological truth in the cliché that clothes make the man (or woman); and there is also a sense in which "makeup," whether lipstick or lumberjack attire, helps the actor to make up a character and to pass it off as real. While costuming is obviously crucial to the performance of certain "exotic" social roles, such as the boundary-transgressing role of the drag queen (Butler 1990), it is no less an ingredient in the performance of more mundane and conventional roles, such as the often highly theatrical role of the heterosexual "regular guy."

～

The theatrical metaphor's popularity and endurance are largely accountable, no doubt, to the ease with which parallels of this kind between theater and ordinary life can be made and understood. But theater and social life are not entirely parallel at every point. Their lines diverge in ways that may be just as revealing as their similarities. Ultimately, theatricality is only one aspect of life, not the whole of it; and the dramaturgical metaphor, like any other, has its limits (Wilshire 1982: 258–81). What, then, are some *disanalogies* between theater and social interaction?

Actor and Audience

In conventional theater the distinction between actor and audience is generally clean and crisp. One is either on stage or seated in the auditorium, but not both at the same time. In ordinary social interaction, by contrast, the distinction between actor and audience is less clear. Imagine, for example, that you are involved in a domestic melodrama (Wallerstein and Blakeslee 1995: 173)—perhaps a heated family discussion around the dinner table. The event is unmistakably theatrical, brimming with impassioned dialogue and histrionic gesture. Where in this family drama does the stage end and the auditorium begin?

Ordinary interaction is a kind of double theater in which we are by turns *both* actor and audience, both participant and observer. Ordinary social interaction thus resembles not so much the conventional theater as the participatory theater (pioneered by the German playwright Berthold Brecht among others), in which the distinction between actor and audience is intentionally subverted. In participatory theater, as in everyday life, the "fourth wall" that separates stage from audience, invisible to begin with, disappears a second time. Actors may address the audience directly, or even venture out into the auditorium to draw audience members (sometimes reluctantly) into the performance, thus turning the entire auditorium into a stage.

Charles Horton Cooley's (1902) notion of the looking-glass self suggests that audiences are like social mirrors in which we monitor and evaluate our own performances. In a more literal sense, Jacques Lacan (1977: 1–8) proposes that the first time children recognize their own images in the mirror is a critical moment in their development, for it is then that they first become the audiences of their own performances. In the mirror, actor and audience are one—an observation worthy of further reflection.

Script and Improvisation

Another noteworthy difference between daily life and theater is that in daily life, action and dialogue almost always arise more extemporaneously than in tightly scripted stage productions. In this respect our daily lives may more nearly resemble improvisational than conventional theater. To be sure, we do rely upon cultural scripts and standard routines to get us through the day, from the general existential scripts that influence our most important life choices (Steiner 1974) to the specific protocols that enable us to drive a car or order a meal in a restaurant (Schank and Abelson 1977; Schank 1990). And we do continually give and receive social cues reminding each other of what we are "supposed to do next" in the scripted interaction rituals of our shared culture (Goffman 1967). Often we are not fully aware of our own cultural scripts until they collide with the alternative scripts or cultural expectations of others, as when we travel abroad in countries whose cultural protocols differ markedly from our own and find ourselves inadvertently insulting our audience.

Some social occasions are less tightly scripted than others, just as some musical performances are scored and carefully rehearsed while others emerge spontaneously in the jam session. The birthing procedure, the athletic contest, the courtroom drama, the surgery, the wedding, the funeral—all of these proceed according to more or less predictable protocols. Yet even these scripted events may contain elements of uncertainty and forced improvisation: the unforeseen complication in the delivery room; the surprise witness in the courtroom; the missing bride or groom. No script, no matter how elaborate, can anticipate every possible contingency. It is these elements of unpredictability and uncertainty that infuse theater and life with emotional drama. Moreover, even the tightest script must afford some room for personal nuance, interpretation, and the filling in of unspecified detail; for just as no two stage actors play Hamlet in exactly the same way, no two social actors interpret and enact the same cultural script identically.

It follows that much of our daily interaction is necessarily improvisational. Ordinary situations demand that we be both actor and author at the same moment (Edie 1967: 225; Brown 1977: 154). Consider again the family argument at dinner. Actors may bring scripted expectations to the table, and they may rehearse their speeches on their mental screens in advance of the performance; but the performance itself is largely extemporized, invented on the spot in response to the unpredictable improvisations of others. The scene is less like a tightly scored composition than it is like an extemporaneous jazz session (cf. Sudnow 1979). There is no written script, no single director, but only the wits of the actors as they spontaneously create dialogue on the fly. In these circumstances, many of the distinctions that define conventional theater seem to collapse. Interaction becomes a kind of primitive or undifferentiated theater in which the usual elements of dramaturgy—written script, director, and the like—implode. Social interaction becomes the theater of the here and now, the one-time-only performance in which every participant may play actor, audience, playwright, and director almost simultaneously. This is the improvisational theater of everyday life.

We have noted that social actors in modern societies, in contrast to those in more traditional societies, enjoy somewhat more freedom and personal control over their life scripts in such matters as marriage, career choice and religious preference. Less firmly rooted in traditional social roles and identities, modern social actors are called upon to be more fluid and flexible than their predecessors, more "mutable" (Zurcher 1977) and "protean" (Lifton 1993) in their responses to an increasingly complex and constantly changing social environment. At least since the 1960s, traditional scripts governing such matters as gender relations, family structure, and religious orthodoxy have come to be widely regarded as options or choices rather than as firm expectations, and those who chafe under the demands of tradition have been freer than ever before, for better or worse, to create their own alternative ways of life. Social life has always arisen from the interplay between cultural script and improvisation; but today we find ourselves relying less on the former and more on the latter. Now, perhaps more than ever, we make life up as we go along in the improvisational society.

These are just a few of the directions in which we may develop the theatrical metaphor. Previous theorists have applied the metaphor in a wide variety of contexts. The anthropologist Marcel Mauss, for instance, has explored the analogy between theater and ritual (Burns 1992: 109), while political theorist Murray Edelman (1988) has analyzed political events as staged spectacles or public dramas constructed through the manipulation of symbols. Philosopher Kenneth Burke (1945) has gone so far as to propose that we may analyze any social phenomenon dramatistically by posing five key questions: What was done (act); when and where was it done (scene); who did it (agent); by what means (agency) and why (purpose)?

Perhaps no social theorist in this century is more renowned for exploring theatrical analogies than the Canadian American sociologist Erving Goffman, on whom we now turn our spotlight. Goffman's style of ethnographic research, known as dramaturgical analysis, has spawned a multitude of fascinating studies analyzing a wide variety of social settings as theatrical venues, including mental hospitals, school classrooms, and gynecological examination rooms (e.g., see Emerson 1970; Henslin and Briggs 1971; Brissett and Edgley 1975).

Goffman's Theater of the Mundane

In *The Presentation of Self in Everyday Life* (1959) and other works (1961a, 1961b, 1963, 1967, 1971, 1974), Goffman develops a view of social life as an intricately staged theatrical production in which social actors attempt to pass themselves off to audiences as the characters they are pretending to be. The pages of Goffman's books are filled with actors seeking—sometimes confidently, sometimes anxiously, sometimes desperately—to secure the validation of others in the ordinary, mundane settings of daily life.

Audiences are powerful in Goffman's world, for they may at any moment notice discrepancies in our performances and call our bluffs, subjecting us to painful embarrassment and humiliation. And so social actors strive to manipulate their audiences skillfully, controlling the information they convey and shrewdly cultivating the arts of "impression management" at every turn. Audiences, for their part, may sometimes assist actors in keeping up appearances. For example, an audience may save a stumbling actor from embarrassment or humiliation by practicing "civil inattention," looking away or pretending not to notice when the actor commits a faux pas or displays a social stigma (Goffman 1963, 1971). Such tender mercies are not entirely altruistic, for audience members know that they too will have their precarious moments onstage, and that they too will depend soon enough upon the kindness of strangers.

Goffman offers a view of social life in which images are as important as reality—indeed, in which image and reality are virtually indistinguishable from one another. Goffman's perspective is in some respects a Machiavellian vision of social life, wherein survival depends less on what one *is* than on what one *appears* to be. It is a vision perfectly suited to a commercial culture such as our own, immersed as we are in the production and consumption of images (Ewen 1988, 1996; Denzin 1991), including advertisements for ourselves (Mailer 1959). Critics of Goffman (e.g., Gouldner 1970; MacIntyre 1984; Manning 1992: 51–55) note that his cool-eyed analysis offers no standpoint from which to construct a moral critique of such a society.

True enough, Goffman is less interested in moralizing than in analyzing how people do in fact assume and maintain their roles. Goffman implies that one's mask, held in place long enough and convincingly enough, at last becomes one's face. In more conventional terms, one's persona (literally "mask") becomes one's personality, or in older parlance, one's character. Eventually, we *are* our masks. We become ourselves, Goffman suggests, by pretending to be ourselves in the affirming presence of others. We invent ourselves in dramatic collaboration with others, and they in turn create themselves in collaboration with us. Social reality is thus a communal creation, an act of collective imagination, a grand illusion that we sustain in the mundane customs, rituals, and maneuvers of daily life.

In Goffman's world we encounter many of the themes of postmodernism. Nothing is entirely solid. There are no fixed, fully unified or perfectly integrated selves. Rather, we are like "holding companies" (1961b: 90) embracing a host of distinct identities appropriate to the various situations we find ourselves in. Now I am a "child," now a "parent," now a "student," now a "teacher," now a "voter," now a "consumer," now a "patient," now a "friend." Which of these roles is the real me? In Goffman's world there seems to be no "real me" in the end, but only a collection of selves administered by a specialized executive self, a kind of faceless personal system administrator whose tedious job it is to decide which mask I should be wearing just now to please the audience of the moment.

Embracing Roles

Goffman examines not only the roles that actors play, but also the attitudes that actors bring to their roles. In some instances social actors hold their roles at a distance in an attitude of cool detachment, refusing to believe very deeply in the performances they give. In other instances actors embrace their roles with such a degree of sincerity that they essentially become what they pretend to be (1959: 17ff, 1961b). In the former instance the mask remains a mask; in the latter, as we have noted, it virtually becomes one's face.[1] Those who were drafted into military service during the Vietnam War, for example, were often less eager to embrace the role of soldier than were those who had volunteered for service. Some recruits only *played* the role of soldier, while others (in their own minds, at least) *became* the role. "To embrace a role," Goffman remarks, "is to be embraced by it."[2]

Most role performances fall somewhere between the poles of role embracement and role distance, belief and disbelief, sincerity and cynicism. Social actors have sometimes been observed to oscillate between these poles in the course of their performances (Goffman 1959: 20–21). Students who enter medical school brimming with idealism, for example, have been observed to grow callous and detached in the course of their arduous training, recovering a measure of their initial idealism only as they approach graduation (Becker and Geer 1958).

Frontstage and Backstage

Goffman is alert to the situational variability of the roles we play, distinguishing "frontstage" from "backstage" performances. Frontstage performances take place in regions within view of an external audience, while backstage performances occur among fellow actors out of eyesight or earshot of their audience, often concealed behind some physical barrier such as a door or wall. Backstage activity is typically more casual and informal than frontstage activity, as actors remove their frontstage masks and share together in the reality behind the staged appearance. "Here the performer can relax; he can drop his front, forgo speaking his lines, and step out of character" (Goffman 1959: 112).

But backstage quickly becomes frontstage again when an intruder enters the scene and actors must scramble to restore public appearances. Goffman illustrates this sudden transformation of backstage into frontstage with an amusing passage from Katherine Archibald's (1947: 159) account of work life in a wartime shipyard. She reports that a group of resting workers, alerted to the approaching presence of a shipyard official, quickly found ways to look busy:

> "Don't let him catch you sitting down," was the universal admonition, and where no work existed a pipe was busily bent and threaded, or a bolt which was already firmly in place was subjected to further and unnecessary tightening. This was the formal tribute invariably attending a visitation by the boss, and its conventions were as familiar to both sides as those surrounding a five-star general's inspection. To have neglected

any detail of the false and empty show would have been interpreted as a mark of singular disrespect.

Backstage and frontstage behaviors are clearly evident in the performance of traditional sex roles. Simone de Beauvoir (1953: 543) contends, for example, that a woman's life becomes more authentic and truthful when she is backstage among other women, removed from the presence of men:

> Confronting man woman is always play-acting; she lies when she makes believe that she accepts her status as the inessential other, she lies when she presents to him an imaginary personage through mimicry, costumery, studied phrases. These histrionics require a constant tension: when with her husband, or with her lover, every woman is more or less conscious of the thought: "I am not being myself." The male world is harsh, sharp edged, its voices are too resounding, the lights are too crude, the contacts rough. With other women, a woman is behind the scenes. For some women this warm and frivolous intimacy is dearer than the serious pomp of relations with men.

Males, for their part, also express different aspects of themselves in backstage situations. In locker room banter, men have been known on occasion to describe women in graphic and predatory terms, expressing sentiments behind the scenes that they would normally be embarrassed to perform on the frontstage of mixed company. But are these backstage utterances necessarily more "real" than the utterances that men make in the intimate company of women? Or is the backstage merely another frontstage, where males feel obliged to perform predatory scripts to gain the approval of other males? The theatrical metaphor raises the intriguing question, "Where in this scenario is the 'real' man?"

We commonly suppose that underneath our social masks lies a more authentic self. In "We Wear the Mask," African American poet Paul Dunbar ([1896] 1993) alludes to a self that lies vulnerable beneath the protective surface of social appearance:

> With torn and bleeding hearts we smile,
> And mouth with myriad subtleties.
> Why should the world be over-wise,
> In counting all our tears and sighs?
> Nay, let them only see us, while we wear the mask.

Dunbar's poem suggests that while social masks are sometimes necessary for survival, there would be less need for them in a more just and humane world. A recent anthology of women's poetry (Howe 1993) raises the banner defiantly: "No More Masks!" But once again, the disturbing question arises whether there is any such real or authentic self beneath our social masks. Is that backstage self only another mask, albeit one that fits more comfortably and requires less exertion to hold in place? Or is it in some sense who we really are?

The metaphor of the mask has other implications as well. Where there is masking, there also may be unmasking. In the social masquerade that Goffman describes, social actors are continually vulnerable to, and fearful of, the humiliating prospect of being unmasked, or publicly shown to be something other than they appear to be. The high public official engaged in an illicit affair, the closeted gay in a hostile milieu, the spy or undercover agent, and the criminal under alias must all fear the social consequences of being "outed" or exposed to public view. But is this not a fear that we *all* share in common as human beings, insofar as we all, at one time or another, seek to disguise or conceal from public view the inevitable discrepancies between who we are and who others expect us to be?

Just as we are all vulnerable to being unmasked, so are we all capable of unmasking others. We ourselves become a source of social anxiety when we set out to strip away the poses and pretensions of others. Professional unmaskers, such as detectives and investigative journalists, do this sort of work for a living, while others hunt hypocrisies on an amateur basis. The aggressive unmasking of moral, religious, political, and other cultural pretensions is by now a dominant motif in the cynical culture of postmodernity (Sloterdijk 1987: 22–100).

The Inner Theater

If all of our social masks were stripped away, what would be left of us? Once again we must ask whether a real or authentic self lies beneath our social masks, or whether our most backstage self is only another mask, albeit one that fits more comfortably than the others. Perhaps we are most "real" when we are not performing for any audience at all, either frontstage or backstage. Perhaps we are most authentic when we are only in the presence of ourselves, immersed in our private soliloquies. Yet even in solitude we discover that we are enacting performances. In our rehearsals before the mirror we are at once both actor and audience. In our secret confessions to ourselves we are both the confessor and the hearer of confession. In our imaginations we are both the creator and consumer of fantasies. And as audiences to our performances—witnessing, evaluating, commenting favorably or critically—we remain, even in solitude, active participants in the inescapable theater of social life.

George Herbert Mead (1934), an important influence on Goffman, was keenly aware that even our most private selves are profoundly social. Our personal identities first take shape through our early and ongoing encounters with various "significant others" (Mead 1934), beginning with our parents, and we carry the introjected images and voices of these significant others with us throughout our lives. These "voices of the mind" (Wertsch 1991) largely constitute who we are.

Our inner theater is crowded with characters.[3] We may imagine ourselves in an angry conversation with a boss, or in a romantic interlude with a lover, or in a brilliant athletic or musical performance before a wildly enthusiastic crowd of thousands. Even when we are talking to ourselves, we hear multiple voices, as when the voice of temptation comes into conflict with the voice of moral restraint and a third voice, the voice of moderation and reasonable compromise, enters to resolve the dispute (or in Freudian terms, when the competing demands of id and superego are mediated by the ego). Mead recognized that this capacity to imagine and perform multiple roles in the inner theater not only is "normal," but is an essential condition of participation in the outer theater of social life. Talking to oneself is, in this view, a sign of social sanity.

Turner and the Drama of History

Goffman confines his intriguing analyses of the social theater mainly to the microdramas of face-to-face interaction. But how much can microanalyses tell us about the larger historical dramas, with casts of thousands or millions, in which most of us are mere bit players? For insight into these larger dramas, we turn to the influential cultural anthropologist Victor Turner.

Unlike Goffman, Turner is interested in the dramatic macronarratives or "big stories"—the political upheavals, the institutional revolutions and cultural transformations—that heave our personal stories to and fro like particles in an oceanic wave. And while Goffman's account of the social theater is generally limited to the examination of life in contemporary Anglo-American culture, Turner brings the wide-angle lens of cross-cultural and historical comparison to his analysis of the social drama. Turner's theory of social drama, expounded in *Dramas, Fields, and Metaphors* (1974) and subsequent works (1982, 1986), centers on the dramatic conflicts that arise among contending social groups within a given society. Based on his analysis of numerous ethnographic and historical case studies, Turner proposes that the drama of social conflict typically unfolds in four rather predictable phases (1974: 37–42).

Phase 1: Breach. A social drama begins when a group, or a person acting in the name of a group, disrupts routine social practices by overtly and deliberately violating some well-established norm. This breach of accepted practice acts as a "symbolic trigger," activating highly charged emotions within and among con-

[handwritten marginalia: Now in Breach]

[handwritten note: Bernie = revolution]
[handwritten note: Trump = bigotry, hateful]

tending groups. One is reminded, for example, of Rosa Park's principled refusal to sit at the back of a city bus in Montgomery, Alabama, in the winter of 1955, a small but highly charged breach of a long-standing tradition inscribed in local custom and law.

Phase 2: Crisis Following the breach phase is a period of mounting social crisis. In the crisis phase, defensive efforts are made to seal off the breach and to restore the previous social order. Failing this, the crisis continues to escalate. Thus, following Rosa Park's symbolic refusal, a young minister named Martin Luther King Jr. and others organized a boycott of the Montgomery bus system. Civil authorities quickly moved to jail Parks and the boycott leaders. Opponents of the boycott bombed four black churches and sent a shotgun blast through the front door of King's home, but these attempts to restore the prior order failed to quell the widening protest, and the crisis escalated (Zinn 1980: 442–43).

The crisis phase represents a moment of danger and high suspense. It is what Turner calls a "liminal" moment—an unstable interval between stable phases. During liminal phases, major social and cultural innovations may come into being. We recall that the Chinese word for "crisis" is formed by combining characters representing "danger" and "opportunity." Like the moment of childbirth, the liminal phase poses dangers, but it also ushers new life and new possibilities into the world.

Phase 3: Redressive action. As a social crisis spreads and as it becomes clear that unrest cannot be readily suppressed, representatives of the disrupted social system move to redress the grievances of the rebellious group and to resolve the conflict through either formal or informal means. Redressive action may include diplomacy, formal negotiation, informal mediation, judicial processes, and public rituals of solidarity. In the Montgomery case, redressive action occurred primarily through the judicial process. A federal court struck down the Montgomery bus segregation ordinance as unconstitutional, establishing an important landmark in U.S. civil rights law. If redressive attempts fail, the system normally regresses to the crisis phase, perhaps taking the form of sullen and smoldering resentment among conflicting factions, or the more violent forms of war, revolution, and the bloody suppression of dissent. If redressive attempts are successful, however, the drama may move forward to a fourth phase.

Phase 4: Reintegration. In this final phase, the society undergoes a restructuring to accommodate the outcomes of redressive action. Turner calls this restructuring "reintegration." New alliances may form, power may shift from one group to another, and the parts of society may be rearranged to reflect new social realities. In some respects, the civil rights movement of the 1950s and 1960s resulted in the reintegration (in Turner's sense) of American social institutions. However, the transformation was far from total. Elements of the old order persisted alongside elements of the new as the nation remained, in many respects, racially divided. Turner notes that when reintegration is unsuccessful, a society may simply endure in a state of chronic factionalism, resigned to an irreparable schism between contending parties, or may proceed toward eventual separation or secession.

Eventually the social system settles down into one or another relatively stable configuration, whereupon the stage is set once again for the next breach, the next crisis, the next redressive action, and the next attempt at reintegration. Thus do social dramas unfold, according to Turner, in a somewhat predictable cycle. Although the particular circumstances may vary from one historical drama to the next, the general pattern of social conflict and resolution displays certain universal (or at least frequently recurring) elements. The actors, the dialogue, the sets, and costumes may vary, but the essential plot remains relatively constant.

Turner's dramaturgical analysis manages to interpret a wide variety of seemingly unique historical events within a single and relatively simple conceptual framework. Within this framework he examines, for example, the historic drama of church and state relations played out in the events surrounding the murder of Thomas Becket, archbishop of Canterbury, by the knights of King Henry II in 1170; the political drama of the Mexican revolution of independence from Spain in 1810 under the leadership of Padre Hidalgo; and the drama of social conflict among the Ndembu of southern Africa. Each of these social dramas is unique in its particulars, and yet all are shown to unfold according to a similar logic that seems to transcend differences of time, place, and culture.

Turner's analysis suggests that human history has a distinctive narrative structure, organized around the themes of conflict and higher-order resolution, with each tentative resolution setting the stage for future conflicts and their resolutions. His theory of social drama resembles in some respects the German philosopher G. W. F. Hegel's dialectical view of history as a continual succession of theses and opposing antitheses (Turner speaks instead of "structures" and "anti-structures"), from which new historical syntheses may emerge. Marx's theory of class conflict similarly relies on the dialectical clash of opposing actors on the stage of history, enacting their stories sometimes as tragedy and sometimes as farce ([1852] 1963: 15). Critics of Turner's theory may object that it presents an excessively tidy view of history, and that the particularities of each culture and historical era cannot be so neatly universalized. But who will deny that dramas of conflict and resolution and renewed conflict have not recurred throughout history and across cultures, or that they will continue to do so as human dramas continue to unfold?

Deep Stories

Whether we view the social drama at the macrolevel of institutional relations (as Turner does) or at the microlevel of interpersonal relations (as Goffman does), we find stories—and stories within stories—unfolding on every hand.[4] Much of the appeal of theatrical metaphors seems to spring from our human need or desire to infuse life with drama and meaning. And so we create dramatic stories for ourselves and act them out for each other on the social stage, playing both actor and audience in the theater of daily life.

We are by nature a narrative species, whose ancestors have been creating and performing stories by the flickering firelight since before the beginning of recorded history (Brockett 1977). While the content of our narratives varies immensely from one culture to another, the general practice of storytelling is culturally universal. But why is this so? What do stories do for us?

Stories serve to connect the bits and pieces of our experience into coherent and meaningful wholes. We could scarcely live without our narratives, for without them our lives would appear as little more than a series of disconnected events with no apparent meaning. Thus, to give a standard example, if I say, "The king died and the queen died," I have merely recited two disconnected facts. But if I say "The king died and the queen died *of grief*," I have told the beginnings of a meaningful story, joining human actors together in a drama of love and suffering.

Psychologists are discovering that stories are essential organizing devices in human cognition and memory, and indeed, that we are virtually incapable of understanding or remembering anything without the aid of unifying narrative structures, which cognitive psychologists call "schemas" or "scripts" (Schank and Abelson 1977; Schank 1990). Unifying stories are especially critical in this age of information overload, wherein we are bombarded daily with a multitude of fragmentary and incoherent messages (Gergen 1991). Stories are also instrumental in teaching the young the core beliefs and values of a culture (Postman 1989), a role that myths and legends have played throughout history.

If these claims are true, then we will not soon outgrow our need for story and mythic narrative. Mythologists such as Mircea Eliade (1975) and Joseph Campbell (1988) have pointed to the essential role that myths continue to play even in advanced scientific cultures such as our own. The term *myth*, which came to imply false or superstitious belief in the rationalist age of Enlightenment, has recently begun to assume a more positive and expansive meaning. Myths are increasingly recognized as powerful symbolic narratives that serve, among other functions, to encode the ideals and aspirations of a culture. They are akin to what Bernard Lee (1995) calls our *deep stories*, the underlying narratives that animate our lives and imbue them with meaning. So intense is our need for deep stories that if we do not inherit dramatic narratives from our culture, we seem to reinvent them on our own. The proliferation of youth gangs in recent decades, with their crude dramatic narratives of territoriality and conquest, may signal the failure of our culture to create and sustain compelling and purpose-giving cultural stories and to communicate these stories effectively to the young. The eagerness with which many children have embraced the *Star Wars* saga and other such epic stories in recent years speaks of a deep and still largely unfulfilled hunger for mythic meaning in our time.

For countless centuries, religions have provided human actors with grand mythic narratives within which to locate themselves and give their lives meaning. In modern times, economic and political ideologies (both capitalist and socialist, both authoritarian and democratic) have often served many of these same functions. Meanwhile, grand scientific narratives ("Once upon a time there was a big bang . . .") have emerged to eclipse ancient stories of creation and to offer dramatic counternarratives of their own.

In the postmodern era, however, these grand narratives of the past are viewed with increasing skepticism, especially among educated elites in Western societies. In the wake of scientific skepticism, many have lost faith in traditional religious narratives. In the wake of fascism and communism, many have lost faith in totalizing ideologies. In the shadow of Hiroshima, Nagasaki, and nuclear proliferation, many have lost faith in the benevolence of science. Thus, some postmodern philosophers, such as Jean-François Lyotard (1984), contend that our faith in the grand narratives of religion, ideology, and science is disintegrating as we survey the carnage and wreckage they have left behind. The age of naive optimism and grandiose certainty is gone. The age of disillusion has arrived. We now rely upon narratives that are more skeptical, more tentative, more local, more temporary, and more modest than the grand narratives of the past.

There is much in this characterization of our times that rings true, particularly as it describes the jaded and cynical attitudes that prevail in many segments of postindustrial societies such as Lyotard's France and the United States. Yet Lyotard may underestimate the depth of the human need for myth and deep story. Even as Lyotard tells his own sweeping story of disillusionment and the loss of grand narratives (itself a grand narrative of sorts), fierce religious and nationalist narratives still flourish in many parts of the world. Ideologies persist in new forms, and the juggernaut of modern science rolls on.

The postmodern world presents us, then, not with a single coherent story, but with a multitude of stories, both large and small, both deep and shallow, articulating the experiences of a multitude of diverse social groups. These intersecting and sometimes clashing narratives are under continual revision as each social faction struggles to reinvent its past, to reimagine its future, and to tell its own story in its own way. And so, for better or worse, we continue to seek meaning and drama in our lives as we strut and fret our hour upon the stage.

Notes

1. The process of learning to play a role with real conviction and credibility was brilliantly explored by the Russian dramatist Konstantin Stanislavski, whose philosophy of acting has altered the course of twentieth-century theater (Funke and Booth 1961; Moore 1976). In such works as *Building a Character* (1949) and *Creating a Role* (1961), Stanislavski spoke out against the forced and mechanical styles of acting that prevailed in the theater of his day. He insisted that good acting, although it transpires on a theatrical stage, should never be overly "theatrical" or "stagey," but is rather the natural expression of the inner "soul and life" of the character (Stanislavski 1963: 95, 158). To enter into the inner life of a role, an actor must, insofar as is possible, *become* the character. Through research into the character's time and place in history, the actor is responsible for creating and enacting an underlying "subtext,"—i.e., the character's deeper thoughts, feelings, and life context. A good actor becomes so fully immersed in a role, and believes so deeply in it, that the part is inside the actor even as the actor is inside the part (1963: 27).

2. Total immersion in an imaginary role has therapeutic as well as theatrical uses. In sociodrama (Sternberg and Garcia 1989) and similar role-playing techniques, participants are asked to assume unfamiliar roles and to act them out vividly, losing their own identities temporarily in order to gain personal insight and discover creative solutions to relational problems.

3. In extreme cases, the proliferation of distinct characters in the inner theater expresses itself pathologically as multiple personality disorder, a condition in which an entire "society" of clearly differentiated characters establishes residence within a single individual. Interestingly, these multiple personas may distinguish themselves from one another not only by adopting different names, ages, and racial and sexual characteristics, but even by requiring different eyeglass prescriptions and responding differently to the same medication (American Psychiatric Association 1987; Chase 1990).

4. Strangely, Goffman has little to say about the stories or social narratives that we create and sustain in our face-to-face interactions. As Sennett (1977: 36) has noticed, Goffman tends to present an image of society in which there are "scenes but no plot."

CHAPTER NINE

~

Society as Discourse

If any single metaphor has come to dominate cultural analysis in recent decades, it is the image of human societies as linguistic creations. The image of society as language—as text, as conversation, as *discourse* in the broadest sense—is by now an established orthodoxy among many theorists in the humanities and cultural studies. Such theorists may differ sharply among themselves in their particular linguistic approaches to the study of social life. Yet despite their differences, they share the conviction that social reality is constructed largely, if not entirely, through the social medium of symbols. Thus, many theorists in recent years have come to call themselves social constructivists or constructionists.

The Postmodern Turn in Social Theory

Social constructionists typically reject conventional notions of an objective reality existing "out there," independently of consciousness and language, in favor of a view of reality as the negotiated consensus agreed upon within particular language communities. Different cultural communities may construct and inhabit different symbolic worlds, and "the only way of knowing a socially constructed world is knowing it from within" (Smith 1990: 22). In this postmodern perspective, the taken-for-granted assumptions of the past are now in quotation marks. One no longer speaks naively of reality (let alone Reality), but rather of multiple alternative "realities" sustained through language. As Anderson (1990) cleverly puts it, "reality isn't what it used to be."

Postmoderns tend to view such symbolically constructed realities as inherently unstable, ambiguous, open to multiple interpretation, and constantly in flux (Tracy 1987). While the term *postmodernism* has been understood in a dizzying multitude of ways (e.g., Lyotard 1984; Denzin 1991; Jencks 1992; Seidman and Wagner 1992; Docherty 1993; Dickens and Fontana 1994; Lemert 1997b;) and has no fixed or authoritative definition (if it did, it wouldn't be postmodern!), most would

163

agree that the term signifies, among other things, a growing skepticism in advanced industrial societies regarding the authority of major social institutions (e.g., religion, politics, and even science) to define stable and universal systems of cultural meaning. Critics of postmodernism fear that this general decline of authority is leading us down a slippery slope toward cultural fragmentation, moral relativism, and social chaos. Its defenders, on the other hand, express the hope that the decentering of authority will open up new opportunities for creative pluralism as local communities of shared interest enjoy the freedom to create and sustain new worlds of meaning and forms of social life.

In its most extreme forms, the constructionist view may risk falling into a kind of linguistic reductionism or "discourse determinism" by attempting to account for all human phenomena as products of language or discourse (Best and Kellner 1991: 27; Lupton and Barclay 1997: 21; Holstein and Miller 1993). Let us grant that some, indeed *many*, phenomena in human experience are constituted in language and could not exist outside of it. The game of chess, for example, is constituted in a system of symbolically encoded rules without which the game would simply not exist. Constructionists argue that the same is true of a multitude of other social games ranging from law, science, and religion to the mundane routines and conventions of everyday life.

But while some realities are indeed linguistically constructed, others do not seem to depend on language or consciousness at all. They cannot be wished or defined or talked away. All but the most unreconstructed constructionist will acknowledge, for example, that gravity is a real force, that it behaves independently of the word *gravity*, and therefore that it is not contingent on our understanding or social construction of it. While *theories* of gravity, and perhaps even some aspects of the subjective *experience* of gravity, are culturally and linguistically defined, gravity itself does not seem to care what we think or say about it as we stumble and fall over the edge of the cliff. Gravity will flatten the constructionist as quickly as it flattens the naive realist.

Linguistic constructionists observe that we can only postulate the existence of a natural world external to language and consciousness (including natural forces such as gravity) from *within* language and consciousness. Following Immanuel Kant and Emile Durkheim, they contend that direct knowledge of an external world is impossible, except as such knowledge is mediated by our categories of thought and language (Brown 1987: 95). Thus, a society that does not share our concepts of gravity and causation will have its own culturally defined understanding and experience of falling. True enough. But this does not mean that the source of the experience is dependent on language. The philosopher John Searle (1995) and others make a persuasive case that we must distinguish between realities that exist independently of language and those that are linguistically and socially constructed, and that we must acknowledge the existence of both kinds of reality.

Some realities are socially constructed and some are not, and still others are somehow a blend of the two. The interesting issues are these: Where do linguistic realities end and nonlinguistic realities begin, and how do the two kinds of reality relate to each other?

Most human phenomena lie somewhere between the extremes of chess and gravity—neither entirely dependent on language nor entirely independent of it. Literary theorist Terry Eagleton (1983: 111), criticizing early versions of linguistic constructionism, asks the right questions: "Was language really all there was? What about labour, sexuality, political power? These realities might themselves be inextricably caught up in discourse, but they were certainly not reducible to it."

In any case, the powers of language have become a central preoccupation of intellectual life in the late twentieth century, and rightly so. Language *is* a powerful force in human life, although not the only one. Where did this fascination with language come from, and where might it be going? A brief historical overview may offer some clues.

Languages about Language

The image of society as a linguistic construction seems to have sprung up in several disciplines at once during the early decades of this century. In hindsight, it was an idea whose time had come. Hilary Lawson (1985) observes that the onset of the postmodern era is marked by the reflexive realization that we live in worlds of language, and that we cannot talk about our language worlds except *in* language—i.e., by creating more language. We are growing ever more acutely aware that we are suspended in webs of meaning that we ourselves have spun (Geertz, 1973: 5) and that there is no viable escape from the web of symbol and interpretation. And so we create languages about language, or "metalanguages," to talk about the largely linguistic nature of social reality.

Language Philosophy

This growing interest in language was evident in both Anglo-American and continental philosophy during the early twentieth century. The emergence of language philosophy in Cambridge, Oxford, and Vienna in the years following World War I marked what Richard Rorty (1967) has called the "linguistic turn" in modern philosophy. One language philosopher in particular, Ludwig Wittgenstein, anticipated linguistic constructionism in his later writings (1953). In his *Philosophical Investigations*, Wittgenstein repudiated his own earlier view of language as a "picture" or "mirror" of objective reality. Instead, he proposed that language actually "creates" reality in a certain sense (Bartley 1985: 139). The meanings of words inhere not in their one-to-one correspondence with an external reality, but rather in their accepted use within the "language games" (conventional rules and usages) of particular cultural communities. Human communities sustain themselves as "forms of life" by creating and maintaining language games, and human language "consists of a multitude of different, often interacting, language games, each with its own 'grammar' or rules of use" (1985: 140). One follower of Wittgenstein, Peter Winch (1958), has urged social scientists to take up Wittgenstein's challenge and to study human communities as life forms through an investigation of their linguistic practices. Another prominent philosopher, Nelson Goodman (1978), has written convincingly of the "world-building" power of language to construct not just images of reality but social realities themselves.

Social Phenomenology

Another group of European philosophers in the early twentieth century was also growing interested in the world-building power of language. Phenomenologists, engaged in the systematic study of the interior structure of consciousness, turned their attention increasingly toward linguistic phenomena. The German philosopher Martin Heiddeger, who famously described language as "the house of Being," noted that the language worlds we inhabit create our sense of reality. Thus, "we Europeans presumably dwell in an entirely different house than Eastasian man" because of fundamental differences in our respective languages, so that "a dialogue from house to house remains nearly impossible," saved only by the prospect that there might be "something [in language] that wells up from a single source" (Heiddeger 1971: 5–8). Across the Atlantic, linguistic anthropologists Edward Sapir and Benjamin Whorf were developing a related view of language based on cross-cultural evidence which suggested that the languages we speak significantly shape our perceptions of reality (Whorf 1956; but for a sharp critique of this view, see Pinker 1994).

Meanwhile, social phenomenologists such as Alfred Schutz (1967) and Peter Berger and Thomas Luckmann (1966) began to explore the ways in which linguistic classifications or "typifications" shape our experience of others and our responses to them. Berger and Luckmann observed, in their influential treatise *The Social Construction of Reality*, that when "I apprehend the other as 'a man,' 'a European,' 'a buyer,' 'a jovial type,' and so on . . . these typifications ongoingly affect my interaction" (Berger and Luckmann 1966: 31). Typifications are like linguistic lenses, determining how we subjectively perceive others, how we expect them to act, and how we in turn react to them. Although typifications shape our subjective perceptions, Berger and Luckmann noted that they have a certain sort of objectivity about them: "Language forces me into its patterns" and "is capable of becoming the objective repository of vast accumulations of meaning and experience, which it can then preserve in time and transmit to following generations" (1966: 37–38). It is largely through such typifications, they argued, that social structures are produced, maintained and passed on (1966: 33).

Symbolic Interactionism

If society is a linguistic construction, as Berger and Luckmann imply, then so are the individual selves and social relations that compose it. Language, in this view, is the very stuff of which our identities are made. The linguistic construction of the self is the special focus of a school of social thought inspired in the 1930s by the pragmatist social philosopher George Herbert Mead (1934) of the University of Chicago, a theoretical tradition which has come to be called "symbolic interactionism" (Blumer 1969).

Mead became convinced that mind, self, and society are all, in a profound sense, products of social interaction, and that our social identities and interactions are everywhere mediated by symbols. If you doubt that your own sense of identity is social and linguistic, you are invited to administer the following simple paper-and-pencil test to yourself. Note that the act of taking this test is itself a symbolic and social act, because the test is composed entirely of symbols and is induced by the communicative act of your reading and responding to the following instructions:

> Write the words "Who am I?" at the top of a blank page. From the top downward, number the page from "1" to "20." In the twenty blanks below, please make twenty different statements in response to the simple question (addressed to yourself), "Who am I?" Answer as if you are giving the answers to yourself, not to somebody else. Write your answers in the order they occur to you. Don't worry about logic or importance. Go along fairly fast. (McPartland 1959)

When you have completed this exercise, known as the Kuhn twenty-statements test, pause for a moment to consider what you have done. As a spontaneous and intuitive subject (what Mead called the "I"), you have taken yourself as a social object (what Mead called the "me") and have described "it" linguistically, in a series of words or phrases. The implicit grammar of the exercise is a grammar of subject and object, joined by a conjugation of the verb "to be": I am this, I am that. Mead believed that the human capacity to take oneself as a linguistic object is fundamental to human consciousness, and to our capacity to develop and reflect upon our identities as social beings. Without socially acquired language, we could scarcely think about ourselves, let alone form complex identities. Symbolic interactionists analyze responses to this test as revealing indicators of our shifting social identities (Zurcher 1977).

The symbolic interactionist notion that our identities are defined and redefined linguistically is the basic premise of *labeling theory* (Lemert 1967; Schur 1980; Gove 1980; Glassner 1982). From the moment of our birth we are affixed with labels of various kinds. First we are categorized as "male" or "female." Then we are given proper names—usually either a "boy's name" or a "girl's name" depending on our genitalia. Gender labels are known to produce marked differences in the way parents and other adults treat infants, a phenomenon amusingly explored in the parable of "Baby X," an infant whose indeterminate sex causes no end of anxiety and confusion in the grown-up world (Seavey et al. 1975).

The point is that we do not know how to behave toward others until we have labeled or typified them. Labeling theorists do not necessarily view this fact in a negative light. Rather, they understand that as linguistic creatures we simply cannot live without applying words to the persons and things we encounter in our daily lives. Particular labels may be either destructive, constructive, or neutral, but labeling of one sort or another is a necessary and unavoidable feature of social interaction. We need our nouns, including nouns that refer to categories of people.

Labeling theorists contend that labels, and social reactions to them, exert a powerful influence on social life. Suppose, for example, that on a dare from friends you commit an act of vandalism. (Labeling theorists would say that you have committed an initial act of "primary deviance.") Now suppose that you are apprehended by police, taken to the station, fingerprinted, booked, brought before a judge, found guilty, given a probated sentence, and released to a parent or guardian. In your journey through the juvenile justice system, you have effectively been labeled a "juvenile delinquent." Labeling theorists caution that you are likely to internalize this label and to begin conforming your self-concept and consequent behavior to the expectations that normally accompany it. Thereafter, you are more likely to commit subsequent acts of "secondary deviance," or deviance influenced by having been labeled.

Deviance is, in a certain sense, created by definition. Every society defines one or another set of behaviors as unacceptable, although what falls outside of the band of respectability varies widely across cultures and even in the same culture through time. In recent years, some behaviors previously stigmatized as deviant, such as bearing children out of wedlock, are more widely tolerated, while other behaviors, such as smoking cigarettes in public, are increasingly deemed unacceptable. Thus, for some behaviors, we have "defined deviancy down" (Moynihan

1993), while for others we have defined deviancy upward by adopting more stringent standards and expectations.

For labeling theorists, social power resides largely in the authority to define who or what is deviant and to enforce these social definitions. In North American culture, the power to define normality and deviance is traditionally located in institutions, such as courts and legislatures, business corporations, religious bodies and the mass media, which have been controlled historically by white, economically advantaged heterosexual males. (Consider, for example, the demographic composition of the U.S. Senate, or of the chief executive officers of Fortune 500 companies.) Not surprisingly, definitions of deviance have traditionally tended to reflect the perspectives and interests of these powerful segments of society. In response to these dominant groups, opposition movements have arisen among racial and ethnic minorities, gays, women, and other marginalized groups to challenge traditional social definitions and to redefine cultural meanings in ways that reflect their own interests. While most such movements have been ideologically liberal or radical, conservative groups also have sought to redefine cultural meanings—for example, by seeking to extend the legal label of "citizen" to include the unborn, and the label "criminal" to include those who perform and receive abortions. Defining and redefining deviance can be an intensely political process, and considerable blood has been shed over words and their cultural meanings.

Labeling theorists contend that, in general, we see ourselves as others see us (or more precisely, as we *believe* others see us) and label ourselves as others label us. This basic principle of symbolic interactionism was advanced a century ago in Charles Horton Cooley's (1902) optical metaphor of the "looking-glass self." Cooley observed that our identities are shaped by the verbal and nonverbal responses we receive from others, and hence that others are like mirrors or looking glasses through which we come to understand ourselves. Following Cooley, labeling theorists have emphasized our tendency to live up to the labels affixed to us, particularly by authority figures. Yet we also may strive to live our labels down— i.e., to resist or reject the labels of others in favor of labels of our own choosing. In many instances, the labels that others impose on us may work not as self-*fulfilling* prophesies (as labeling theorists generally predict), but rather as self-*denying* prophesies (Merton [1948] 1968: 475–90). But in either case we are responding to the labels that others have applied to us, confirming the power of language to shape our actions.

As we grow older we may choose to accept or reject the identities that others have fitted us with, and to compose alternative identities for ourselves. The anthropologist Mary Catherine Bateson (1989) explores this process in *Composing a Life*, developing the metaphor of the self as a musical or literary composition. Bateson follows the life stories of five women as they improvise their identities, "editing" and "rewriting" when necessary, in collaboration with others—a process similar to Berger's (1963: 54–65) notion of biographical reconstruction, wherein we continually reinterpret our past in light of present needs and interests.

Symbolic interactionists take an interest not only in how we define our identities, but also in how we define the situations in which we find ourselves. The Thomas theorem famously states that if we "define situations as real, they are real in their consequences" (Thomas and Thomas 1928: 572). This theorem suggests that the meanings we attach to situations may be more important to an understanding of human behavior than what is "objectively" true, for we act on the basis of what we *believe* to be true, irrespective of what is actually the case. Consider the women caught up in witch-hunts of the Middle Ages. Accused of possession by Satan, many were sentenced to death and executed by the religious and civil authorities of their time. The belief of their accusers in the reality of satanic possession was enough to seal their fates, irrespective of Satan's actual existence or nonexistence. In this instance as in countless others, symbolic interactionists observe that the definitions of the powerful generally prevail over those of the powerless.

It is actually a mistake to speak of *the* definition of a situation, as symbolic interactionists sometimes have, because in any given situation there may be a multitude of possible interpretations of the same scene, or as Goffman (1974, 1981) puts it, many possible interpretive "frames." Even a single actor may alternately view the same scene through several different interpretive frames. In a postmodern world of multiple interpretations and multiple identities, Cooley's looking-glass self comes to look ever more like a moving figure in a house of mirrors.

Ethnomethodology

Like symbolic interactionism, ethnomethodology is a body of theory and research concerned with how people construct meanings. Ethnomethodology means literally the systematic study (*ology*) of people's (*ethno*) methods, and more specifically, their methods of producing and making sense of the mundane activities of everyday life. Ethnomethodologists have their own distinctive methods of uncovering the methods of others. A favorite research strategy is to disrupt or "breach" the taken-for-granted assumptions that normally prevail in a given situation and to observe how people respond to the social rupture. In his path-breaking *Studies in Ethnomethodology* (1967), Harold Garfinkel describes one such natural experiment or demonstration in which he instructed his UCLA students, returning home for holiday visits, to conduct themselves as if they were strangers in their own homes and to report the responses of others. Students returned to report that their behavior had elicited responses of "astonishment, bewilderment, shock, anxiety, embarrassment, and anger," prompting accusations "that the student was mean, inconsiderate, selfish, nasty, or impolite" (1967: 47).

Demonstrations of this kind dramatize the precariously fragile nature of the social order that we normally take for granted. When the "normal" order of things is disrupted, we commonly respond with signs of disorientation and distress and set about to restore the situation to normalcy. In a certain (not necessarily political) sense, Garfinkel's demonstrations suggest that there is a deeply conservative strain in human nature toward maintaining order and stability in daily life.

Garfinkel's research also suggests that the human need for meaning is so intense that we create meanings even where none exist. In a classic demonstration, Garfinkel paired volunteer students with a "counselor" (actually an experimenter). Each student was separated from the counselor by an opaque screen and was instructed to ask the counselor questions that could be answered "yes" or "no." Here is a strip of conversation transcribed from the experiment:

Subject: I happen to be of the Jewish faith and I have been dating a Gentile girl. . . . [Dad] never said don't date her, but at the same time he will come up with digs and sayings that make me feel very ill at ease about dating the girl. . . . Do you feel that I should continue dating this girl?

Experimenter: My answer is no.

Subject: No. Well, that is kind of interesting. . . . Maybe it is easier for an outsider to see certain things that I am blind to at this moment. . . . I would like to ask my second question now. . . . Should I have further discussion with Dad over this subject about dating the Gentile girl?

Experimenter: My answer is yes.

Subject: Well, I feel that is reasonable. . . . (Garfinkel 1962: 80–81)

While the student believed that the counselor was responding thoughtfully to his questions, the counselor's responses were in fact being generated from a table of random numbers. Thus, the student was unwittingly fabricating his own meanings. This demonstration and others like it (e.g., McHugh 1968; Blum and McHugh 1971) suggest that we are by nature "meaning-makers," to the point of making sense of the nonsensical and finding meaningful messages where there really are none.

Some ethnomethodologists believe that we construct meanings according to certain deep rules or interpretive procedures that resemble grammatical rules. Aaron Cicourel (1970, 1974: 80) proposes that just as there may be deep-structural grammatical rules that allow us to generate meaningful sentences (Chomsky

1965), there may also be basic rules or interpretive procedures that enable us to respond appropriately in varied social situations. In ordinary conversations with close friends, for example, we employ such procedures intuitively when we make sense of each others' fragmentary and shorthand expressions, or when we make smooth transitions from one topic of conversation to another. Conversational analysts have examined in fine detail, sometimes with the aid of video technology, a wide range of unspoken rules and methods that ordinary people use daily to construct ordinary conversations, including norms governing the duration, sequencing, and permissible interruption of conversation (Handel 1982; Heritage 1987; Tannen 1990, 1994; Silverman 1998). Through studies of this kind, linguistically oriented sociologists hope to uncover the hidden syntax or grammatical structure of social life.

Hermeneutics

While ethnomethodologists have been interested mainly in conversational or face-to-face interaction, a much older and more established scholarly tradition has focused on the interpretation of written texts. Hermeneutics, the art and craft of interpretation, is named in honor of the legendary Greek figure Hermes, messenger of the gods. Hermeneutics arose in Germany in the early nineteenth century as a historical approach to the interpretation of sacred scriptures. Today its methods are applied to all manner of texts, but especially to "classic" texts both sacred and secular, ancient and modern (Mueller-Vollmer 1989; Tracy 1981).

A leading figure in contemporary hermeneutics is the German theorist Hans Georg Gadamer. In *Truth and Method* (1975), Gadamer proposes that the reading of a classic text is a kind of conversation with the past, and that every such conversation is historically situated. Every text is written from within some historically specific "horizon" of understandings and concerns. Likewise, every reader comes to the text from within his or her own particular horizon of understandings and concerns. Every authentic attempt at interpretation therefore requires a "fusion of horizons" across the temporal and cultural distances that normally separate a reader from a text. Thus, when I encounter the Platonic dialogues or the teachings of Buddha, I inevitably bring my own "pre-understandings," prejudices, and present-day concerns to the act of reading a text that was produced in a culturally and historically distant context. Gadamer insists that we cannot do otherwise. In the act of reading I encounter understandings and concerns different from my own. I confront the "otherness" of persons who have lived in other places and times (1989: 270), and I am challenged to expand my own horizon in order to understand the other on the other's own ground.

Gadamer is especially critical of the scientific Enlightenment's skepticism toward traditional worldviews and its contempt for the "prejudices" of the past. He notes that Enlightenment rationality is itself an interpretive tradition with its own distinctive prejudices, not the least of these being a self-contradictory prejudice against prejudices. Even the Enlightenment rationalist's skepticism toward tradition is an interpretive tradition (and a rather dogmatic one at that). There is finally no escape from the "hermeneutic circle" of interpretation, wherein we understand the parts of a text in relation to the whole and the whole in relation to its parts from within some historically specific tradition of interpretation. We may give a text a hostile reading, seeking to "unmask" its hidden motives and interests (what Ricoeur has called the "hermeneutics of suspicion"), or a generous and sympathetic reading (the "hermeneutics of recovery") (Ricoeur 1970, 1981). But in either case the meaning of the text emerges from the encounter between text and reader—informed not only by what the text brings to the reader, but also by what the reader brings to the text. Literary theorists in recent decades have been enormously interested in the complex relations among author, text, reader, and interpretive community within the historical *contexts* (literally "with-texts") that surround them (e.g., Fish 1980; Eagleton 1983).

Gadamer's approach to the interpretation of texts may be applied more broadly to the interpretation of cultural phenomena in general, although Gadamer offers no simple, mechanical method for doing so (Bleicher 1982). Classic texts and other complex cultural artifacts are far too subtle for that. As Anthony Giddens (1984) notes, cultural analysis is extraordinarily complex because it demands a "double hermeneutic." Not only must we interpret the outward, "objective" manifestations of society, but we also must attempt to reconstruct the inner interpretations of its members—a methodological principle traditionally known as *Verstehen* or interpretive understanding (Weber [1904–17] 1949). Geologists can study rocks without studying how rocks interpret and thereby modify their own conditions of existence. In contrast to natural scientists, social scientists face a much more complicated task, because the subjective interpretations of social actors are deeply implicated in the seemingly objective structures that they create and sustain. For social scientists (indeed, for social actors in general) there is simply no escape from interpretation, or from the interpretation of interpretation.

Structuralism and Semiotics

While hermeneutics has its origins in German religious and philosophical scholarship, French structuralism is an intellectual movement inspired largely by modern linguistics. The emergence of linguistics as a twentieth-century science has opened up a vast new range of suggestive analogies between the properties of social systems and the properties of language systems. The French structuralist-anthropologist Claude Lévi-Strauss, whose work came to prominence in the 1950s, was among the first to recognize these new possibilities.

Drawing on the structural linguistics of Ferdinand Saussure and Roman Jakobson, Lévi-Strauss sought the origins of human culture in the linguistic structures encoded in the neural pathways of the human brain. Cultural systems, Lévi-Strauss believed, are generated by unconscious systems of linguistic rules. Here he relied on Saussure's ([1916] 1966) distinction between language as an abstract system of rules (*la langue*) and the actual speech performances (*la parole*) governed by these rules. A chess analogy may help to clarify this distinction (Harland 1987: 12). When we watch a game of chess, we cannot understand the series of moves that players make until we first understand the rules of chess that make these moves meaningful. By the same token, we cannot understand the speech and action of social actors without first understanding the system of structural rules that generate their actions. By treating observable social phenomena as manifestations of deeper linguistic systems, Lévi-Strauss hoped to uncover the fundamental (but largely unconscious) structures of the human mind.

Saussure and Jacobson had argued that language is essentially a system of differences. Every element of language—its sounds, words, grammars, and meanings—is defined by what it is not. Thus, for example, the sound *oh* is distinct from *ah* and every other sound, and the word *green* is defined in contrast to everything that is "not green." Language may be viewed, in short, as a system of binary oppositions: X's and not X's, Y's and not Y's. Lévi-Strauss carried this insight one step further, arguing that human cultures are organized around just such binary oppositions (male/female, sacred/profane, raw/cooked, and the like). Our capacity to make binary distinctions and to categorize reality according to these distinctions is fundamental to human mind and culture, whether we live in "primitive" or "modern" societies. The emergence of human culture out of nature, Lévi-Strauss argued, is accomplished by classifying the world into systems of binary opposition such as these.

Lévi-Strauss and others (e.g., Leach 1970, 1976) have analyzed a broad range of cultural phenomena, including kinship systems, food practices, and mythologies, through the lens of structural linguistics. Lévi-Strauss argued, for example, that when we view a society as a system of communication, we see that "the rules of kinship and marriage serve to insure the circulation of women between groups" just as "linguistic rules [ensure] the circulation of messages" (1968: 83; Clarke 1981: 157–83), establishing relationships of reciprocity and cooperation among groups. Similarly, Lévi-Strauss analyzed mythologic systems as elaborate linguistic constructions based on binary oppositions. Myths, he believed, are powerful mental models, expressed in symbolic form, that generate cultural performances in somewhat the same way that a musical score may be said to generate an orchestral performance.

Numerous anthropological, sociological, and literary studies have sought to analyze cultural phenomena in binary terms. Mary Douglas's *Purity and Danger* (1966) makes the case, for example, that many cultural classification systems are organized around the distinction between the "clean" and the "dirty," associating order with cleanliness and disorder or chaos with dirt. More recently, Pierre Bourdieu (1984), in his massively documented *Distinction*, analyzes the French social class system in terms of binary oppositions, charting in remarkable detail the specific tastes and practices that mark one's class membership. As Pierre Bourdieu (1984: 6–7) critically observes:

> Taste classifies, and it classifies the classifier. Social subjects, classified by their classifications, distinguish themselves by the distinctions they make between the beautiful and the ugly; the distinguished and the vulgar [by displaying their] preferences in music and food, painting and sport, literature and hairstyle . . . . The denial of lower, coarse, vulgar, venal, servile—in a word, natural enjoyment, which constitutes the sacred sphere of culture, implies an affirmation of the superiority of those who can be satisfied with the sublimated, refined, disinterested, gratuitous, distinguished pleasures forever closed to the profane.

In short, Bourdieu's is a critique of social class display organized around the binary distinction between "high" culture and "low" or "vulgar" nature.

Semiotics, the study of signs and symbol systems, has close affinities with French structuralism and has itself become something of a high art form in French intellectual circles. Its leading practitioner, literary theorist Roland Barthes, has analyzed a wide assortment of cultural phenomena as though they were "texts" to be read and analyzed in the manner of literary criticism. Barthes's semiotic analyses (e.g., 1972) have included studies of such diverse phenomena as wrestling matches; Hollywood movies; fashions in hair, food, and clothing; children's toys; striptease; and advertisements for laundry detergent—all of these analyzed as systems of symbols. (If you would like to try your own hand at semiotic analysis, try analyzing and comparing the symbol systems that Americans of varied social backgrounds typically associate with Halloween, Thanksgiving, Christmas, Three Kings Day, Easter, Juneteenth, and the Fourth of July.) The literary tools of semiotics, carried over into the social studies, open up a variety of interesting new possibilities for the analysis of cultural systems (Hodge and Kress 1988).

Deconstruction and Poststructuralism

By the 1960s, French structuralism had become a major force in anthropological theory, but it would also soon become a major target of criticism (e.g., Kurzweil 1980; Clarke 1981; Harland 1987). Lévi-Strauss had seemed to say that the mental and linguistic models that underlie culture are in some sense more real than the cultural phenomena they generate. Some critics complained that Lévi-Strauss's theory, with its focus on mental models, ignored empirical phenomena that inconveniently contradicted these models. One major critic, the French literary theorist Jacques Derrida (1976, 1978), took a different tack, challenging the structuralist doctrine of binary oppositions that lay at the very core of Lévi-Strauss's theory. Lévi-Strauss had viewed binary oppositions as more-or-less stable structures underlying cultural systems. Derrida observed, however, that when we look closely at binary oppositions such as nature/culture or speaking/writing, these seemingly sharp and crisp dichotomies become blurred, ambiguous and unstable. Under close critical scrutiny, such oppositions may even collapse like a house of cards.

Derrida coined the term *differance* to name the shifting and unstable relationship between the two terms of a binary opposition. In French, *differance* creates a complex pun. When we make distinctions, we imply not only a *difference* between opposing terms, but also a relationship of *deference* between them, privileging one term over the other. Moreover, when we call binary oppositions into question, we *defer* or postpone indefinitely any final determination of their meaning. Derrida observed that most distinctions (e.g., higher/lower, male/female, white/black) tacitly, and without warrant, imply the superiority of one term over the other. Invidious distinctions of this kind typically reflect the interests of those who make them. Thus, for instance, it is in the interest of upper-class white males to preserve invidious distinctions that imply their own superiority, and thus fortify their positions of privilege through the subtle power of language.

Derrida advocates the interrogation or calling into question of traditional distinctions. We may begin to *deconstruct* such invidious distinctions by inverting the respective positions of the terms—for example, privileging female over male, or black over white. But this only reproduces the conventional order of things in reverse mirror image. A more radical move is to deny the meaningfulness of the binary distinction in the first place (Norris 1987). To deconstruct a prevailing distinction, then, is not merely to invert the distinction, but to question its very existence. It is not merely to challenge what is said, but also to reveal what has been concealed and give voice to what has been silenced by conventional ways of writing and talking. Deconstruction thus radically challenges the authority of traditional ways of conceptualizing the world. Following the linguist Saussure, Derrida holds that the relationship between signifier (e.g., a word) and signified (e.g., the idea or experience it names) is inherently loose, slippery, and context dependent. The upshot of Derrida's analysis is that the meanings preserved in language are inherently unstable, "undecidable," and always open to multiple readings and to the free play of language.

Critics fear that this view of language is subversive and even anarchic in its cultural implications. They accuse Derrida of promoting a radical relativism in which all meanings are contingent on the reader's interpretive interests, no interpretation is better than any other, and hence nothing is true. Some sympathetic readers of Derrida contend that this caricature of his position is a political polemic, driven less by a serious consideration of Derrida's writings than by a zeal to defend privileged traditions of interpretation. Other defenders seem gleefully to embrace the subversive, transgressive, anarchic impulses in Derrida's thought. Meanwhile, the moral and political implications of Derrida's writings remain (aptly enough) murky, ambiguous, and open to multiple interpretation (Lilla 1998).

Derrida's critique of structuralism has ushered in a poststructuralist era in literary and cultural studies. He, along with the late social historian Michel Foucault, remains a looming presence in poststructuralist theory. Foucault was a historical scholar of extraordinary range and depth, driven by a fascination with the discourses that have informed cultural history. As Foucault used the term, a *discourse* is a body of language pertaining to some particular domain of knowledge. As a unit of language, discourse is larger than a word, larger than a sentence, larger than a paragraph or book. It represents all of the ways in which a particular language community thinks, writes, and speaks about a given range of phenomena in a particular time and place in history. Throughout his career Foucault investigated discourses in such varied domains as medicine, penology, and sexuality. His studies, based on detailed examinations of archival records from successive historical periods, trace deep shifts (reminiscent of the massive shifts of tectonic plates that occur deep beneath the surface of the earth) in the ways people have conceptualized these domains. Throughout his work, moreover, Foucault (1980, 1984, 1990) has focused on the intimate and inseparable connection between knowledge (inscribed in specialized discourses) and power.

In *Madness and Civilization* (1965), for example, Foucault examines discourses reflecting changing conceptions of insanity since the Middle Ages. In medieval Europe, the insane were not usually locked up but were often allowed to roam free in the countryside. Conceptions of madness shifted in the age of scientific Enlightenment, when madness came to be understood in binary opposition to reason. Enlightened reason demanded the separation and restraint of irrational forces in society. Thus, by the eighteenth century, the insane were typically separated from the "normal" populace and confined to asylums, where they could be brought under rational, systematic, and centralized control. By the nineteenth and twentieth centuries, the discourse on madness had shifted again, this time toward a medical model of insanity as a mental "illness" to be "treated" in psychiatric hospitals by medical professionals practicing under the banner of science. Foucault shows how the transformations of discourse on madness correspond to the transfer of power into the hands of scientific experts in modern societies, with scientific discourse serving as the medium through which these new forms of power are exercised.

In *Discipline and Punish* (1977), Foucault examines changing conceptions of crime and punishment. He observes that in the eighteenth century, with the rise of scientific reason, authorities sought new and more efficient means of controlling crime and punishing offenses. Medieval torture and execution gave way to newer and more "enlightened" methods of control. In keeping with the scientific and rationalist spirit of the times, the English utilitarian philosopher Jeremy Bentham proposed the design of a new kind of prison, the *panopticon*, a circular structure from which guards in a central watchtower could observe every prisoner, and prisoners could in turn observe each other, thus keeping their fellow prisoners under constant surveillance. Bentham's scientific design was adapted also to schools, military barracks, and hospitals, embodying in architectural form the combined ideals of external discipline and internal self-control that accompanied the rise of the modern state. For Foucault, the panopticon symbolizes the modern state's attempt to surveil and police a growing and increasingly diverse population, using scientific rationality as an efficient instrument of power.

In *The History of Sexuality* ([1978] 1990), Foucault turns his gaze toward the discourses of the erotic. He observes that sexual discourse during the Middle Ages was organized under the unified language of the church and was couched in the vocabulary of carnal sin, confession, and penance. In the modern era, by contrast, we have witnessed the proliferation of multiple sexual discourses ([1978] 1990: 33–35). Traditional religious ways of thinking and talking about sexuality survive alongside the modern secular discourses of law, medicine, popular culture, and its sexual subcultures. There are now more kinds of talk and writing about sexuality than ever before, including elaborate scientific classifications of sexual behavior. Only in recent centuries, Foucault argues, has sexuality come to be classified as a distinct and separate sphere of life, and subclassified according to formal categories such as "homosexual" and "heterosexual." The scientific classification of sexuality, he notes, has served to "medicalize" sexuality, bringing it under the control of "experts." Meanwhile, dissident groups have sought to resist the growing power of medical and legal discourse to define and control sexuality by developing "counter discourses" of their own ([1978] 1990: 101), such as the languages of feminism and of gay rights, which speak on behalf of the controlled and in their own terms.

Throughout Foucault's work we discern the recurring theme of power (and, less often, resistance to power) accomplished through the subtle, almost invisible medium of language. As in George Orwell's *1984* (1949), the subjugated often assist in their own subjugation by absorbing the discourse of their masters. But

Foucault's analysis seems to suggest a further possibility: that discourses exercise power over the masters as well, controlling the thoughts and actions of the controllers as well as the controlled. We are all controlled by our own rhetoric at times, and thus we are all, in Fredric Jameson's (1972) phrase, inmates in the "prison-house of language."

Foucault's analysis, like Gadamer's, suggests that we do not speak our languages so much as they speak us. We may seek escape from the prison-house of language by creating counterdiscourses to challenge the discourses of those who dominate us; and yet we have not escaped the constraints of language. We have only traded one regime of discourse for another. And so we go on creating discourses and counterdiscourses (and discourses-about-discourse à la Foucault) ad infinitum. In human life there is no escape from historically situated discourse. We may mourn this realization or we may celebrate it, but for better or worse we live in language, and it lives in us.

Foucault calls up two striking metaphorical images to describe his approach to the history of discourse. In his earlier work (e.g., Foucault 1972) he envisions his historical studies as a kind of "archaeology of knowledge," as though discourses were layered through time like geological strata. Reconstructing the history of ideas is seen as a kind of archeological dig in which we encounter both continuities and abrupt breaks in "discourse formations" as we trace the history of an idea from its origin in the past toward the surface of the present. Later, Foucault shifts to a genealogical metaphor, borrowed from the philosopher Friedrich Nietzsche. In this view, we begin with present concerns and interests, tracing the history of an idea backward or downward through the alien discourses of the past, but with no presumption that an idea has any single or definitive origin. But in either case, Foucault is interested in the discontinuities of discourse—those points in history when ways of thinking, talking, and writing seem to have undergone startling breaks or transformations. Foucault believes that such transformations typically reflect fundamental shifts in relations of power, sensitively registered in the language through which knowledge is articulated and control is exercised.

In recent years, discourse analysis has become something of a cottage industry in the historical and cultural studies (During 1993). Thanks in part to Foucault's example, new ways of writing social history are emerging. In contrast to traditional "great man" approaches to the study of history, which focus on the importance of monumental events and the exploits of powerful individuals (such as Napoleon at Waterloo), the new social history seeks to reconstruct the ways in which ordinary people have lived their daily lives through the centuries, with special attention not only to their material conditions of existence (e.g., Braudel 1973), but also to the social discourses that have defined their understandings of the world and of themselves. Edward Said (1978), for example, has critically examined the discourse, which he calls "orientalism," through which the West has historically categorized and colonized the diverse cultures of the East, caricaturing them as exotic and mysteriously sinister. Indeed, the very binary opposition of "West" and "East," he observes, is largely an arbitrary cultural construction serving the political interests of its creators.

In our own time, Foucault finds a great profusion of social discourses operating simultaneously, even within a single society. There is no longer any single, central organizing discourse in the postmodern world, as there was, for example, in the age of medieval European theocracies. In the postmodern era, discourse and power are now more decentered, diffuse, and dispersed than they once were. Others have similarly characterized the postmodern era as a time of crumbling philosophical foundations (Rorty 1979) and collapsing faith in grand narratives and discourses of every sort, whether philosophical, religious, political, or scientific (Lyotard 1984). The postmodern world is fraught with uncertainty and danger. Yet fluid and unstable though it is (and precisely because it is fluid and unstable), the present era creates an opening for promising new forms of language and politics to emerge—or so Foucault might have hoped.

Postmodern Feminism

Among the most significant developments in social theory during the last half of the twentieth century was the growing presence and influence of feminist thought in intellectual and political life. Contrary to the caricatures of some of its detractors, feminism has never been a monolithic movement. The women's movement has developed in several alternative directions simultaneously (Donovan 1994), with internal divisions often breaking along class and ethnic lines. African American feminist bell hooks (1984), has argued, for example, that fundamental differences in the historical and contemporary experiences of black and white women have sometimes produced differing feminist understandings and agendas. Yet despite their internal differences, feminists of all kinds have questioned traditional patriarchal justifications of male authority and privilege through history.

Feminists of the postmodern variety, keenly attentive to the power and politics of language, have sought to shake the foundations of patriarchy by deconstructing the basic assumptions that underlie masculist culture. Susan Hekman (1990) has lucidly analyzed these assumptions as a series of dubious binary oppositions or false dichotomies. Her analysis of patriarchy nicely illustrates the application of poststructuralist concepts within a feminist context.

1. *Rationality/Irrationality.* Hekman begins by noting that our culture has traditionally portrayed men as rational beings, while representing women as

irrational and fickle. Feminist responses to this characterization go beyond merely asserting that women can be as rational as men. They challenge our very notions of rationality itself. Hekman remarks that as long as "the association between the rational and the masculine, the irrational and the feminine is maintained, feminine ways of knowing will forever be conceptualized as inferior" (1990: 39). Feminist scholarship on the relationship between gender and cognition (e.g., Belensky et al. 1986; Gilligan 1982) suggests the need to rethink our conventional understandings of reason, making more room for intuitive and compassionate ways of knowing than are allowed for in traditional male conceptions of rationality-as-formal-abstraction.

2. *Subject/Object.* Another traditional dichotomy portrays men as the central subjects of history, while women are viewed largely as passive objects in their service. A woman is defined not by what she is, but by what she is not: not man, the other, a residual category of humanity (Beauvoir 1953; Hekman 1990: 74). Psychoanalytic theorist Julia Kristeva (1986) proposes to undermine this traditional subject/object relationship by creating discourses in which women reconstitute themselves as subjects—not as fixed subjects, but as complex and diverse subjects in a perpetual process of self-transformation.

3. *Nature/Culture.* A third traditional dichotomy links women with nature and men with culture or civilization (Hekman 1990: 105–51). Not only are women, as mothers, traditionally thought to be closer to nature than men, but they are also presumed to possess an "essential nature" as helpmates, as caregivers, and as followers. To challenge these natural roles, according to the traditional view, is to defy the very law and order of the universe. Feminists have generally been sharply critical of the doctrine of essential nature, arguing that gender roles are defined primarily by language and culture rather than biology. If the narratives of women's lives are defined more by culture than by nature, and have been authored largely by men, then they can be rewritten—and this time by women in control of their own stories.

Other false dichotomies criticized by feminists include those that equate the masculine with power and the feminine with powerlessness. Marilyn French, in *Beyond Power*, observes that "Western thought is profoundly dual, which is to say that in the West difference is more important than similarity." The presumed superiority of dominant groups (including men) "rests on their differences from other humans" (1985: 500–504). When we realize that men and women are in fact more alike than different, the basis of male claims to superiority is undermined, and with it the traditional hierarchies of patriarchal power.

Sandra Bem (1977) goes a step further, envisioning the possibility that one day the very masculine/feminine dichotomy itself might be transcended, and that each person will be allowed and encouraged to develop her or his positive human potential in all directions, irrespective of whether these directions are traditionally defined as masculine or feminine. The ultimate deconstruction of gendered oppositions, she seems to say, is the deconstruction of the very notion of gender itself.

Gays and lesbians, in their own efforts to challenge traditional dichotomies of gender, have employed many of the same deconstructionist strategies used by postmodern feminists. Consider "queer theory" (Seidman 1996), for example. The very choice of this term as a theoretical self-description is a witty, ironic inversion of the traditional binary opposition which sets straight against gay and privileges the former over the latter. As Charles Lemert (1997b: 67) observes, queer theory "subvert[s] the epithet often hurled at gay, lesbian or bisexual people in order to call attention to the queer nature" of sexual bigotry—in effect, ridiculing the ridiculers in their own terms until such time as the antagonistic opposition between the two is at last rendered culturally obsolete. Postmodern theorists emphasize that such antagonistic oppositions as gay/straight and masculine/feminine are largely social or cultural constructions, and as such, can be redefined, reinvented, repudiated, or transcended through time.

The male/female opposition is, of course, only one of many binary oppositions in which women's lives are imbedded. Patricia Hill Collins, in *Black Feminist Thought* (1991), examines not only dichotomies of gender, but of race and class as well from a perspective influenced by postmodern feminism. As an African American woman from a working-class background, Collins chooses to turn traditional hierarchies on their heads and to place traditionally marginalized social categories at the very center of her analysis. Thus, she develops an explicitly Afrocentric feminist analysis that diverges from analyses of race, gender, and class written from traditional Eurocentric, male, and economically privileged standpoints.

Similarly, Dorothy Smith (1987) develops an explicitly feminist sociology that takes the lived experiences of women as its point of departure, upending traditional patriarchal sociologies that analyze social life (often unconsciously) from the standpoint of male experiences, interests, and perspectives. Smith (1999: 96–130) appears to be more critical of postmodern forms of feminism than Collins, fearing that in their preoccupation with abstract, disembodied discourse (and discourse about discourse) they run the risk of losing touch with the everyday, earthbound lives and concerns of embodied women.

There is more to life, after all, than discourse. There are also, among other things, the things of the body, long neglected in a dualistic culture that separates body from mind and privileges the latter over the former. Feminists and other social theorists in recent years have grown increasingly interested in the social significance of the body and its desires (e.g., Boston Women's Health Book Collective 1973; Ussher 1997; Williams and Bendelow 1998; Bartkowski 1999). Discussions of embodiment frequently center on the provocative writings of postmodern feminist and queer theorist Judith Butler (1990, 1993), who contends that sex and gender roles are social/linguistic constructions that we create and recreate daily in the very act of performing them. Butler deconstructs the conventional biological concepts of "male" and "female," arguing that rigid binary sex-typing is a socially constructed fiction (1993: 5)—just one of the many ways in which culture inscribes its meanings on our bodies. Even our material existence itself, she seems to say, is a kind of cultural fabrication. Philosopher Martha Nussbaum (1999) and other critics, however, have severely questioned whether Butler, as a feminist "floating high above all matter" (1999: 42), can begin to address the real material concerns of women around the world from a perspective that seems to reduce the body to an abstract discourse. It seems clear that we experience our bodies, at least in part, in prelinguistic (e.g., during infancy) and extralinguistic ways (e.g., Lupton and Barclay: 21–24). While Sigmund Freud certainly exaggerated when he remarked that biology is destiny, it would be an equal and opposite exaggeration to suggest that our bodies are wholly under the control of language and culture. Yet in Butler's behalf, neither can we deny that our bodily experiences, postures, gestures, and sexualities are regulated by linguistic and semiotic systems from an early age, nor that every physical performance is simultaneously a cultural performance.

Critical Theory and the Defense of Reason

While Western social theory has generally neglected the body, it has prized the mind and its capacity to reason. More recently, however, deconstruction and other postmodern intellectual movements have challenged the traditional "logocentrism" or reason-centeredness that runs throughout Western intellectual history from the ancient Greeks through the modern scientific Enlightenment. Challenging this enthronement of reason, postmoderns in general, and especially those influenced by Nietzsche, typically view reason skeptically as a set of verbal and cognitive ploys that we use to pursue what we desire. If reason is the servant of desire, then individuals and groups with varying interests and desires will, like cynical courtroom lawyers, fabricate very different "rational" accounts of reality to suit their needs. A typically postmodern question is: *Which* rationality, and *whose*? (MacIntyre 1988).

But the romance of reason is not yet dead. The old modernist Enlightenment faith in reason survives in many quarters, and especially in scientific communities. Among social theorists, the defenders of reason (critically understood) include a group of German social theorists associated with the Institute for Social Research in Frankfurt, commonly known as the Frankfurt school of critical sociology (Connerton 1976; Dreitzel 1979; Arato and Gebhardt 1990; Agger 1998: 78–98), whom we previously encountered in chapter 4. This group, whose early leaders included Max Horkheimer, Theodor Adorno, and Herbert Marcuse, first emerged during the worldwide economic depression of the 1930s to challenge both fascism and capitalism. As a socialist movement, influenced by Karl Marx but opposed to dogmatic and domineering forms of Marxism (such as Stalinism), the Frankfurt school struggled to maintain an Enlightenment commitment to the emancipatory potential of reason. Its leaders envisioned the possibility of an authentically rational society which might yet free humanity from the false ideologies and oppressive political and economic systems of past and present.

Critical theorists of the Frankfurt school have strongly challenged scientific and technological abuses of reason, and particularly the instrumental use of reason as a tool of domination. They have abhorred the employment of rational means in the pursuit of immoral ends, exemplified in the technically advanced barbarism of the Third Reich, with its efficient factories of death. Yet despite strains of cultural pessimism, they have remained hopeful of reason's liberating possibilities. Threats to reasoned discourse, critical theorists warn, may come from many directions, including fascism and Nazism, instrumental capitalism, authoritarian state-socialism, shallowly positivistic and technocratic forms of science, and more recently, antirationalist varieties of postmodernism.

Among contemporary Frankfurt theorists, Jürgen Habermas in particular has pursued an interest in the linguistic and communicative dimensions of social life. Habermas has continued and extended the work of his predecessors, elaborating their critiques of domination, instrumental rationality, and the perils of the "totally administered society" governed by a scientifically trained but ethically illiterate technocratic elite. His *Theory of Communicative Action* (1984/1988) makes a formidable attempt to synthesize theoretical insights from such diverse figures as Marx, Weber, Mead, and the philosophers of language. Habermas is especially interested in the conflict between large-scale social systems (such as capitalism and state bureaucracy) and the small-scale personal and communal "life worlds" of ordinary human beings. His analysis suggests that these abstract social systems bear down on the lives of ordinary people and threaten to crush their humanity.

In response to this threat, Habermas seeks to develop an ethics of discourse (to which we will return shortly) that would expand the capacity of ordinary people to participate meaningfully, rationally, and democratically in the decisions that affect their lives. Habermas is now perhaps the leading defender of the modern

Enlightenment ideal of rational discourse. Caught between premodern traditionalists on the one hand and postmodern cynics on the other, Habermas continues to defend on both fronts the embattled ideals of reason.

⌒

The theoretical traditions we have examined thus far in this chapter, from symbolic interactionism to structuralism, and from poststructuralism to critical theory, differ among themselves in significant ways. Yet they all share a common fascination with language, taking discourse as their point of poetic departure. In recent decades linguistic metaphors have come to dominate cultural studies in both the humanities and the social sciences. In these final pages we will consider some current developments of linguistic metaphor in social theory and some promising new directions for the future.

Society as Text

In our survey of linguistic images of society we may observe two distinct but related metaphorical themes. If we take *written* discourse as our metaphorical model of society, we arrive at an image of society as a kind of "text" to be authored, read, edited, revised, erased, and the like. If, on the other hand, we take *spoken* discourse as our metaphorical point of departure, a society comes to sound more like a vast and intricate "conversation" or "dialogue" among a multitude of diverse voices through time. Let us explore the implications of each of these alternative linguistic images—text and talk—in its turn.

The fascination with writing and text that marked hermeneutics, semiotics, structuralism, and poststructuralism has given rise to the metaphorical notion that human society is itself a kind of text, inscribed in sign and symbol and capable of being "read" intelligently by those who possess its hidden codes. As the writings of continental theorists (and especially the French post structuralists) became available in English translation, many British and North American theorists soon began to explore this new way of thinking and writing about the composition of society.

The image of society as text is particularly fitting in the heavily text-dependent information societies of the post-industrial world. Dorothy Smith (1999: 33) astutely observes that virtually all social relations in such societies are mediated by texts—"by written, printed, or otherwise inscribed words and images (on television and movie screens, on the computer monitor)." In nearly every sphere of our lives, from home and school to work organization and political forum, our knowledge and daily practices are grounded in textual symbols and images. Thus we find our lives increasingly shaped by and organized around the textual mate-

186 ⁓ Chapter Nine

rials that we consume, process, produce, and disseminate to others. Even our personal relations, mediated as they often are by memos, e-mails, legal documents, and the like, are increasingly textual relations. We define ourselves, in part, through the texts that we author; for there is a sense in which "we are what we write [and] we write what we are" (Agger 1989: 303).

Among North American theorists, Richard Harvey Brown (1977, 1987, 1989, 1992a, 1992b) has been a particularly prolific advocate of text as a societal metaphor. Brown describes himself as a "symbolic realist," insisting that shared symbols are the very stuff of human consciousness and being. "As constitutive of human experience, symbols are *real* in the fullest sense of the word" (1989: 162). And because symbols are real, they have real social, political, and moral consequences.

In his critique of contemporary culture, Brown challenges not only the naive positivist rhetoric of value-neutral science, but also the individualist rhetoric of selfhood that prevails in North American culture. The rhetoric of individualism, he argues, conceals our social connectedness, privatizes our understanding of morality, and thus prevents us from assuming moral responsibility for the well-being of the *polis* or public community. The result, as we see at every turn, is the disintegration of communities and the impoverishment and degradation of civic discourse. How can we counteract these destructive tendencies in our culture? We can begin, Brown believes, by rethinking our images of society in ways that revitalize our public moral philosophy. Neither the premodern image of society as an unfolding organism nor the modern industrial image of society as a vast and complex machine operated by a technocratic elite is adequate to the task of constructing a meaningful philosophy of public participation and responsibility in the postmodern era. For this we need an image of society that honors our capacity to author, to interpret, and to rewrite the human story. We need an image of *society as text*, and more particularly, as moral narrative. Brown and others in this genre (e.g., Denzin 1990; Klein 1992; Agger 1989, 2000) employ the term *text* in a spacious and poetic way. As Julie Klein observes:

> The idea of a text is no longer confined to a written representation of "reality" or, more narrowly, a work of literature. Any statement of experience—any oral or written record, any theory or method, any natural or human science—is a discursive practice that can be "read." A text might be . . . a work of art or tool, a ritual or painting, a social action or public policy. Indeed, culture itself is seen as an "ensemble of texts" [Geertz 1973: 452]. Texts are no longer the province of English departments, metaphor the business of literary critics, or narrative the stuff of fiction. (Klein 1992: 10)

How, then, is a society like a text? The crux of the text metaphor resides in the relationship between writer and reader. Just as the game metaphor features the relationship between player and opponent, and the dramaturgical metaphor the relationship between actor and audience, the text metaphor focuses on the interplay of author and reader in the inscription or fixation of meaning (Geertz 1983: 30–31). This process of inscription is not confined to literal writing and reading, but extends by analogy to every aspect of social life when viewed as text.

Let us explore the analogy point for point. Like a written text, human society is constituted through symbols and could have no conceivable existence outside of them. Creative agents (authors) combine and recombine symbols according to cultural rules and conventions (analogous to grammatical rules), permitting a multitude of possible symbolic combinations or permutations. Thus Brown (1989: 8, 161) writes of the "human authorship of the world . . . a making of the world through language." The symbols of text and society become meaningful only through acts of interpretation. Symbols do not interpret themselves. They require the active engagement of readers/interpreters to bring them to life. Both textual and social symbol systems are capable of being edited, revised, and rewritten, interpreted and reinterpreted almost endlessly. Brown hopes that the textual metaphor's emphasis on the power and possibilities of human authorship and interpretation might inspire us to rewrite the world in more humane terms, coauthoring a less technocratic, less individualistic, more democratic, and more communal moral narrative.

The textual metaphor has its limitations. It is dangerously misleading if it implies that we can author *any* sort of world we wish. There will always be external constraints on our power to remake the world to conform to our poetic fantasies. Precisely where such constraints (physical, biological, economic, etc.) lie, and how tight or unalterable they are, is, of course, a matter of legitimate dispute. To complicate matters further, authors themselves often have radically conflicting ideas about what kind of story to tell, so that coauthoring the world often turns out to be a contentious and even bloody process. In this postmodern age of contested knowledge (Seidman 1998) and multiple authorship, we had better not expect the social text to be perfectly harmonious and coherent—nor should we suppose that it has ever been so in the past.

Textual metaphors can be overly cerebral and pretentious at times, especially when they are encrypted in the esoteric jargon of postmodernism. Postmodern jargon lends itself readily to parodies and hoaxes. A satirical analysis of the television comedy *Gilligan's Island*, for instance, finds that "Gilligan himself represents the transgressive potentialities of the decentered ego," and that the television movie, *Escape from Gilligan's Island*, "represents a reactionary attempt to totalize what had been theorized in the series as an untotalizable heteroglossia, a *bricolage*" (Morton 1990). One physicist (Sokal 1996) publicly prides himself on having defrauded the editors of the journal *Social Text* by persuading them to publish his bogus essay entitled "Transgressing the Boundaries: Toward a Transformative Hermeneutics of Quantum Gravity," written as a parody of the intellectually fashionable language of postspeak.

Yet despite its liabilities, the textual metaphor has brought some excitement to social theory in recent decades by creating "a new metalanguage in the human sciences, which opens up behaviors, cultures, and even entire historical epochs to reading as texts" (Klein 1992: 10). It allows us to read social reality in new ways, and even to write some new social reality of our own. Much of its appeal resides in its promise of the possibility that we may creatively author ourselves and our societies, a possibility that other metaphors (and especially deterministic models drawn from the natural sciences) cannot so readily promise.

Society as Conversation

An alternative linguistic metaphor projects the image of society as an ongoing conversation. Numerous theorists in this century, from the symbolic interactionists onward, have observed that we create social life largely through face-to-face dialogue. Thus we may choose to view human societies, metaphorically if not literally, as elaborate networks of intersecting and sometimes conflicting conversation.

Literal conversations have been the subject of extensive research in recent decades. Symbolic interactionists, ethnomethodologists, sociolinguists, and linguistic anthropologists have examined in fine detail the dynamics of conversation within and across cultures (e.g., Hymes 1964; Dreitzel 1979; Craig and Tracy 1983; Atkinson and Heritage 1984; Shotter 1993; Silverman 1998). Deborah Tannen (1990, 1994), for example, has undertaken detailed research on male/female differences in conversational style. Meanwhile, Sherry Turkle (1984, 1995) has closely observed interactions in the electronic chatrooms of the Internet, where conversational players create imaginary alternative identities in the relative freedom and anonymity of cyberspace.

From the world of conversation comes the metaphor of "voice," employed particularly by those who write on behalf of groups that have been historically marginalized or oppressed through history, and whose voices have been silenced or ignored in public discourse. Carol Gilligan in A Different Voice (1982), aptly chooses the conversational metaphor to make her point that male-dominated psychology has devalued and neglected women's approaches to moral reasoning. Dorothy Smith (1987: 29–36) challenges the institutionalized "authority of the male voice" as an embodiment of patriarchal power and privilege. Similarly, Gayatri Chakravorty Spivak (1988) reaches for a conversational metaphor when she asks, "Can the Subaltern Speak?" in an essay that reflects on postcolonial struggles for self-determination among subordinated peoples in the developing world, including Spivak's native India. Among social theorists in general, there is growing acknowledgment of the inherently multicultural nature of social reality itself, and of the need to widen the circle of discourse to encompass voices that have heretofore been systematically excluded from political and intellectual conversation (Anderson and Collins 1992; Lemert 1993). Accordingly, we find growing attention to the experience of being "the other" (Levinas 1989; Madrid 1988), and to the critical role that cultural translators and other go-betweens play in interpreting one cultural world to another (e.g., Castañeda 1996). At last, we are realizing that from one cultural vantage or another we are *all* the other, the foreigner, the alien, the stranger in a strange land.

Feminist theorists have noted that women in particular tend to favor the metaphor of the voice. Mary Field Belenky et al. (1986: 16) observe a "tendency for women to ground their epistemological premises in metaphors suggesting speaking and listening," in contrast to the visual metaphors (e.g., knowledge as illumination, knowing as seeing, truth as light) more commonly favored by traditional men of science and philosophy. Patricia Hill Collins (1991: xi., 113, 214) shares this view. She herself speaks of the struggles of black women (particularly from working-class backgrounds like her own) to find or regain their voices as they strive to define their own identities in the face of daunting obstacles and controlling cultural images that seek to define them externally. Her own analysis of black feminist thought is explicitly open to "multiple voices [which highlight] the diversity, richness and power" of African American women's intellectual community (1991: xiii.). Collins speaks poetically of "the journey from silence to language to action" (1991: 112), a process through which subjugated knowledges are given expression and silenced voices are finally heard.

Closely related to the metaphor of the voice is the metaphor of dialogue. The dialogue as a literary form is at least as ancient as the *Upanishads* and is extraordinarily developed in the Socratic dialogues of Plato. Literary interest in dialogue has been stimulated by the rediscovery of the Russian literary critic Mikhail Bakhtin (1981), whose dialogical analyses of novels as polyphonic or "many-voiced" constructions were suppressed in the monological culture of Stalinism. Indeed, we find growing interest in the phenomenon of dialogue not only among literary theorists, but also among social philosophers, educators, religious ecumenists, psychotherapists, negotiaters, and mediators. What is it about our time in history that seems to call forth an urgent interest in the problems and possibilities of dialogue?

Interest in dialogue arises in part from the experience of living in a fragmented world of human differences marked by destructive antagonisms along economic, political, racial and ethnic, religious, sexual, and other lines. While conflicts of these kinds have existed for millennia, never before have they occurred in the presence of such advanced technologies of violence. In such a world, the search for alternatives to violence as a means of resolving conflicts takes on a special urgency. Winston Churchill's (1954) dictum that "to jaw, jaw is always better than to war, war" has never been more apt. The need to overcome social fragmentation is perhaps most clearly apparent in highly diverse societies, such as the United States, that manifest strong individualist tendencies (Bellah et al. 1985).

Dialogical Communities: The Socratic Paradigm

We live, then, in a world of dangerous divisions. This is the historical context within which the social philosopher Richard Bernstein (1983: 223–31) pleads for the construction of *dialogical communities*—communities of serious and sustained conversation based on mutual respect and a willingness to listen across differences. Bernstein imagines the possibility of communities that are richly diverse, yet nonetheless unified around a common commitment to the conversation. Dialogue by its very definition requires a diversity or plurality of voices and an acknowledgment of the "otherness" of others (Gurevitch 1988; Levinas 1989), for dialogue without difference would be nothing more than collective monologue. But authentic dialogue goes beyond the mere acknowledgment of difference. It also requires a strong communal commitment to the conversation, and to shared rules of discourse that make that conversation possible.

But what should these rules of discourse be? One possible answer may be sought in the dialogues of Plato (in Hamilton and Cairns 1961), which purport to recount conversations between Socrates and his fellow Athenians more than two millennia ago. If we examine these dialogues carefully, we can discern a well-developed paradigm for creating and sustaining communities of dialogue. While the Platonic dialogues, and their depiction of Socrates, are semifictional and highly idealized, there is little doubt that they were inspired by real Socratic encounters that Plato witnessed as a young man. Gadamer (1980: 126) observes that the Socratic dialogues "engaged the participants for whole days at a time and established a living community among them," and Brann (1979: xxxvii) contends that this "establishment of dialogic community is itself *the* Socratic accomplishment." Through a close textual analysis of the dialogues, the Socratic paradigm can be shown to include at least the following principles or rules of discourse:

1. *Let us seek to tell the truth.* Authentic dialogue demands honesty. Socrates' view of the aim of dialogue as the honest pursuit of truth stands in sharp

contrast to the more cynical, pragmatic, and relativistic views of his sophist rivals, who (by his account) are less interested in truth than in the manipulation of argument for their own ends.

2. *Let us strive not to contradict ourselves.* Socratic dialogue typically begins with a question, such as "What is justice?" (*Republic*) or "Can virtue be taught?" (*Protagoras*), and proceeds in search of a conclusion that withstands the test of noncontradiction. Ultimately, Socratic dialogue rejects both the conservative authority of tradition and the democratic authority of public opinion in favor of the higher authority of reason. For Socrates, rational self-consistency, pursued through the procedure of question-and-answer, is essential to achieving the Athenian ideals of personal and social harmony.

3. *Let us listen carefully to those with whom we differ.* Something akin to a principle of free speech is operative in the Socratic dialogues, at least for those privileged enough to gain access to the conversation. Every view may have the floor, although not every view will be judged to have equal merit (*Protagoras*, in Segal 1986: 165). (It is no small irony, incidentally, that the freedom of speech that Socrates himself enjoys is severely curtailed in his proposed republic.)

4. *Let us attend carefully to the details of our conversation.* Socrates draws frequent analogies to the skilled manual crafts by way of illuminating the craft of discourse. He shows particular concern for the careful naming of things. Definitions are not to be advanced lightly; and when they are advanced, their consequences are to be pursued to the end.

5. *Let us proceed by establishing points of common agreement.* Whether a given argument will be abandoned or allowed to stand is determined by a consensual principle of progress-by-agreement—i.e., by the rational and uncoerced consent of participants. In addition, Socrates recommends a periodic review of agreements, a "taking stock of where things stand" in the conversation (*Symposium* and *Gorgias,* in Segal 1986: 262, 303). This principle of progress-by-agreement is a ratchetlike mechanism for pushing the conversation to ever higher levels of consensus while at the same time preventing it from slipping backward too easily.

6. *Let us sublimate our aggressions.* Socrates warns against displays of excessive aggression or competitiveness. There is, to be sure, a gamelike quality to Socratic dialogue not unlike that found in an intense game of chess. An opening gambit is followed by strategic moves and countermoves by the respective players. Like a chess master, Socrates is adept at anticipating his adversary several moves in advance. Yet authentic dialogue must be more than a mere game of words, a verbal domination game whose

ultimate object is to compel the submission of others (Gouldner 1965: 261–62; Hamilton and Cairnes 1961: xxiv.). Excessive competition subverts the higher goal of dialogue as a communal search for truth.

Timely and graceful displays of diplomacy, tact, and modesty aid in the sublimation of aggression. Thus, Socrates seeks to cool an overheated exchange with the headstrong Callicles by offering these soothing and deferential (if ironic) words to his scornful adversary: "And please, my gifted friend, try to teach me my primer in a milder tone, so that I won't run away from your school" (*Gorgias*, in Segal 1986: 297). This sort of dialogical etiquette has a disarming effect, diplomatically bringing the adversary back into the community of shared purpose.

7. *Let us risk being changed by the conversation.* This principle of risk points to the essential open-endedness of dialogue. Socratic dialogue is transformative with respect both to participants themselves and to their understanding of the objects of discourse. To enter Socratic dialogue is to risk the possibility of being changed by the conversation.

8. *Let us reevaluate the rules of discourse when the conversation fails.* Interestingly, one of the implicit rules of discourse in Socratic dialogue is that the rules of discourse are themselves subject to renegotiation and change. In *Protagoras* (Segal 1986: 163ff), for example, dialogue breaks down over the issue of how long each party may speak. The dialogue resumes only after a new rule of discourse is agreed upon, limiting the duration of speech and appointing an umpire to enforce the time limit.

   The theoretical point is that some rule systems contain within themselves metarules (or rules-about-rules) permitting the system's self-transformation. The rules of Socratic discourse, like the amendment provisions in democratic constitutions, are clearly reflexive in this sense. They are not given once and forever, but evolve in response to unanticipated problems or crises such as the dialogical breakdown described above.

9. *Let us agree to stay in the conversation.* In the Socratic ideal, dialogical community entails a commitment to stay in the conversation for better or worse, renegotiating the rules of discourse when necessary, in order to keep the conversation going. Because Socratic dialogue insists on the priority of the question over the answer (Gadamer 1975, 1980), it is an infinite game (Carse 1986), resisting closure and allowing for an indefinite continuation of play. The truth is approached but never finally captured.

Nowhere is the commitment to dialogue as a way of life more poignantly expressed than in Socrates' principled refusal to flee the city of Athens to escape his own death sentence (*Crito*). To his last breath, Socrates is committed to staying in serious conversation with his fellow Athenians. The unspoken promise of the Socratic paradigm is that if we faithfully observe these basic rules of dialogue, the quality of our public discourse and the quality of our communal and personal lives will be deepened and enriched. Empirically, we cannot say to what degree this promise is fulfilled in practice, so rarely has the paradigm been tried in the world outside of Plato's mind.

Beyond the Socratic Paradigm

Many elements of the Socratic paradigm still remain intact as normative ideals in twentieth-century conceptions of dialogue. Even the postmodern American pragmatist Richard Rorty (1979), famed for his all-out assault on classical and modern attempts to establish absolute and changelesss philosophical foundations, speaks approvingly of the "Socratic virtues" and reaffirms the Socratic commitment to "keep the conversation going." Yet in certain respects, our understanding of dialogue has undergone significant changes since the time of Socrates. Many are skeptical of the existence of universal and eternal truths, or of our human capacity to know them definitively even if they exist. We now seem to take a more pragmatic view of dialogue as a tool for problem solving and conflict resolution as we "seek to discover some common ground to reconcile differences" in the face of the "irreducibility of conflict grounded in human plurality" (Bernstein 1983: 223). This problem-solving orientation toward dialogue is evident in a rapidly expanding body of literature on mediation, negotiation, and conflict resolution (e.g., Fisher and Ury, 1983; Folberg and Taylor, 1984; Dunlop, 1984; Lemmon, 1985; Moore, 1986; Fisher and Brown, 1988). This literature reports a wide range of dialogical procedures designed to aid conflicting parties in reaching workable solutions to problems that might otherwise escalate into potentially destructive conflict, from the microlevel of the family to the macrolevel of international relations.

To be sure, the classical understanding of dialogue as a search for ultimate truth still survives today in some quarters. It can be found, for example, in Robert M. Hutchins's (1952) introduction to the *Great Books of the Western World*, dedicated to the "Great Conversation" of Western Civilization, which Hutchins characterizes (grandly and without a touch of historical irony) as the "Civilization of Dialogue." But this loftier conception of dialogue now coexists alongside a more earthbound view of dialogue as a tool in the struggle for mutual survival. If there is a moral imperative in our own time, it is to find ways to live together in all of our glorious and hideous plurality without degrading or annihilating each other. In the struggle for survival, dialogical strategies may be useful tools in the prevention of mutual destruction.

Another important difference between classical and contemporary conceptions of dialogue lies in their respective attitudes toward democracy. Plato was candidly and unapologetically critical of the institutions of Athenian democracy. Contemporary conceptions of dialogue, by contrast, usually point toward the possibility of greater inclusiveness and democratic participation in public discourse. Richard Bernstein's notion of dialogical community, for example, is explicitly democratic, calling for a communal life in which decisions are arrived at through pluralistic discourse and reasonable persuasion. In contrast to the Platonic vision of a static and harmonious social order, democracy is by its nature a dynamic, messy, and contentious process. Bernstein shares Hanna Fenichel Pitkin's and Sara M. Schumer's (1982: 47) view of democratic politics as an "encounter among people with differing interests, perspectives, and opinions—an encounter in which they reconsider and mutually revise opinions and interests, both individual and common." Democratic decision making occurs in an environment of conflict, imperfect knowledge, and uncertainty. Democratic outcomes "are always more or less temporary, subject to reconsideration, and rarely unanimous." Conflicts, as they inevitably arise, are resolved through open discussion and persuasion— i.e., through a political form of dialogical community (cf. Carter and Kobylka, 1986). Bernstein deplores the fact that "much of humanity has been systematically excluded and prevented from participating in such dialogical communities" (1983: 226).

The democratization of dialogue is also an important theme in Gouldner's (1979) analysis of the "culture of critical discourse" in advanced industrial societies. Gouldner contends that a new class of intelligentsia is ascending to power in these societies, armed with a shared ideology which demands that public claims be justified by reason and evidence. In some respects the culture of critical discourse is elitist, favoring the interests of the most educated, literate, and articulate segments of society. But in other respects it is egalitarian, because it demands that every claim be justified without reference to the speaker's societal position or authority, and is in principle open to anyone. Many who have heretofore been excluded from critical discourse may now join the conversation.

The impulse to democratize dialogue finds its sharpest political expression in the theory and practice of the Brazilian educator Paulo Freire (1982, 1998; Freire and Macedo, 1987). Freire's "pedagogy of the oppressed" is a radically dialogical form of education in which teacher and learner are mutually engaged in developing literacy and critical social analysis simultaneously (Freire, 1982; Freire and Macedo, 1987; Walker 1981). Freire relies on Martin Buber's (1958, 1965) notion of the I/Thou relationship to characterize the dialogical community of coteachers and colearners. The point of dialogue, for Freire, is not merely to reach a meeting of minds and hearts, but to forge the tools for a dialogical transformation of oppressive economic and political structures.

Paradoxically, we see in the modern era not only a progressive *democratization* of dialogue, but also an increasing *bureaucratization* of dialogue in which conversants are not individuals speaking for themselves, but rather teams of agents speaking for large organizational entities. Thus we now refer to dialogues among nation-states ("Arab-Israeli dialogue"), between capital and labor in contract negotiations, and the like. Within organizations as well, dialogue among contending parties now frequently occurs within the matrix of formal administrative hearings and grievance procedures.

In an age of postmodern cynicism, many doubt whether dialogue across differences is ultimately possible at all. Derrida (1989), for example, in a sharp encounter with Gadamer, frankly doubts that we can ever achieve common understanding in dialogue. Other postmodern writers, such as Lyotard (1984: 10–11), tend toward the cynical view that manipulation and deceit are inevitable features of dialogue. Lyotard describes the "game of dialogue" as a contest of domination, a "balance of power" in which each move provokes a defensive/reactive or (better yet) an inventively aggressive countermove. The object of the game is to displace or disorient one's opponent with an unexpected move that throws the other off balance. There are cynical tendencies as well in exchange theories of interpersonal communication (Roloff 1981: 25–27) and in the writings of Goffman (1959, 1970), who sometimes seems to view sincerity itself as a self-protective, self-aggrandizing maneuver.

But in the dialogue about dialogue we can hear more idealistic voices as well. Consider, for example, Buber's (1958, 1965) influential writings on dialogue as an authentic encounter between an I and a Thou. In the I/Thou relationship, persons encounter each other in their totality, distinguishing this relationship from the segmented, instrumental relationship between I and It. In authentic dialogue, "heart speaks to heart" (Kaufmann, 1967: 668). Though Buber's conception of dialogue is less reason-centered than that of Socrates, they share a faith in the possibility of sincere encounter.

More recently, Habermas has restated the Socratic principle of sincerity in his theory of communicative competence (1970, 1979, 1984/1988). Habermas observes that much of what passes for authentic communication is in fact pseudocommunication, in which reciprocal misunderstandings are not recognized as such "due to the pretense of pseudoconsensus" (1970: 117). Pseudocommunication is systematically distorted by coercive structures of domination that give one speaker a privileged position of power over another. In response to this problem, Habermas outlines the conditions of an "ideal speech situation" that would allow authentic communication to occur (1979: 1–68; see also Gusdorf 1965, Grice 1975; and Mura 1983 on the ethics of discourse). For Habermas, the ultimate aim of rational discourse is for speaker and hearer to reach consensus or common understanding, uncontaminated by the effects of illegitimate power, coercion, manipulation, or deceit. Reasoned argument, not social position or the authority of tradition, should carry the day (Calhoun 1992: 2). And neither Habermas, nor Buber, nor Socrates is prepared to abandon the hope that authentic communities of dialogue can be achieved.

But is dialogic civility really possible in a cynical age? This is the core question posed by Ronald C. Arnett and Pat Arneson (1999) in a recent and wide-ranging survey of dialogical thought. In our own view, the perennial debate between cynics and idealists is untestable in thought alone. We simply do not know whether, or under what circumstances, authentic dialogue is possible until we have tested its possibilities and limitations in the natural laboratory of social practice. The point, finally, is not merely to theorize about communities of dialogue but to attempt to build them into the world, and to reflect candidly on our successes and failures.

It is arguable that communities of dialogue similar to those envisioned by Bernstein (1983) and others already exist. Habermas (1989) maintains that early modern prototypes of such communities could be found in the coffee houses of London and the salons of Paris 300 years ago, although these public spaces were mainly reserved for members of the propertied elite. Today, the circle of public discourse is somewhat wider and more inclusive. Elements of dialogical community, however imperfect, may be found in the institutions of liberal democracy, in universities, in international forums such as the United Nations, in ecumenical religious bodies, and in the emerging institutions of mediation and negotiation (e.g., Fisher and Ury, 1983; Fisher and Brown, 1988; Marks, 1989). In the academic sphere, Smith (1999: 133–56) envisions the emergence of a more fully dialogic sociology in which many diverse voices, grounded in many different modes of social experience, receive a respectful hearing. Meanwhile, Tannen (1998) finds some hopeful signs of a shift in American society away from a deeply adversarial or "argument culture" and toward a culture of dialogue.

Creating dialogical structures capable of spanning economic, political, ethnic, religious, sexual, or other social chasms is certainly no panacea. Indeed, in some instances face-to-face encounters among conflicting parties may only harden differences. Dialogue is also hard work; the effort must be mutual and all parties must be prepared to persist relentlessly (Howe 1963: 3). But even the cynic must acknowledge that when the alternative to dialogue is mutual destruction, there is little to lose in the attempt.

Dialogical experiments are by nature open-ended and risky. Their outcomes are never wholly reducible to what conversants bring to the conversation, but are emergent in the conversation itself (Gadamer 1975). Therein lies the possibility of mutual transformation that makes dialogue more than merely a tool for solving problems or resolving conflicts among fixed positions. In the task of building communities of dialogue, the Socratic virtues seem as essential now as they have ever been: careful speaking and listening, persistence in the search for agreement, sublimation of aggression through tact and diplomacy, tenacious commitment, and a willingness to be changed by the conversation.

Closing Words

If a society is a vast and intricately complex conversation (or conversation *among* conversations) through time, the same is true of social theory as well, for social theory does not exist outside of society. Rather, it is one set of conversations among the multitude of conversations that constitute our social life. Theorists have come and theorists have gone, but the conversation has endured through centuries. It is a conversation conducted largely through metaphor, with each metaphor representing a distinctive voice and viewpoint. The conversation began long before Socrates and will not end until the last human or posthuman breath is drawn.

In the past century we have seen a deep shift in the metaphors that dominate social theory. Nineteenth-century social theorists favored metaphors that mimicked the more successful natural sciences, selecting analogies mainly from biology, chemistry, and physics. Social scientists, modeling themselves after physical scientists, sought to discover the natural "laws" of society and history. In recent decades, however, the ground has shifted. Today, the positivist dream of a social physics seems, if not dead, at least dormant. Meanwhile, Clifford Geertz (1983: 21) observes, "the move toward conceiving of social life as organized in terms of symbols . . . has grown by now to formidable proportions."

Geertz goes on to note that theorizing (scientific or otherwise) has always proceeded mainly through metaphor or analogy—a way of seeing one thing as another and thereby achieving a "comprehension of the less intelligible by the more." Thus the scientific imagination has conceived that "earth is a magnet, the heart is a pump, light is a wave, the brain is a computer, and space is a balloon." Social theory has likewise been a story told in metaphors and analogies. To nineteenth-century theorists, the social world looked very much like an organism or a machine. Today theorists are more apt to see it as "a serious game, a sidewalk drama, or a behavioral text" (Geertz 1983: 23). Increasingly our societal metaphors have come not from the sciences but from the humanities. One wonders where the social and cultural studies would be today if Auguste Comte's dream had been to establish not a "social physics," but rather a "social linguistics" or a "social aesthetics."

Geertz may somewhat exaggerate the decline and fall of scientific metaphors.

In chapter 2 we noted a growing interest among social theorists in metaphors borrowed from evolutionary biology and ecology. Meanwhile, the rapid development of computer and information sciences has opened up some intriguing metaphorical opportunities for scientifically minded theorists. Information processing models already dominate cognitive psychology, and they may grow increasingly prominent in the social sciences as well.

The metaphors we create and embrace do not merely describe social reality, but also may subtly influence its course of development. Thus, if we conceive social life as a war and act upon that assumption, we are apt to create a rather different world than if we conceive social life as a conversation or a game or a legal code. Every metaphor and every social theory implies its own distinctive assumptions about reality, its own objects of focus, its own characteristic methods of research, and its own political and moral consequences (Brown 1977; Sjoberg and Nett 1997). Each metaphor leads us down a different path of understanding to a different destination. Therefore, we had better choose our metaphors carefully. Remaining unconscious of our metaphors (the sleepwalker's option) is also a choice, with its own comatose consequences.

Sociology has been described as "an ultimately vain but irresistible search for a single general theory" capable of making all social phenomena intelligible (Wallace 1969: 59). In recent years many social analysts have reached the conclusion that there can probably never be any such unified theory. Like William Shakespeare, we employ a multitude of metaphors, and it will be difficult or impossible to reconcile these competing images of society. Thus, Brown concludes that "we can have either no general theory or several general theories, but we cannot with consistency have only one general theory" (1992b: 226)—not even the theory of society as discourse which Brown himself favors.

And so the blind sages continue to dispute the nature of the social elephant—a very peculiar creature of which they themselves are a part. Each sage describes the beast from the distinctive angle of a particular metaphor. Each metaphor is partial and biased in its own special ways, concealing some aspects of the whole as it reveals others. Each is a way of seeing and a way of not seeing. And although each metaphor may correct the excesses of the others, none can do the elephant full justice. For in the end, an elephant—and especially one as massive, many-sided, and rapidly mutating as ours—is like nothing but itself.

~

A Guide to
Metaphorical Analysis

For those who would like to try their own hands at metaphorical analysis, this guide provides a more advanced discussion of the cognitive and cultural uses of metaphor, together with some proposed criteria for evaluating their theoretical merits in the social sciences. In chapter 1 we described metaphor as a mode of thought wherein we interpret one domain of experience through the language of another, creating a fusion of images and associations between the two. We distinguished metaphor ("A *is* B") from simile ("A *is like* B") and analogy ("A is like B with respect to attributes *x*, *y*, and *z*"). We went on to distinguish positive analogy (the likenesses between A and B) from negative analogy or disanalogy (the differences between A and B) and neutral analogy (those respects in which we do not yet know whether A and B are alike or different) (Hesse 1966). The scholarly literature on metaphor, simile, and analogy is vast and growing rapidly.[1] We cannot begin to do it justice here. Thus, as we continue our discussion of metaphor, we will touch only upon those points that seem especially relevant to our focus on social theory.

The Dynamics of Metaphor

Throughout the literature on metaphor we find a recurring emphasis on its creative and dynamic qualities. One interesting debate concerns whether metaphors are based on properties that exist "objectively" between two phenomena (a commonsense view), or whether metaphors actually "create" such similarities in our minds. Most contemporary literary theorists tend toward the latter view. In a classic statement, Max Black (1962: 37) notes that it "would be more illuminating in some cases to say that the metaphor creates the similarity than to say that it formulates some similarity antecedently existing." Similarly, Eugene Miller

199

(1979) distinguishes between a "verificationist" tradition that advocates the systematic testing of metaphorical claims against objective reality and a "constitutivist" tradition, which emphasizes the ways in which metaphors create realities of their own. In the latter tradition, the poet Wallace Stevens describes metaphor as "the *creation* of resemblance by the imagination" (in Brogan 1986: 15; emphasis added).[2]

Consider this example. When William Shakespeare writes that all the world is a stage, is he merely *discovering* common properties of theater and social life, or is he, in the very act of making metaphor, *inventing* a more dramatic world for his readers? We live in a world both found and made, and the place where the finding ends and the making begins is sometimes difficult to discern. Perhaps we may say that while some metaphors do little more than call our attention to familiar similarities, others (the more poetically interesting metaphors) create new and unexpected connections among the elements of our experience—connections that would not otherwise have come into being.

Douglas Hofstadter (1985: 550) notes that metaphors and analogies arise when one thing reminds us of another, triggering an association between present and past experience. This suggests that the logic of analogy is "conservative" in a certain sense, pressing new experience into the preexisting and established categories within which we have sorted past experience. Like the Procrustean bed in Greek legend, an analogy may amputate potential new meanings that do not fit conveniently within its framework. Yet paradoxically, the logic of analogy may in some instances have radical or revolutionary implications as well, especially when a fresh analogy leads us to see things in new and unexpected ways (Sjoberg and Nett 1997: 246–48; Schön 1967). The logician Charles S. Peirce ([1932] 1957) was among the first to recognize the power of analogy (or what he called "abduction") as a creative source of new hypotheses[3] and hence an essential tool in the logic of discovery (Kaplan 1964). Peirce's early insight has been vindicated. Metaphors and analogies are now generally acknowledged as the creative inspiration for numerous theoretical insights and models in both the physical and social sciences.[4]

Literary theorists often speak of metaphors as having a direction of movement or impact. When Shakespeare says that all the world's a stage, for instance, the main movement of the metaphor is from B (the domain of theater) to A (the world of everyday life). Yet the movement of meaning may flow in the opposite direction as well. As the two domains "interact," each may alter our perception of the other (Richards 1936; Black 1962). Thus, Shakespeare's theatrical metaphor may dramatically alter our perception of the larger social world, but it may subtly alter our perception of theater as well.[5]

Interactions among meanings within a metaphor are often exceedingly complex. Consider the fact that most words have multiple meanings, or at least shades of meaning. Furthermore, their meanings include both their literal denotations and their connotations (i.e., the emotional and other psychological associations that often accompany words). Thus, when we bring A and B together to create a metaphor, all of the meanings and shadings of A may potentially interact with all of the meanings and shadings of B. The more we analyze, the more we realize that there is probably no such thing as a simple metaphor.

Just as the terms within a metaphor interact with each other, so does the metaphor as a whole interact with its social or cultural environment. A metaphor does not come from nowhere. It comes from particular people situated in particular social groups in particular places, times, and cultural settings. Once a metaphor is created, it may then shape the thoughts, feelings, and actions of people and groups, thus feeding back into the social context from which it emerged and altering that context in the process. Metaphors have many socially relevant uses: they organize and categorize experience; they control meanings and motivate actors; they articulate shared values and beliefs; in short, they are essential devices in the construction of the social world (St. Clair 1994). The dynamic interaction between ideas (including metaphors) and their social contexts is the main focus of that fascinating branch of social theory known as the sociology of knowledge (Mannheim 1936; Merton [1948] 1968: 510–62; Berger and Luckmann 1966).

Finally, we must note that the meanings of metaphors often vary through time and across cultures. The metaphor of society-as-war may mean one thing in the age of muskets and another in the age of nuclear missiles. The metaphor of the eagle as a revered national symbol has one set of meanings and historical associations in the United States and another in Mexico. Metaphors may even have different meanings to different segments of the same society. Thus, while whiteness may connote purity and goodness to most Anglo-American speakers of English, the color white has had less pure and noble connotations among African American social critics such as Malcolm X (1964: 188f) and Toni Morrison (1992: 59). In short, the meanings of metaphors are not universal and static, but rather multiple and changing. Like puns, they have more than one sense and can be appreciated on more than one level. Accordingly, a single metaphor may be developed in a multitude of different and even opposing directions.

The Metaphorical Construction of Culture

Metaphors are not the exclusive province of poets and theorists. Considerable evidence from the cognitive sciences suggests that human beings in general are by nature metaphorical or analogical thinkers (Holyoak and Thagard 1995), a trait that may be found at a more rudimentary level in chimpanzees (Goodall 1991: 22) and perhaps other species as well.

Why must we make metaphors? Because without them, we could scarcely make sense of our sense data. We are bombarded with sensory input at every moment of our lives. These billions of bits of experience would seem chaotic and meaningless if we could not sort them according to their recurring features and compare them with previous experiences. Thus, we continually and actively process bits of experience by selecting, sorting, arranging, comparing, analyzing, and synthesizing them. Among these basic cognitive processes is our capacity to forge connections, often unconsciously, among seemingly unrelated experiences through the use of metaphors and analogies.

Metaphors are deeply imbedded in the languages we speak. When we examine the etymological roots of our vocabularies, we soon discover that most words are in fact "faded," "frozen" or "dead" metaphors (which are, of course, metaphors about metaphors). The term *etymological roots*, for instance, figuratively suggests that words are like growing plants. The word *metaphor* is itself a metaphor, from a Greek root meaning "to carry over or transfer," as though metaphors literally moved meanings from one place to another. Many clichés and proverbs are metaphors. Thus "a stitch in time saves nine" is more than a sewing lesson, and the proverbial "bird in the hand" is usually something other than a bird. We often invoke familiar metaphors of this sort without fully realizing it, like the man who did not know he had been speaking prose all of his life.

As basic tools of the mind, metaphors, similes, and analogies are instrumental in the continual construction of culture. A growing body of anthropological scholarship suggests that the metaphorical construction of culture occurs in diverse societies around the world, and not just in Western civilizations (Sapir and Crocker 1977; Fernandez 1991; Tilley 1999). Consider the range of cultural domains in our own society in which metaphors are at work. The realm of political discourse, for instance, is replete with metaphors and analogies (Lakoff 1996; Tannen 1998). Much of our political vocabulary is made of figurative language borrowed from athletic competition (as when we speak of a political "race") and warfare (a political "campaign"). Political editorialists rely on historical metaphors when they warn of ominous parallels between our time and times past, drawing dubious analogies to such dire events as the rise of Nazism, the onset of the Great Depression, the fall of the Roman Empire, or the coming of the Dark Ages, or when they caution that the next foreign policy decision could lead to "another Munich" or "another Vietnam." While it is natural to interpret new experiences in the light of prior experiences by drawing analogies to the past, we must remain constantly aware that such analogizing, even in the hands of capable historians, is fraught with dangers (Fischer 1970: 243–59).

Metaphors and analogies are also basic to legal reasoning (Levi 1949). Courtroom arguments commonly assert that if the facts of one case are sufficiently analogous to the facts of another in relevant respects, then the legal principle that applied in the former case should hold in the latter as well. Thus, trial attorneys frequently invoke metaphors and analogies to convince judges and juries that a particular legal precedent is relevant to the case at hand.

The power of metaphors is readily apparent in religious discourse as well (McFague 1982; Lee 1993). Jewish and Christian theologies traditionally draw upon family metaphors that picture ultimate reality as a strong father figure. Taoist texts, by contrast, call upon the imagery of water, at once both the gentlest and most powerful of substances, while Zen Buddhist teachings associate the ultimate nature of things with deep silence. Like the blind sages in the Indian fable, religious thinkers of all faiths have been guided by metaphors in their explorations of sacred mysteries, although their respective metaphors have often seemed to point in rather different directions.

It almost goes without saying that literature and the arts are saturated with metaphors. These are their stock-in-trade. Less obvious, perhaps, is the prevalence of metaphor and analogy in science. While such poetic devices were once regarded as inherently unscientific, contemporary philosophers and historians of science now generally acknowledge the crucial role that metaphors and analogies have often played in the process of scientific discovery, even in the most rigorous physical sciences (Hesse 1966; Weisberg 1993). It is well known, for example, that Niels Bohr constructed his model of the atom from an analogy to the solar system. Friedrich Kekule's discovery of the structure of benzene rings came to him in a dream in which he visualized the remote analogy of a snake seizing its own tail, while James Watson and Francis Crick's model of DNA as a double helix was inspired by a near analogy to Linus Pauling's helical model of protein (Weisberg 1993: 106, 156). Much of our knowledge of the body derives from technological metaphors: the heart as mechanical pump, respiration as combustion, or the brain as computing machine (Jonathan Miller 1978). Among philosophers of science the interesting question is not whether metaphors and analogies can be useful in developing scientific theories (for this is no longer in doubt), but whether they are essential infrastructures of theory or mere scaffoldings that can be safely taken down once formal theories are firmly in place.

Metaphors and analogies also have played an indisputable role in the history of technological invention, from the development of winged aviation—literally the process of becoming a bird—to the design of the printing press by analogy to the wine press (Weisberg 1993: 42, 125–49). The history of technology is brimming with examples of this kind (Koestler 1964; Schön 1967; Boden 1992).

Metaphors also play a critical role as persuasive devices in commerce, as teaching devices in education (Pugh et al. 1992), and as interpretive devices in psychotherapy (Kopp 1995). We may well ask: In what social institution are metaphors *not* important? In every sphere of life our ability to think, to imagine, and to create culture depends on our capacity to generate and interpret metaphors. Indeed, it begins to seem that human culture is, to a surprising degree, a metaphorical construction. This is not to say, of course, that metaphor is the *only* means of constructing culture. There are many mental tools besides metaphor; yet there are none that can replace it.

Our thesis throughout this book has been that social theory, as one special domain of culture, is created largely through metaphor. This raises a thorny question: "Are all metaphors in social theory equally valid, or are some more insightful and valuable than others?" Making complex judgments about the adequacy of competing metaphors is the task of metaphorical analysis. The following protocol may be helpful to those who wish to pursue this distinctive form of cultural criticism.

Evaluating Metaphors in Social Theory

Metaphors and analogies are not all created equal. Some are frankly more interesting than others. (With apologies to Forrest Gump, life is not, after all, terribly much like a box of chocolates—at least not for me.) Literary and cultural critics have proposed a variety of criteria for evaluating the quality of metaphors and analogies (e.g., Booth 1979: 53–56; Brown 1977: 99–107), distinguishing the better ones from the worse. As we try to make such judgments within the context of social theory, here are some questions we will want to ask. Together, these questions constitute a preliminary protocol for metaphorical analysis in the social and cultural studies.

1. *Does the metaphor have heuristic value? Does it show promise of yielding unexpected new insights?*
2. *Is the metaphor adequately developed or explicated?*
3. If our interests are primarily scientific, *does the metaphor lead to the discovery of general explanatory principles?*
4. Relatedly, *does it generate any testable hypotheses or predictions?*
5. If our interests are primarily aesthetic, *is the metaphor particularly creative or elegant or poetically insightful?*
6. And if our concerns are primarily moral or ideological, *does the metaphor serve rhetorically to advance some desirable end in a persuasive way? Moreover, whose interests does the metaphor serve?*

Let us consider each of these criteria of judgment in further detail.

1. Heuristic Potential

Metaphors and analogies in the social sciences may be judged first by their heuristic potential—i.e., by their capacity to produce new discoveries and insights. A heuristic metaphor is fertile with possibilities for further development. Every major metaphor in social theory, from "society as organism" to "society as discourse," contains within itself a multitude of divergent possibilities for analogical development. Mary Hesse (1966) has noted that an analogy's heuristic potential resides mainly in what she calls the "neutral analogy"—those points at which the analogy's validity is unknown and in need of deeper inquiry (cf. Peirce's notion of abduction as discussed in note 3).

One might suppose that the most valuable analogies are those that establish the highest degree of isomorphism (i.e., the strongest possible resemblance) between two domains, but this is not necessarily so (Brown 1977: 101–2). The heuristic value of an analogy often depends on a high degree of apparent dissimilarity between the domains in question. It is not isomorphisms per se, but rather unnoticed or unexpected isomorphisms that make an analogy interesting. A heuristic analogy is one that has the capacity to surprise us with a fresh view of a familiar subject, to suggest fruitful new concepts, and to generate novel lines of inquiry.

The heuristic potential of an analogy is not limitless. Fredric Jameson (1972: v) observes that analogical models typically undergo a predictable series of developmental stages through which their heuristic potientials are gradually depleted. In the initial stage, an analogical model triggers an explosion of intellectual energies by offering a fresh and exciting perspective on the world, presenting old problems in new dress and bringing a host of new problems into view. In the second stage, the analogy's inadequacies gradually become apparent and the model itself is readjusted to bring it into line with its object of study. Finally, its opportunities exploited and its limitations apparent, the weary analogy is abandonded in favor of some fresh new analogy, whereupon the cycle recommences. There are clear parallels between this view of the rise and fall of analogical models and Thomas Kuhn's (1972) more general discussion of the rise and fall of paradigms in the history of science.

2. Adequacy of Explication

Ideally, a metaphor is economical and concise, offering an "elegantly efficient integration of a broad range of diverse phenomena" (Brown 1977: 104). Metaphors and similes are not very informative, however, until we begin to explicate the points of resemblance that they leave implicit. In so doing, we transform metaphors and similes into analogies. To explicate an analogy is to specify, to the point of diminishing returns, the set of relevant attributes shared by A and B (the positive analogy) as well as the set of relevant attributes that differentiate them (the negative analogy).

Metaphors and analogies tend to train our focus on the positive similarities between A and B while subtly suppressing our awareness of their differences (Morgan 1997). In the social sciences, positive analogies are often advanced uncritically and haphazardly, while negative analogies are almost entirely ignored. Early efforts to develop Darwinian models of social change (Hofstadter 1944; Degler 1991), for example, often resulted in the uncritical transfer of biological terminology into the social sciences with little attention focused on the significant differences between organic evolution and sociocultural change. It is unfortunate that the negative analogy is so regularly neglected, for it may in some instances be as theoretically enlightening as the positive. Even a "weak" analogy is useful if it forces us to articulate the grounds of its inadequacy, for in so doing we are made to bring our hidden assumptions and preconceptions to the level of conscious awareness and public criticism.

How can we do a better job of explicating our analogies? Suppose, for example, that someone suggests that "racism is a cancer in the body social" (Brown 1977: 105). This seemingly simple metaphor, derived from the image of society as organism, packs a great deal of information and implication into eight little words. We begin to explicate its meaning by asking "In what respects is this so?" Precisely how is a society like a living body? Precisely how is racism like a cancer? Precisely how is the relationship between racism and society like the relationship between cancer and the body? What, if any, are the social analogues of radiation, chemotherapy, and surgery? Who will perform the treatments? And upon whom or what? In what respects are racism and cancer *dis*analogous (the negative analogy)? And in what respects does it remain unclear, pending further investigation, whether the two are alike or not (the neutral analogy)?

To explicate this metaphor thoroughly, it may be useful to draw up a glossary of key terms and relationships from the field of oncology (e.g., carcinogens cause tumors; tumors may be either benign or malignant; carcinomas may metastasize, etc.). From this base we may then attempt to "map" the language of cancer onto the domain of race relations, being careful to note those points at which correspondences are either forced or apparently nonexistent.

The problem of explication is complicated by the fact that a single metaphor or simile often contains within itself multiple possibilities for development. Two theorists, working from the same metaphorical base, may arrive at very different (though not necessarily contradictory) analogical outcomes. In developing the dramaturgical metaphor, for instance, it will make a considerable difference whether we adopt scripted or improvisational theater as our base model, or whether we choose to view life as comedy or tragedy.

The process of explicating a metaphor must end somewhere. We may profitably analyze a metaphor to the point of diminishing returns, but there is little to be gained from doggedly and mechanically analyzing it to death. In any case, a good metaphor exhausts us long before we have exhausted it.

3. Explanatory Power

Social scientists in the positivist tradition have long sought to model the social studies after the physical sciences in the hope of duplicating the impressive achievements of the latter and sharing in their prestige. Social scientists in this tradition will be particularly interested in the power of analogies to generate scientific explanations and testable predictions.

Analogies may be useful as a means of discovering general explanatory principles. Let us return for a moment to Richard Brown's "racism as cancer" example (1977: 105). Brown states that if we are persistent and insightful enough in developing the analogy between racism and cancer, we will eventually exhaust the relevant points of comparison between the two phenomena. Either we will have learned everything that medicine can teach us about racism, thus exhausting the metaphor's heuristic potential, or we will move in the direction of developing a general explanatory theory of "systems breakdown" that encompasses *both* cancer *and* racism—a theory that transcends the metaphor by subsuming both of its terms under a more general and literal set of explanatory concepts. At this more general level, bodies and societies are not seen to be *like* systems; they simply *are* particular instances of systems and are governed by the same set of general systemic laws.

Social scientists have frequently attempted to proceed from analogy to general explanatory law in the manner outlined above. Donald Campbell (1965) argues, for example, that similarities between biological evolution and cultural change are so striking that they may be subsumed under a common set of general evolutionary principles. He remarks (1965: 26) that the "analogy to cultural cumulations will not be from organic evolution per se, but rather from a general model of adaptive fit . . . for which organic evolution is but one instance." Similarly, George Homans (1961: 68–70) examines the analogy between economic exchange and other forms of social transaction, concluding that "the similarities in the propositions of the two shine through the differences" and that the "Law of Supply [in economics is] equivalent to—we dare say identical with—our proposition: The more valuable the reward gotten by an activity, the more often a man will emit it." In each case the identification of positive analogies between the principles of one domain and those of another leads to the discovery of a set of more general principles that purport to explain phenomena in either domain.

The use of analogy for explanatory purposes need not imply that one term in the analogy is necessarily "reduced" to the other. Many influential social theorists, including Emile Durkheim and Talcott Parsons, have made use of biological analogies while at the same time staunchly resisting any suggestion that sociocultural phenomena are reducible to biological principles. In some respects, analogy actually represents an *alternative* to the reductionist strategy. Ludwig von Bertalanffy (1968: 48) suggests that a "unitary conception of the world may be based, not upon the possibly futile and certainly farfetched hope finally to reduce all levels of reality to the level of physics, but rather on the isomorphy of laws in different fields." Thus, if we were to discover general explanatory principles that hold good at both the biological and social levels of analysis (e.g., see James Miller 1978 for an ambitious attempt in this direction), these principles would not be the exclusive property of either biologists *or* social scientists. We would have no good reason to say that one field had been "reduced" to the other.

4. Predictive Power

Social scientists, and particularly those in the positivist tradition, are interested not only in the explanatory power of theories, but also in their capacity to generate testable hypotheses or predictions. Consider, for example, the case of gravity models in demography. John Stewart (1948) proposed that the Newtonian gravity equation (in which the gravitational attraction between two bodies is equal to the product of their masses divided by the squared distance between them) might be used to predict the volume of interaction (e.g., transportation or communication) among cities. Stewart's model had clear test implications and generated subsequent research that led, in turn, to the refinement of the model. The model offers a clear example of Charles Peirce's ([1932] 1957) logic of abduction, or analogy, in its capacity as a creative source of theories and hypotheses (see note 3).

Note that the analogy between Newtonian gravity and urban interaction does not pretend to subsume gravitation and migration under a common set of explanatory principles. The resemblance is purely formal or mathematical, not substantive. Thus, there is apparently no "deep analogy" that would lead us to believe that gravity and migration are separate manifestations of the same underlying process. The analogy is valuable nonetheless, for while it may fail to *explain* urban interaction, it is still useful for the purpose of *prediction*. Rarely are the predictive consequences of analogical models so clearly developed in the social sciences.

5. Aesthetic Value

While scientists will be interested mainly in the explanatory and predictive power of metaphors, those educated in the humanities are likely to pay more attention to their artistic or aesthetic merits. Thus, Brown (1977), in a book aptly entitled *A Poetic for Sociology*, urges us to judge the value of metaphors and analogies in social theory, at least in part, with an eye toward their cognitive aesthetics— their poetic insight, their elegance, and their capacity to create and recreate the world through symbol.

The cognitive aesthetics of a model, Brown notes, need not be viewed as a radically unscientific or antiscientific standard of judgment. Considerations of elegance do sometimes play a part in the judgment of scientific theories and mathematical proofs, if only as tie-breakers between competing products that are otherwise equally satisfactory. An analogy that organizes vast bodies of information in a satisfying and parsimonious way commands more than a purely scientific appreciation; it calls forth certain artistic appreciation as well.

Social scientists are not always so artful in their use of metaphor. Mixing metaphors is usually considered poor form in literary circles, but among social theorists it appears to be a mark of high ambition. The prominent American social theorist Talcott Parsons, for instance, sought to incorporate physical, biological, economic, and other metaphors into a grand and cumbersome theoretical system (Brown 1977:117). The danger, of course, is that when social theorists attempt to integrate metaphors from many different domains, the result may be both aesthetically and intellectually incoherent.

Aesthetic judgments are subject to immense variability—beauty residing in the unique relationship between beholder and beheld—and therefore, it is unlikely that we will ever arrive at universally accepted criteria for evaluating the aesthetic worth of metaphorical models. But this is not an argument for aesthetic obtuseness. It is an impaired soul indeed that cannot appreciate the music of metaphor and the architecture of analogy.

6. Moral and Ideological Value

A similar problem arises with respect to the moral and ideological evaluation of metaphorical models—namely the problem of the cultural relativity of values. Some have tried to side-step the problem by arguing that scientific knowledge of the social world can and should be entirely "value free" with respect to moral and ideological issues (Weber [1918] 1958). Knowledge is neutral, so the argument goes, and what we choose to do with that knowledge is a moral or political judgment, separate and distinct from scientific judgments about what is or is not empirically true. According to this line of thought, the moral or political consequences of a model should have no bearing on its validity.

This image of science as a morally neutral and value-free enterprise still lives in the popular culture, but the naiveté of this view is now generally apparent to those who reflect seriously on the social context of science, for reasons that we discussed in chapter 3. Scientific knowledge *is* a form of power in the modern world, an insight reached four centuries ago by Sir Francis Bacon and reaffirmed by such contemporary social critics as Jürgen Habermas (1970, 1971), Michel Foucault (1980), and Stanley Aronowitz (1988). If knowledge is power, it can hardly fail to have moral and political implications. Metaphorical models in the social sciences—in mathematical game theory, for instance—often have profound moral or political policy consequences, and to ignore these would be not only naive but intellectually dishonest. Therefore, when we assess metaphorical models in social theory, we must ask: "What human values and interests are favored by this model, and what values and interests are hindered or suppressed?" Normative and ideological questions are by no means the only consideration in judging the worth of a metaphor, but neither can they be honestly ignored.

It is a fundamental axiom in the sociology of knowlege that one's perception of social reality is conditioned strongly by one's location in the social order. Our views of the world, including our favored metaphors and analogies, are likely to reflect our own limited experiences of the social whole. Thus, the experience of riding atop the social elephant and attempting to guide its movements is rather different from the experience of being trampled under its prodigious weight. The rider comes to one understanding of society, the trampled to another.

Karl Mannheim (1936: 274–75), a founder of the sociology of knowledge, observed that metaphorical images of society are sometimes selectively appropriated by various economic classes and political factions in accordance with their respective social positions and interests. Mannheim demonstrated, for example, that the image of society as an organic entity expressed the conservative interests of the landed nobility in nineteenth-century Germany, while the commitments and interests of the left were better reflected in atomistic and mechanistic models of society, which implied that the component elements of the social structure can be disassociated and recombined to form new social compounds.

Closer to home, the endorsement of social Darwinism by powerful business interests in the late nineteenth and twentieth centuries (Hofstadter 1944; Degler 1991) reminds us that models of society are sometimes embraced or rejected on the basis of the values and interests they support. Claiming that a given set of social arrangements is "natural" or "inevitable," for example, is often used to promote conservative political objectives on the presumption that "if something is natural, then efforts to change it will be futile" (Wolfe 1993: 172).

We see, then, that metaphors are rarely ideologically neutral, but that they often carry a hidden cargo of assumptions from one domain of discourse to another. Moreover, the subtle implications of such domain assumptions (Gouldner 1970) are often embraced unconsciously and uncritically. One task of metaphorical analysis is to bring these assumptions and implications to the surface of awareness and public discussion.

Metaphors may be not only ideologically biased, but gender biased as well. Different metaphors may resonate the differing sensibilities of men and women. Carol Gilligan (1982) and others (e.g., Belenky et al. 1986) have argued that women and men tend to exhibit differing "ways of knowing," including differing ways of approaching moral questions. Thus, Gilligan finds that in their moral judgments, men are more likely than women to reason according to formal or abstract principles, while women are more apt to process moral issues with an affective concern for community, connectedness, and the giving of care. If such differences exist, we should expect to find corresponding differences in the metaphors that men and women invoke to talk about our lives together as human beings. In general, women may be more inclined than men to embrace organic and communicative metaphors of social life (for example, the images of society as ecosystem, as theater, or as dialogue), while men may generally show a stronger affinity for mechanistic and competitive metaphors (society as machine, as market, or as game). This is, in any case, a testable hypothesis.

Contemporary political and moral rhetoric is thick with metaphor (Lakoff 1996). We often hear, for example, that our society has lost its "moral compass" (mechanistic metaphor) and is teetering on a crumbling "moral foundation" (architectural/mechanistic metaphor), and is therefore in need of "moral rearmament" and "cultural warfare" (military metaphors) against the forces of "moral decay" that are devouring it like a "cancer" (biological metaphors). We also hear references to an intricately woven "social fabric," often in the context of divisive attacks against those elements of society that are presumed to be fraying its edges or ripping it apart. Less often do we hear that the diverse groups that constitute our society share an "interwoven destiny" (Cisneros 1993)—a textile metaphor of a different texture.

In some instances, metaphors and analogies portray images of what we believe a good society ought to be like, not what societies are like in actuality. The image of society as a well-functioning biological organism may appeal especially to those who yearn for a perfectly harmonious society, whether such a thing could actually exist or not. Similarly, metaphors may in some instances reflect the personal inclinations of those who make and consume them. The image of society as a computer or cybernetic system may appeal especially to those with an interest in science, high technology, and the electronic future. The image of society as theater or text may appeal especially to those with literary interests, while the image of society as war may attract those drawn to issues of domination and subordination. Judgments concerning what constitutes a "good metaphor" in such instances may say as much about the values and interests of the evaluator as they do about the metaphor itself.

Herein lies the chief dilemma in evaluating metaphors and analogies against moral or ideological criteria. In a radically and self-consciously pluralistic world there is little agreement about what such criteria should be. In the postmodern situation we may hesitate to claim absolute or universal status for our own moral and ideological notions; and yet we can no longer pretend (as advocates of value-neutrality once did) that metaphors, analogies, or any other representations of reality are morally or ideologically neutral. Perhaps the best we can do in this situation is to state our moral and political commitments candidly, to give our reasons for embracing them, and then to offer theoretical critiques in the light of these openly acknowledged commitments.

In any case, those who practice metaphorical analysis will perform a signal service by helping to raise cultural awareness to a new level, giving us a subtler understanding of the poetry and rhetoric of our public discourse. It is one thing to create and use metaphors. This is something we all do. It is another thing entirely to reflect carefully on our metaphors and to probe their deeper implications. This, a much rarer skill, is the essential task of metaphorical analysis.

Notes

1. For contemporary philosophical and psychological research on metaphor, see especially Sacks (1979), Lakoff and Johnson (1980), and Ortony (1993). Classic statements include those of Vaihinger (1925), Richards (1936), Black (1962), Turbayne (1962), and Ricoeur (1977). For recent work on analogy, see Holyoak and Thagard (1995), Gelernter (1994), and Hofstadter (1985, 1995).

2. Brogan (1986) offers a thoughtful analysis of the relationship between metaphor and simile. She argues that metaphor, by inviting us to see two things as one, is a unifying force in language. It works toward connection and coherence, answering a human yearning for unity. At the opposite extreme, deconstructive theories of language (e.g., Derrida 1976, 1978) picture language as a system of differences, with every word defined against that which it is not and every sign forever distinct from what it signifies. In this view, the very nature of language tends toward disintegration. Brogan maintains that simile lies between these extreme poles of unity and fragmentation, drawing its power from both poles "just as it is necessary to have positive and negative poles in order to have a current of electricity" (1986: 25). Simile thus allows for the "interplay of opposing forces in language," the forces of convergence and divergence (1986: 182).

3. Logic textbooks normally classify analogy as a weak form of inductive reasoning. However, Peirce ([1932] 1957) argued that analogy, or "abduction" as he termed it, is

distinct from both induction and deduction. While deduction involves reasoning "downward" from the general to the particular and induction involves reasoning "upward" from the particular to the general, analogy involves reasoning "across" from one realm of experience to another, or as Peirce says, "from facts of one kind to facts of another" ([1932] 1957: 129). For example, the chemist Van't Hoff, having noted that "the osmotic pressure of a number of chemical substances was inversely proportional to their atomic weights, thought that perhaps the same relation would be found to exist between the same properties of any other chemical substance" ([1932] 1957: 236). Peirce was careful to note that abduction is a weaker form of inference than either deduction or induction. It commits us to nothing; it merely "causes a hypothesis to be set down on our docket of cases to be tried" by induction. Peirce was impatient with forced or untestable analogies in science. He recommended that the predictive consequences of an analogy be stated clearly and distinctly in advance, and that its failures as well as its successes be noted honestly after subsequent testing.

4. There has been some debate in recent decades—largely semantic—about the relationships among the terms *theory*, *analogy*, and *model*. At one extreme are those, following Herbert Simon and Allen Newell (1956), who treat all theories as models and all models as analogies. Others, such as David Willer (1967), prefer to treat analogy as one of several types of models and to treat models as way stations toward the development of formal theory. Our own view, closer to Willer's, is to see metaphors and analogies as an inspirational source of many formal models and theories, without which the latter might never have been conceived.

5. Koan: To the most avid fan, is baseball a metaphor for life, or is life a metaphor for baseball?

Bibliography

~

Abell, Peter. 1992. "Is Rational Choice Theory a Rational Choice of Theory?" In *Rational Choice Theory: Advocacy and Critique*, ed. by J. S. Coleman and T. J. Fararo. Newbury Park, Calif.: Sage.

———. 1996. "Sociological Theory and Rational Choice Theory." In *The Blackwell Companion to Social Theory*, ed. by B. Turner. Oxford, UK: Blackwell.

Abrahamson, Mark. 1978. *Functionalism*. Englewood Cliffs, N.J.: Prentice-Hall.

Adams, Richard N. 1975. *Energy and Structure*. Austin: University of Texas Press.

Addams, Jane. [1907] 2000. "Utilization of Women in City Government." In *Social Theory: Roots and Branches*, ed. by P. Kivisto. Los Angeles: Roxbury.

Adler, Alfred. 1930. "Individual Psychology." In *Psychologies of 1930*, ed. by C. Murchison. Worcester, Mass.: Clark University Press.

Adorno, Theodor W., Else Frenkel-Brunswik, Daniel Levinson, and R. Nevitt Stanford. 1950. *The Authoritarian Personality*. New York: Harper.

Agger, Ben. 1989. *Socio(onto)logy: A Disciplinary Reading*. Urbana: University of Illinois Press.

———. 1998. *Critical Social Theories: An Introduction*. Boulder, Colo.: Westview.

———. 2000. *Public Sociology: From Social Facts to Literary Acts*. Lanham, Md.: Rowman & Littlefield.

Aldrich, Howard E. 1979. *Organizations and Environments*. Englewood Cliffs, N.J.: Prentice-Hall.

Alexander, Jeffrey, ed. 1985. *Neofunctionalism*. Beverly Hills, Calif.: Sage.

American Psychiatric Association (APA). 1987. *Diagnostic and Statistical Manual of Mental Disorders*, 3d ed. Washington, D.C.: APA.

Anderson, Margaret, and Patricia Hill Collins, eds. 1992. *Race, Class and Gender: An Anthology*. Belmont, Calif.: Wadsworth.

Anderson, Walter Truett. 1990. *Reality Isn't What It Used to Be*. San Francisco: Harper & Row.

Appelbaum, Richard. 1970. *Theories of Social Change*. Chicago: Markham.

Arato, Andrew, and Elke Gebhardt, eds. 1990. *The Essential Frankfurt School Reader*. New York: Continuum.

Archibald, Katherine. 1947. *Wartime Shipyard*. Berkeley and Los Angeles: University of California Press.

Arendt, Hannah. [1951] 1979. *The Origins of Totalitarianism*. San Diego: Harcourt.

———. 1963. *Eichmann in Jerusalem: A Report on the Banality of Evil*. New York: Viking.

Aristotle. [ca. 330 B.C.E.] 1935. *Poetics*. New York: Modern Library.

Arnett, Ronald C., and Pat Arneson. 1999. *Dialogic Civility in a Cynical Age*. Albany: SUNY Press.

215

Aronowitz, Stanley. 1988. *Science as Power*. Minneapolis: University of Minnesota Press.

Arrighi, Giovanni. 1978. *The Geometry of Imperialism*. London: NLB.

Arrow, Kenneth. 1951. *Social Choice and Individual Values*. New Haven: Yale University Press.

Atkinson, J. M., and John Heritage, eds. 1984. *Structures of Social Action: Studies in Conversation Analysis*. Cambridge, UK: Cambridge University Press.

Axelrod, Robert. 1984. *The Evolution of Cooperation*. New York: Basic.

Bailey, Kenneth D. 1994. *Sociology and the New Systems Theory*. Albany: SUNY Press.

Bakhtin, M. M. 1981. *The Dialogic Imagination*, ed. by M. Holquist. Austin: University of Texas Press.

Barash, David. 1991. *Introduction to Peace Studies*. Belmont, Calif.: Wadsworth.

Barthes, Roland. 1972. *Mythologies*. New York: Noonday.

Bartkowski, John. 1999. Review of P. Mellor and C. Schilling, *Re-forming the Body*; and S. Coakley, ed., *Religion and the Body*. *Review of Religious Research* 41: 279–81.

Bartley, W. W., III. 1985. *Wittgenstein*. LaSalle, Ill.: Open Court.

Barzun, Jacques. 2000. *From Dawn to Decadence*. New York: HarperCollins.

Bateson, Mary Catherine. 1989. *Composing a Life*. New York: Penguin.

Baudrillard, Jean. 1983. *Simulations*. New York: Semiotext(e).

———. 1988. *America*, trans. by C. Turner. London: Verso.

Bauer, Raymond. 1966. *Social Indicators*. Cambridge: MIT Press.

Beauvoir, Simone de. 1953. *The Second Sex*. New York: Knopf.

Becker, Gary. 1976. *The Economic Approach to Behavior*. Chicago: University of Chicago Press.

———. 1991. *A Treatise on the Family*. Chicago: University of Chicago Press.

Becker, Howard S., and Blanche Geer. 1958. "The Fate of Idealism in Medical School." *American Sociological Review* 23: 50–56.

Beeghley, Leonard. 1989. *The Structure of Social Stratification*. Boston: Allyn & Bacon.

Belenky, Mary Field, Blythe McVicker Clinchy, Nancy Rule Goldberger, and Jill Mattuck Tarule. 1986. *Women's Ways of Knowing*. New York: Basic.

Bell, Daniel. 1973. *The Coming of Post-industrial Society*. New York: Basic.

———. 1976. *The Cultural Contradictions of Capitalism*. New York: Basic.

Bellah, Robert N. 1970. *Beyond Belief*. New York: Harper & Row.

———, Richard Madsen, William M. Sullivan, Ann Swidler, and Steven M. Tipton. 1985. *Habits of the Heart*. Berkeley: University of California Press.

———, Richard Madsen, William M. Sullivan, Ann Swidler, and Steven M. Tipton. 1991. *The Good Society*. New York: Knopf.

Bem, Sandra. 1977. "Beyond Androgyny." In *Family in Transition*. 2d ed., ed. by A. S. Skolnick and J. H. Skolnick. Boston: Little, Brown.

Bennett, William J. 1994. *Index of Leading Cultural Indicators*. New York: Simon & Schuster.

Berger, Peter. 1963. *An Invitation to Sociology*. Garden City, N.Y.: Anchor Doubleday.

———. 1967. *The Sacred Canopy*. Garden City, N.Y.: Doubleday.

———, and Thomas Luckmann. 1966. *The Social Construction of Reality*. Garden City, N.Y.: Doubleday.

Berliner, David C., and Bruce J. Biddle. 1995. *The Manufactured Crisis*. Reading, Mass.: Addison-Wesley.

Bernays, Edward L. 1947. "The Engineering of Consent." *Annals of the American Academy of Political and Social Science* 250: 113–20.

Berne, Eric. 1964. *Games People Play*. New York: Grove.

Bernstein, Richard J. 1976. *The Restructuring of Social and Political Theory*. Philadelphia: University of Pennsylvania Press.

———. 1983. *Beyond Objectivism and Relativism*. Philadelphia: University of Pennsylvania Press.

Berry, Thomas. 1988. *The Dream of the Earth*. San Francisco: Sierra Club Books.

Bertalanffy, Ludwig von. 1968. *General System Theory*. New York: Braziller.

Best, Steven, and Douglas Kellner. 1991. *Postmodern Theory*. New York: Guilford.

Binmore, Ken. 1992. *Fun and Games*. Lexington, Mass.: Heath.

Bjork, Daniel. 1993. *B. F. Skinner: A Life*. New York: Basic.

Black, Max. 1962. *Models and Metaphors*. Ithaca: Cornell University Press.

Blau, Peter. 1964. *Exchange and Power in Social Life*. New York: Wiley.

Bleicher, Joseph. 1982. *The Hermeneutic Imagination*. London: Routledge and Kegan Paul.

Bloch, Marc. 1964. *Feudal Society*. Chicago: University of Chicago Press.

Bloom, Allan. 1987. *The Closing of the American Mind*. New York: Simon & Schuster.

Blum, Alan, and Peter McHugh. 1971. "The Social Ascription of Motives." *American Sociological Review* 36: 98–109.

Blumer, Herbert. 1969. *Symbolic Interactionism*. Englewood Cliffs, N.J.: Prentice-Hall.

Bly, Robert. 1996. *The Sibling Society*. Reading, Mass.: Addison-Wesley.

Boden, Margaret A. 1992. *The Creative Mind*. New York: Basic.

Bonner, John. 1986. *Introduction to the Theory of Social Choice*. Baltimore: Johns Hopkins University Press.

Booth, Wayne C. 1979. "Metaphor as Rhetoric: The Problem of Evaluation." In *On Metaphor*, ed. by Sheldon Sacks. Chicago: University of Chicago Press.

Boston Women's Health Book Collective. 1973. *Our Bodies, Ourselves: A Book by and for Women*. New York: Simon & Schuster.

Boulding, Elise. 1992. *The Underside of History: A View of Women through Time*. Revised ed. Newbury Park, Calif.: Sage.

Boulding, Kenneth. 1962. "An Economist's View of 'Social Behavior: Its Elementary Forms.'" *American Journal of Sociology* 67: 458–61.

Bourdieu, Pierre. 1984. *Distinction*. Cambridge: Harvard University Press.

Bowles, Samuel, and Herbert Gintis. 1976. *Schooling in Capitalist America*. New York: Basic.

Brann, Eva. 1979. "Introduction." In Plato's *The Republic*, ed. and trans. by R. Larson. Arlington Heights, Ill.: Harlan Davidson.

Braudel, Fernand. 1973. *Capitalism and Material Life, 1400–1800*. New York: Harper & Row.

Brissett, Dennis, and Charles Edgley, eds. 1975. *Life as Theater: A Dramaturgical Sourcebook*. Chicago: Aldine.

Brockett, Oscar G. 1977. *History of the Theatre*, 3d ed. Boston: Allyn & Bacon.

Brodie, Richard. 1996. *Virus of the Mind*. Seattle: Integral Press.

Brogan, Jacqueline Vaught. 1986. *Stevens and Simile: A Theory of Language*. Princeton: Princeton University Press.

Brown, Richard Harvey. 1977. *A Poetic for Sociology*. Cambridge, UK: Cambridge University Press.

———. 1987. *Society as Text*. Chicago: University of Chicago Press.

———. 1989. *Social Science as Civic Discourse*. Chicago: University of Chicago Press.

———, ed. 1992a. *Writing the Social Text*. New York: Aldine DeGruyter.

———. 1992b. "Social Science and Society as Discourse." In *Postmodernism and Social Theory*, ed. by S. Seidman and D. G. Wagner. Cambridge, UK: Blackwell.

Browning, Barbara. 1998. *Infectious Rhythm: Metaphors of Contagion and the Spread of African Culture*. New York: Routledge.

Buber, Martin. 1958. *I and Thou*, 2d ed. New York: Collier/Macmillan.

———. 1965. *Between Man and Man*. New York: Macmillan.

Buchanan, James M., and Gordon Tullock. 1962. *The Calculus of Consent*. Ann Arbor: University of Michigan Press.

Buckley, Walter. 1967. *Sociology and Modern Systems Theory*. Englewood Cliffs, N.J.: Prentice-Hall.

Burke, Kenneth. 1945. *A Grammar of Motives*. New York: Prentice-Hall.

Burns, Tom. 1992. *Erving Goffman*. London: Routledge.

Buss, David. 1998. *Evolutionary Psychology: The New Science of the Mind*. Needham Heights, Mass.: Allyn & Bacon.

Butler, Judith. 1990. *Gender Trouble*. New York: Routledge.

———. 1993. *Bodies That Matter*. New York: Routledge.

Calhoun, Craig. 1992. "Introduction." In *Habermas and the Public Sphere*, ed. by C. Calhoun. Cambridge: MIT Press.

Calvin, William H. 1990. *The Ascent of Mind*. New York: Bantam.

Campbell, Bernard. 1966. *Human Evolution*. Chicago: Aldine.

Campbell, Donald. 1960. "Blind Variation and Selective Retention in Creative Thought as in Other Knowledge Processes." *Psychological Review* 67: 380–400.

———. 1965. "Variation and Selective Retention in Sociocultural Evolution." In *Social Change in Developing Areas*, ed. by H. R. Barringer, G. I. Blanksten, and R. Mack. Cambridge, Mass.: Schenkman.

———. 1975. "On the Conflicts between Biological and Social Evolution and between Psychology and Moral Tradition." *American Psychologist* 30: 1103–26.

Campbell, Joseph. 1988. *The Power of Myth*. New York: Doubleday.

Campion, Jane (screenwriter and film director). 1992. *The Piano* (film). Los Angeles: Miramax.

Cannon, Walter B. 1932. *The Wisdom of the Body*. New York: Norton.

Caplan, Arthur L., ed. 1978. *The Sociobiology Debate*. New York: Harper.

Capra, Fritjof. 1982. *The Turning Point*. New York: Simon & Schuster.

Carlin, George. 1997. *Brain Droppings*. New York: Hyperion.

Carse, James P. 1986. *Finite and Infinite Games: A Vision of Life as Play and Possibility*. New York: Ballantine.

Carson, Rachel. 1962. *Silent Spring*. New York: Knopf.

Carter, Bradley Kent, and Joseph F. Kobylka. 1986. "The Dialogic Community: Education, Leadership and Participation in James Madison's Thought." Paper presented at the annual meetings of the Southwestern Political Science Association, San Antonio, Texas.

Cassidy, John. 2000. "The Fountainhead." *New Yorker* (April 24/May 1): 162–75.

Castañeda, Antonia. 1996. "Language and Other Lethal Weapons: Cultural Politics and the Rites of Children as Translators of Culture." In *Mapping Multiculturalism*, ed. by A. F. Gordon and C. Newfield. Minneapolis: University of Minnesota Press.

Casti, John. 1989. *Paradigms Lost*. New York: Avon.

Chaplin, Charlie (director and actor). 1936. *Modern Times* (film). Hollywood, Calif.: United Artists.

Chase, Truddi. 1990. *When Rabbit Howls*. New York: Jove.

Chase-Dunn, Christopher. 1989. *Global Formation*. Cambridge, Mass.: Blackwell.

Chodorow, Nancy. 1978. *The Reproduction of Mothering*. Berkeley: University of California Press.

Chomsky. 1965. *Aspects of the Theory of Syntax*. Cambridge: MIT Press.

Churchill, Winston. 1954. Speech at White House, in *New York Times*, June 27: 1.

Cicourel, Aaron. 1970. "Basic and Normative Rules in the Negotiation of Status and Role." In *Recent Sociology No. 2: Patterns of Communicative Behavior*, ed. by H. P. Dreitzel. New York: Macmillan.

———. 1974. *Cognitive Sociology*. New York: Free Press.

Cisneros, Henry. 1993. *Interwoven Destinies*. New York: Norton.

Clark, Arthur C. 1968. *2001: A Space Odyssey*. New York: New American Library.

Clarke, Simon. 1981. *The Foundations of Structuralism*. Totowa, N.J.: Barnes & Noble.

Clausewitz, Karl von. [1834] 1962. *On War*. London: Routledge.

Coleman, James S. 1990. *Foundations of Social Theory*. Cambridge: Belknap/Harvard University Press.

———, and Thomas J. Fararo, eds. 1992. *Rational Choice Theory: Advocacy and Critique*. Newbury Park, Calif.: Sage.

Collier, James Lincoln. 1991. *The Rise of Selfishness in America*. New York: Oxford University Press.

Collins, Patricia Hill. 1991. *Black Feminist Thought*. New York: Routledge.

Collins, Randall. 1975. *Conflict Sociology*. New York: Academic.

———. 1988. *Theoretical Sociology*. San Diego: Harcourt Brace Jovanovich.

———. 1994. *Four Sociological Traditions*. New York: Oxford University Press.

Commoner, Barry. 1971. *The Closing Circle*. New York: Knopf.

Comte, Auguste [1830–42] 1998. "The Positive Philosophy of Auguste Comte," trans. by H. Martineau. In *Auguste Comte and Positivism: The Essential Writings*, ed. by Gertrude Lenzer. Chicago: University of Chicago Press.

Connerton, Paul, ed. 1976. *Critical Sociology*. Harmondsworth, UK: Penguin.

Cooley, Charles Horton. 1902. *Human Nature and the Social Order*. New York: Scribner.

Coontz, Stephanie. 1992. *The Way We Never Were*. New York: Basic.

———. 1998. *The Way We Really Are*. New York: Basic.

Coser, Lewis. 1956. *The Functions of Social Conflict*. New York: Free Press.

———. 1971. *Masters of Sociological Thought*. New York: Harcourt Brace Jovanovich.

Craig, Robert T., and Karen Tracy. 1983. *Conversational Coherence*. Beverly Hills, Calif.: Sage.

Cross, Stephen J., and William R. Albury. 1987. "Walter B. Cannon, L. J. Henderson, and the Organic Analogy." *Osiris*. 3(2d series): 165–92.

Csikszentmihalyi, Mihaly. 1990. *Flow: The Psychology of Optimal Experience*. New York: HarperCollins.

Dahrendorf, Ralf. 1988. *The Modern Social Conflict*. New York: Weidenfeld & Nicolson.

Daly, Mary. 1973. *Beyond God the Father*. Boston: Beacon.

———. 1985. *The Church and the Second Sex*. Boston: Beacon.

Darwin, Charles. [1859] 1964. *On the Origin of Species*. Cambridge: Harvard University Press.

Davis, Kingsley, and Wilbert E. Moore. 1945. "Some Principles of Stratification." *American Sociological Review* 10: 242–49.

Davis, Morton D. 1970. *Game Theory*. New York: Basic.

Dawkins, Richard. 1976. *The Selfish Gene*. New York: Oxford University Press.

———. 1982. *The Extended Phenotype*. New York: Oxford University Press.

———. 1987. *The Blind Watchmaker*. New York: Norton.

———. 1989. *The Selfish Gene*. New ed. New York: Oxford University Press.

Degler, Carl. 1991. *In Search of Human Nature: The Decline and Revival of Darwinism in American Social Thought*. New York: Oxford University Press.

Demerath, N. J., III, and Richard A. Peterson, eds. 1967. *System, Change and Conflict*. New York: Free Press.

Dennett, Daniel C. 1991. *Consciousness Explained*. Boston: Little, Brown.

Denzin, Norman K. 1990. "Reading Cultural Texts." *American Journal of Sociology* 95: 1577–80.

———. 1991. *Images of Postmodern Society*. London: Sage.

Derrida, Jacques. 1976. *Of Grammatology*. Baltimore: Johns Hopkins University Press.

———. 1978. *Writing and Difference*. Chicago: University of Chicago Press.

———. 1989. "Three Questions to Hans-Georg Gadamer." In *Dialogue and Deconstruction*, ed. by D. P. Michelfelder and R. E. Palmer. Albany: SUNY Press.

Dickens, David R., and Andrea Fontana, eds. 1994. *Postmodernism and Social Inquiry*. New York: Guilford.

Docherty, Thomas, ed. 1993. *Postmodernism: A Reader*. New York: Columbia University Press.

Donno, Daniel. 1981. "Introduction." In N. Machiavelli, *The Prince*. New York: Bantam Classic.

Donovan, Josephine. 1994. *Feminist Theory*. New York: Continuum.

Douglas, Mary. 1966. *Purity and Danger*. New York: Praeger.

———. 1980. "Introduction: Maurice Halbwachs (1877–1945)." In M. Halbwachs, *The Collective Memory*. New York: Harper & Row.

Downs, Anthony. 1957. *An Economic Theory of Democracy*. New York: Harper & Row.

Dreitzel, Hans Peter, ed. 1979. *Recent Sociology No. 2: Patterns of Communicative Behavior*. New York: Macmillan.

Du Bois, W. E. B. [1908] 1970. "Race Friction between Black and White." In *W. E. B. Du Bois: A Reader*, ed. by M. Weinberg. New York: Harper & Row.

Dunbar, Paul Laurence. [1896] 1993. "We Wear the Mask" (poem). In *The Collected Poetry of Paul Laurence Dunbar*, ed. by J. M. Braxton. Charlottesville: University Press of Virginia.

Dunlop, John T. 1984. *Dispute Resolution*. Dover, Mass.: Auburn House.

During, Simon, ed. 1993. *The Cultural Studies Reader*. London: Routledge.

Durkheim, Emile. [1893] 1947. *The Division of Labor in Society*. Glencoe, Ill.: Free Press.

———. [1895] 1958. *The Rules of Sociological Method*. New York: Free Press.

———. [1897] 1966. *Suicide*. New York: Free Press.

Eagleton, Terry. 1983. *Literary Theory*. Minneapolis: University of Minnesota Press.

Edelman, Murray J. 1988. *Constructing the Political Spectacle*. Chicago: University of Chicago Press.

Edgerton, Robert B. 1992. *Sick Societies: Challenging the Myth of Primitive Harmony*. New York: Free Press.

Edie, James. 1967. "Comments on Maurice Natanson's Paper 'Man as Actor.'" In *Action: The Second Lexington Conference on Pure and Applied Phenomenology*. Pittsburgh: Duquesne University Press.

Ehrlich, Paul. 1968. *The Population Bomb*. New York: Ballantine.

Ekeh, Peter P. 1974. *Social Exchange Theory: The Two Traditions*. Cambridge: Harvard University Press.

Eliade, Mircea. 1975. *Myths, Rites, Symbols* (2 vols.), ed. by W. C. Beane and W. G. Doty. New York: Harper & Row.

Elias, Norbert. [1939] 1978. *The Civilization Process*. New York: Urizen.

Elshtain, Jean Bethke. 1995. *Democracy on Trial*. New York: Basic.

Elster, Jon, ed. 1986. *Rational Choice*. New York: New York University Press.

———. 1989. *Nuts and Bolts for the Social Sciences*. Cambridge, UK: Cambridge University Press.

———, and Aanund Hylland, eds. 1986. *Foundations of Social Choice Theory*. Cambridge, UK: Cambridge University Press.

Emerson, Joan. 1970. "Behavior in Private Places." In *Recent Sociology* No. 2, ed. by Hans Peter Dreitzel. New York: Macmillan.

Engels, Friedrich. [1878] 1970. *Anti-Dühring*. New York: International.

Etzioni, Amitai. 1968. *The Active Society*. New York: Free Press.

———. 1993. *The Spirit of Community*. New York: Crown.

Ewen, Stuart. 1988. *All Consuming Images*. New York: Basic.

———. 1996. *PR!: A Social History of Spin*. New York: Basic.

Faludi, Susan. 1991. *Backlash: The Undeclared War against American Women*. New York: Doubleday Anchor.

Fernandez, James W., ed. 1991. *Beyond Metaphor: The Theory of Tropes in Anthropology*. Stanford: Stanford University Press.

Feyerabend, Paul. 1978. *Against Method*. New York: Schocken.

Fine, Gary Alan. 1996. *Talking Sociology*. Needham Heights, Mass.: Allyn & Bacon.

Fiorenza, Elisabeth Schussler, and M. Shawn Copeland. 1996. *Feminist Theology in Different Contexts*. London: Concilium/SCM Press.

Fischer, David Hackett. 1970. *Historians' Fallacies*. New York: Harper & Row.

Fish, Stanley. 1980. *Is There a Text in This Class?* Cambridge: Harvard University Press.

Fisher, Roger, and Scott Brown. 1988. *Getting Together*. Boston: Houghton Mifflin.

———, and William Ury. 1983. *Getting to Yes*. New York: Penguin.

Folberg, Jay, and Alison Taylor. 1984. *Mediation*. San Francisco: Jossey-Bass.

Foucault, Michel. 1965. *Madness and Civilization*. New York: Random House.

———. 1972. *The Archaeology of Knowledge and the Discourse on Language*. New York: Pantheon.

———. 1977. *Discipline and Punish*. New York: Pantheon.

———. [1978] 1990. *The History of Sexuality: An Introduction*. Vol. I. New York: Vintage.

———. 1980. *Power/Knowledge*, ed. by C. Gordon. New York: Pantheon.

———. 1984. *The Foucault Reader*, ed. by P. Rabinow. New York: Pantheon.

———. 1990. *Michel Foucault: Politics, Philosophy, Culture*, ed. by L. D. Kritzman. New York: Routledge.

France, Anatol. [1894] 1991. *The Red Lily*. Quoted from *The Oxford Dictionary of Modern Quotations*, ed. by T. Augarde. Oxford, UK: Oxford University Press.

Frank, André Gunder. 1993. *The World System*. London: Routledge.

Franzoni, David (screenwriter). 1992. *Citizen Cohn* (film screenplay based on book by Nicholas Von Hoffman). New York: HBO Films.

Freire, Paulo. 1982. *Pedagogy of the Oppressed*. New York: Continuum.

———. 1998. *Pedagogy of Freedom*. Lanham, Md.: Rowman & Littlefield.

———, and Doñald Macedo. 1987. *Literacy*. South Hadley, Mass.: Bergin and Garvey.

French, Marilyn. 1985. *Beyond Power*. New York: Summit.

———. 1992. *The War against Women*. New York: Summit.

Freud, Sigmund. 1930. *Civilization and Its Discontents*, trans. by Joan Riviere. London: Hogarth.

Friedan, Betty. 1963. *The Feminine Mystique*. New York: Norton.

————. 1981. *The Second Stage*. New York: Summit.

Friedman, Milton. 1953. *Essays in Positive Economics*. Chicago: University of Chicago Press.

Fudenberg, Drew, and Jean Tirole. 1991. *Game Theory*. Cambridge: MIT Press.

Fukuyama, Francis. 1995. *Trust: Social Virtues and the Creation of Prosperity*. New York: Free Press.

Funke, Lewis, and John E. Booth, eds. 1961. *Actors Talk about Acting*. New York: Avon.

Gadamer, Hans-Georg. 1975. *Truth and Method*. New York: Continuum.

————. 1980. *Dialogue and Dialectic*. New Haven: Yale University Press.

————. 1989. "The Historicity of Understanding." In *The Hermeneutics Reader*, ed. by Kurt Mueller. New York: Continuum.

Gamson, William A. 1972. *SIMSOC: Simulated Society*, 2d ed. New York: Free Press.

Gardner, Howard. 1985. *The Mind's New Science: A History of the Cognitive Revolution*. New York: Basic.

Garfinkel, Harold. 1962. "Common Sense Knowledge of Social Structures." In *Theories of the Mind*, ed. by J. Scher. New York: Free Press.

————. 1967. *Studies in Ethnomethdology*. Englewood Cliffs, N.J.: Prentice-Hall.

Gates, Bill, with Collin Hemingway. 1999. *Business @ the Speed of Thought: Using a Digital Nervous System*. New York: Time Warner.

Gates, Henry Louis, Jr. 1992. *Loose Canons: Notes on the Culture Wars*. New York: Oxford University Press.

————, and Cornel West. 1996. *The Future of Race*. New York: Knopf.

Geertz, Clifford. 1973. *The Interpretation of Cultures*. New York: Basic.

————. 1983. "Blurred Genres: The Refiguration of Social Thought." In *Local Knowledge*. New York: Basic.

————. 1988. *Works and Lives: The Anthropologist as Author*. Stanford: Stanford University Press.

Gelernter, David. 1991. *Mirror Worlds*. New York: Oxford University Press.

————. 1994. *The Muse in the Machine*. New York: Free Press.

Gerard, R. W., Klyde Kluckhohn, and Anatol Rapoport. 1956. "Biological and Cultural Evolution: Some Analogies and Explorations." *Behavioral Science* I : 6–34.

Gergen, Kenneth J. 1991. *The Saturated Self*. New York: Basic.

Gibbon, Edward. [1776–1788] 1974. *The History of the Decline and Fall of the Roman Empire*. New York: AMS Press.

Gibbs, Jack P. 1989. *Control: Sociology's Central Notion*. Urbana: University of Illinois Press.

Giddens, Anthony. 1984. *The Constitution of Society*. Cambridge, UK: Polity Press.

Gilligan, Carol. 1982. *In a Different Voice*. Cambridge: Harvard University Press.

Gillman, Charlotte Perkins. [1898] 2000. *Women and Economics*. Selection reprinted in *Social Theory: Roots and Branches*, ed. by P. Kivisto. Los Angeles: Roxbury.

Gladwell, Malcolm. 1996. "The Tipping Point." *New Yorker* (June 3): 32–38.

————. 2000. *The Tipping Point*. Boston: Little, Brown.

Glassner, Barry. 1982. "Labeling Theory." In *The Sociology of Deviance*, ed. by M. Rosenberg, R. Stebbins, and A. Turowetz. New York: St. Martin's.

Gleick, James. 1987. *Chaos: Making a New Science*. New York: Penguin.

Glendon, Mary Ann. 1991. *Rights Talk*. New York: Free Press.

Goffman, Erving. 1959. *The Presentation of Self in Everyday Life*. New York: Macmillan.

————. 1961a. *Asylums*. New York: Doubleday.
————. 1961b. *Encounters*. Indianapolis: Bobbs-Merrill.
————. 1963. *Stigma*. Harmondsworth, UK: Penguin.
————. 1967. *Interaction Ritual*. New York: Anchor.
————. 1970. *Strategic Interaction*. Oxford, UK: Basil Blackwell.
————. 1971. *Relations in Public*. New York: Basic.
————. 1974. *Frame Analysis*. New York: Harper.
————. 1981. *Forms of Talk*. Philadelphia: University of Pennsylvania Press.
Goldberg, David E. 2000. "Illinois Genetic Algoriths Laboratory." URL: gal4.ge.uiuc.edu (June 7, 2000).
Goldberg, David Theo. 1999. "Call and Response: Sports, Talk Radio and the Death of Democracy." In *The Soundbite Culture*, ed. by D. Slayden and R. K. Whillock. Thousand Oaks, Calif.: Sage.
Goldfarb, Jeffrey C. 1991. *The Cynical Society*. Chicago: University of Chicago Press.
Golding, William. 1954. *Lord of the Flies*. New York: Putnam.
Goodall, Jane. 1991. *Through a Window: My Thirty Years with the Chimpanzees of Gombe*. Boston: Houghton Mifflin.
Goodman, Nelson. 1978. *Ways of Worldmaking*. Indianapolis: Hackett.
Gouldner, Alvin. 1965. *Enter Plato*. New York: Basic.
————. 1970. *The Coming Crisis of Western Sociology*. New York: Basic.
————. 1979. *The Future of Intellectuals and the Rise of the New Class*. New York: Seabury.
Gove, Walter, ed. 1980. *The Labeling of Deviance*. Beverly Hills, Calif.: Sage.
Gramsci, Antonio. 1971. *Prison Notebooks: Selections*. New York: International.
Grandjean, Burke D. 1975. "An Economic Analysis of the Davis-Moore Theory of Stratification." *Social Forces* 53: 543–52.
Grant, David, and Cliff Oswick, eds. 1996. *Metaphor and Organizations*. London: Sage.
Green, Donald P., and Ian Shapiro. 1994. *Pathologies of Rational Choice Theory*. New Haven: Yale University Press.
Grice, H. P. 1975. "Logic and Conversation." In *Syntax and Semantics, Vol. 3: Speech Acts*, ed. by P. Cole and J. L. Morgan. New York: Academic.
Grotowski, Jerzy. 1968. *Towards a Poor Theatre*. New York: Simon & Schuster.
Gurevitch, Z. D. 1988. "The Other Side of Dialogue." *American Journal of Sociology* 93: 1179–99.
Gusdorf, Georges. 1965. *Speaking (La Parole)*. Evanston: Northwestern University Press.
Habermas, Jürgen. 1970. *Toward a Rational Society*. Boston: Beacon.
————. 1971. *Knowledge and Interests*. Boston: Beacon.
————. 1979. *Communication and the Evolution of Society*. Boston: Beacon.
————. 1984/1988. *The Theory of Communicative Action*. 2 vols. Boston: Beacon.
————. 1989. *The Transformation of the Public Sphere*. Cambridge: MIT Press.
Haken, Hermann, Anders Karlqvist, and Unbo Swedin, eds. 1993. *The Machine as Metaphor and Tool*. Berlin: Springer-Verlag.
Hall, Calvin S., and Lindzey, Gardner. *Theories of Personality*, 2d ed. New York: Wiley.
Hamilton, Edith, and Huntington Cairns, eds. 1961. *The Collected Dialogues of Plato*. Princeton: Princeton University Press.
Hammer, Michael, and James Champy. 1993. *Reengineering the Corporation*. New York: Harper Business.
Hampden-Turner, Charles. 1981. *Maps of the Mind*. New York: Macmillan.
Handel, Warren. 1982. *Ethnomethodology*. Englewood Cliffs, N.J.: Prentice-Hall.

Hardin, Garrett. 1968. "The Tragedy of the Commons." *Science* 162: 1243–48.

Harland, Richard. 1987. *Superstructuralism*. London: Methuen.

Heath, Anthony. 1976. *Rational Choice and Social Exchange*. Cambridge, UK: Cambridge University Press.

Hechter, Michael. 1987. *Principles of Group Solidarity*. Berkeley: University of California Press.

Heidegger, Martin. 1971. *On the Way to Language*. San Francisco: Harper & Row.

Heilbroner, Robert. 1972. *The Worldly Philosophers*, 4th ed. New York: Simon & Schuster.

Heims, Steve Joshua. 1993. *Constructing a Social Science for Postwar America: The Cybernetics Group, 1946–1953*. Cambridge: MIT Press.

Hekman, Susan J. 1990., *Gender and Knowledge*. Boston: Northeastern University Press.

Henig, Jeffrey R. 1994. *Rethinking School Choice: Limits of the Market Metaphor*. Princeton: Princeton University Press.

Henslin, James M., and Mae A. Briggs. 1971. "Dramaturgical Desexualization." In *Studies in the Sociology of Sex*, ed. by James M. Henslin. New York: Appleton-Century-Crofts.

Heritage, John C. 1987. "Ethnomethodology." In *Social Theory Today*, ed. by A. Giddens and J. H. Turner. Stanford: Stanford University Press.

Herman, Edward S., and Noam Chomsky. 1988. *Manufacturing Consent*. New York: Pantheon.

Hesse, Hermann. 1949. *Magister Ludi*. New York: Ungar.

Hesse, Mary. 1966. *Models and Analogies in Science*. Notre Dame: University of Notre Dame Press.

Hindess, Barry. 1988. *Choice, Rationality and Social Theory*. London: Unwin Hyman.

Hobbes, Thomas. [1651] 1964. *Leviathan*. New York: Washington Square Press.

Hodge, Robert, and Gunther Kress. 1988. *Social Semiotics*. Ithaca: Cornell University Press.

Hofstadter, Douglas. 1985. *Metamagical Themas*. New York: Basic.

———, and the Fluid Analogies Research Group. 1995. *Fluid Concepts and Creative Analogies*. New York: Basic.

Hofstadter, Richard. 1944. *Social Darwinism in American Thought*. Philadelphia: University of Pennsylvania Press.

Holloway, Karla F. C. 1992. *Moorings and Metaphors*. New Brunswick, N.J.: Rutgers University Press.

Holstein, James A., and Gale Miller, eds. 1993. *Reconsidering Social Constructionism*. New York: Aldine de Gruyter.

Holyoak, Keith J., and Paul Thagard. 1995. *Mental Leaps: Analogy and Creative Thought*. Cambridge: MIT Press.

Homans, George. 1958. "Social Behavior as Exchange." *American Journal of Sociology* 63: 597–606.

———. 1961. *Social Behavior: Its Elementary Forms*. New York: Harcourt, Brace & World.

———. 1964. "Commentary." *Sociological Inquiry* 34: 229–31.

———. 1974. *Social Behavior: Its Elementary Forms*. Revised ed. New York: Harcourt Brace Jovanovich.

hooks, bell. 1984. *Feminist Theory: From Margin to Center*. Boston: South End Press.

Horkheimer, Max, and Theodor Adorno. [1944] 1990. *Dialectic of Enlightenment*. New York: Continuum.

Horowitz, David. 1999. *The Art of Political War*. Los Angeles: Committee for a Non-Left Majority.

Horowitz, Irving Louis. 1993. *The Decomposition of Sociology.* Oxford, UK: Oxford University Press.

Howe, Florence, ed. 1993. *No More Masks: An Anthology of Twentieth-Century American Women Poets.* New York: HarperCollins.

Howe, Reuel L. 1963. *The Miracle of Dialogue.* Minneapolis: Seabury.

Hubbard, Elbert. 1899. "A Message to Garcia" (pamphlet). West Aurora, N.Y.: Roycroft Press.

Huizinga, Johan. [1938] 1950. *Homo Ludens: A Study of the Play Element in Culture.* Boston: Beacon.

Hunter, James Davison. 1991. *Culture Wars.* New York: Basic.

Hutchins, Robert M. 1952. *The Great Conversation,* Vol I., *Great Books of the Western World.* Chicago: Britannica.

Hymes, Dell, ed. 1964. *Language in Culture and Society.* New York: Harper & Row.

Iannaccone, Laurence R. 1995. "Risk, Rationality and Religious Portfolios." *Economic Inquiry* 33: 285–95.

James, William. 1890 [1950]. *The Principles of Psychology.* Vol. 1. New York: Dover.

———. 1911. "The Moral Equivalent of War." In *Memories and Studies.* New York: Longmans.

Jameson, Fredric. 1972. *The Prison-house of Language.* Princeton: Princeton University Press.

Jary, David, and Julia Jary. 1991. *The HarperCollins Dictionary of Sociology.* New York: HarperCollins.

Jencks, Charles, ed. 1992. *The Postmodern Reader.* New York: St. Martin's.

John Paul II. 1993. *The Splendor of Truth* (papal encyclical). Boston: St. Paul Books and Media.

Johnson, Paul. 1983. *Modern Times.* New York: Harper & Row.

Jordan, John M. 1994. *Machine-age Ideology.* Chapel Hill: University of North Carolina Press.

Kanter, Donald, and Philip H. Mirvis. 1989. *The Cynical Americans: Living and Working in an Age of Discontent and Disillusion.* San Francisco: Jossey-Bass.

Kaplan, Abraham. 1964. *The Conduct of Inquiry.* San Francisco: Chandler.

Kaplan, Robert D. 1994. "The Coming Anarchy." *Atlantic* (February): 44–76.

Kaufmann, Walter. 1967. "Buber's Religious Significance." In *The Philosophy of Martin Buber,* ed. by P. A. Schilpp and M. Friedman. LaSalle, Ill.: Open Court.

Kearl, Michael, and Daniel Rigney. 1995. "Moral Relativism and Moral Health." *Second Opinion* (April): 73–83.

Keeley, Lawrence H. 1996. *War Before Civilization: The Myth of the Peaceful Savage.* New York: Oxford.

Keesing, Roger, and Felix Keesing. 1971. *New Perspectives in Cultural Anthropology.* New York: Holt, Rinehart & Winston.

Kennan, George. 1977. *Cloud of Danger.* Boston: Little, Brown.

Kidder, Rushworth M. 1994. "Universal Human Values: Finding an Ethical Common Ground." *The Futurist* (July/August): 8–13.

Kilpatrick, William. 1992. *Why Johnny Can't Tell Right from Wrong.* New York: Simon & Schuster.

King, Martin Luther. 1963 [1970]. "Letter from Birmingham Jail." In *Great Documents in Black American History,* ed. by G. Ducas. New York: Praeger.

Kivisto, Peter. 2000. *Social Theory: Roots and Branches.* Los Angeles: Roxbury.

Klein, Julie Thompson. 1992. "Text/Context: The Rhetoric of the Social Sciences." In *Writing the Social Text*, ed. by R. H. Brown. New York: Aldine de Gruyter.

Koestler, Arthur. 1964. *The Act of Creation*. New York: Dell.

——, and J. R. Smythies, eds. 1969. *Beyond Reductionism*. Boston: Beacon.

Kopp, Richard R. 1995. *Metaphor Therapy*. Philadelphia: Brunner/Mazel.

Kormondy, Edward J. 1976. *Concepts of Ecology*. Englewood Cliffs, N.J.: Prentice-Hall.

Kristeva, Julia. 1986. *The Kristeva Reader*, ed. by Toril Moi. New York: Columbia University Press.

Kropotkin, P'etr. [1902] 1972. *Mutual Aid*. New York: New York University Press.

Kuhn, Thomas. 1972. *The Structure of Scientific Revolutions*, 2d ed. Chicago: University of Chicago Press.

Kurian, George Thomas, ed. 1991. *New Book of World Rankings*. New York: Facts on File.

Kurzweil, Edith. 1980. *The Age of Structuralism*. New York: Columbia University Press.

Kuttner, Robert. 1997. *Everything for Sale*. New York: Knopf.

Lacan, Jacques. 1977. *Ecrits: A Selection*. New York: Norton.

Lakoff, George. 1996. *Moral Politics*. Chicago: University of Chicago Press.

——, and Mark Johnson. 1980. *Metaphors We Live By*. Chicago: University of Chicago Press.

Lakoff, Robin Tolmach. 2000. *The Language War*. Berkeley: University of California Press.

Laqueur, Walter, and Barry Rubin, ed. 1989. *The Human Rights Reader*. New York: Meridian/New American Library.

Lasch, Christopher. 1977. *Haven in a Heartless World*. New York: Basic.

——. 1978. *The Culture of Narcissism*. New York: Norton.

Lasswell, Harold. [1936] 1951. "Politics: Who Gets What, When, How." In *The Political Writings of Harold D. Lasswell*. Glencoe, Ill.: Free Press.

Latour, Bruno, and Steve Woolgar. 1979. *Laboratory Life: The Social Construction of Scientific Facts*. Beverly Hills, Calif.: Sage.

Lawson, Hilary. 1985. *Reflexivity: The Post-modern Predicament*. LaSalle, Ill.: Open Court.

Leach, Edmund. 1970. *Claude Lévi-Strauss*. New York: Viking.

——. 1976. *Culture and Communication*. Cambridge, UK: Cambridge University Press.

Leavitt, Gregory. 1977. "The Frequency of Warfare: An Evolutionary Perspective." *Sociological Inquiry* 14: 49–58.

LeBon, Gustav. 1896. *The Crowd*. New York: Macmillan.

Leder, Drew. 1993. "Live from the Panopticon: Architecture and Power Revisited." *Lingua Franca* (July/August): 30–35.

Lee, Bernard. 1993. *Jesus and the Metaphors of God*. New York: Paulist Press.

——. 1995. *The Future Church of 140 B.C.E.* New York: Crossroads.

Lee, Alfred McClung. 1978. *Sociology for Whom?* New York: Oxford University Press.

Lehrer, Tom. 1965. "Wernher Von Braun," on *That Was the Year That Was* (phonograph record). Reprise/Warner Brothers.

Lemert, Charles, ed. 1993. *Social Theory: The Multicultural and Classic Readings*. Boulder, Colo.: Westview.

——. 1997a. *Social Things: An Introduction to the Sociological Life*. Lanham, Md.: Rowman & Littlefield.

——. 1997b. *Postmodernism Is Not What You Think*. Malden, Mass.: Blackwell.

Lemert, Edwin M. 1967. *Human Deviance, Social Problems, and Social Control*. Englewood Cliffs, N.J.: Prentice-Hall.

Lemmon, John Allen. 1985. *Family Mediation Practice*. New York: Free Press.

Lenski, Gerhard, and Jean Lenski. 1982. *Human Societies*, 4th ed. New York: McGraw-Hill.

———. 1987. *Human Societies*, 5th ed. New York: McGraw-Hill.

Lerner, Robert, Standish Meacham, and Edward McNall Burns. 1988. *Western Civilizations*, 11th ed. New York: Norton.

Levi, Edward H. 1949. *An Introduction to Legal Reasoning*. Chicago: University of Chicago Press.

Lévi-Strauss, Claude. 1968. *Structural Anthropology*. London: Allen Lane.

Levinas, Emmanuel. 1989. *The Levinas Reader*, ed. by Sean Hand. Oxford, UK: Blackwell.

Levy, Steven. 1992. *Artificial Life*. New York: Vintage.

Lewin, Kurt. 1951. *Field Theory in Social Science*. New York: Harper.

Lewontin, R. C., Steven Rose, and Leon J. Kamin. 1984. *Not in Our Genes*. New York: Pantheon.

Liebow, Eliot. 1967. *Tally's Corner*. Boston: Little, Brown.

Lifton, Robert Jay. 1993. *The Protean Self*. New York: Basic.

Lilla, Mark. 1998. "The Politics of Jacques Derrida." *New York Review of Books*, XLV: 36–41.

Lindsay, Peter H., and Donald A. Norman. 1977. *Human Information Processing*, 2d ed. New York: Academic.

Locke, John. [1690a] 1965. *Two Treatises on Government*. New York: New American Library.

———. [1690b] 1959. *An Essay Concerning Human Understanding*. New York: Dover.

Lorenz, Konrad. 1977. *Behind the Mirror*. New York: Harcourt Brace Jovanovich.

Lovejoy, Arthur O. 1964. *The Great Chain of Being*. Cambridge: Harvard University Press.

Lovelock, James. 1979. *Gaia: A New Look at Life on Earth*. Oxford, UK: Oxford University Press.

Luhmann, Niklas. 1982. *The Differentiation of Society*. New York: Columbia University Press.

Lumsden, Charles J., and Edward O. Wilson. 1981. *Genes, Mind and Culture*. Cambridge, UK: Harvard University Press.

Lundberg, George. 1961. *Can Science Save Us?* New York: McKay.

Lupton, Deborah, and Lesley Barclay. 1997. *Constructing Fatherhood: Discourses and Experiences*. London: Sage.

Lyman, Stanford M., and Marvin B. Scott. 1975. *The Drama of Social Reality*. New York: Oxford University Press.

Lynch, Aaron. 1996. *Thought Contagion*. New York: Basic.

Lynd, Robert S. 1939. *Knowledge for What?* Princeton: Princeton University Press.

Lyotard, Jean-François. 1984. *The Postmodern Condition*. Minneapolis: University of Minnesota Press.

———, and Jean-Loup Thebaud. 1985. *Just Gaming*. Minneapolis: University of Minnesota Press.

Maccoby, Michael. 1976. *The Gamesman: The New Corporate Leaders*. New York: Simon & Schuster.

Machalek, Richard. 1992. "Why Are Large Societies Rare?" *Advances in Human Ecology* 1: 33–64.

Machiavelli, Niccolò. [1521] 1964. *The Art of War*. In *Machiavelli: The Chief Works and Others*, ed. and trans. by A. H. Gilbert. Durham: Duke University Press.

———. [1532] 1981. *The Prince*. Toronto: Bantam.

MacIntyre, Alistair. 1984. *After Virtue*. Notre Dame: University of Notre Dame Press.
————. 1988. *Whose Justice? Which Rationality?* Notre Dame: University of Notre Dame Press.
Madrid, Arturo. 1988. "Missing People and Others: Joining Together to Expand the Circle." *Change* (May/June): 55–59.
Mailer, Norman. 1959. *Advertisements for Myself*. New York: Putnam.
Malcolm X. 1970. *By Any Means Necessary*. New York: Pathfinder.
————, with Alex Haley. 1964. *The Autobiography of Malcolm X*. New York: Ballantine.
Malinowski, Bronislaw. 1922. *Argonauts of the Western Pacific*. London: Routledge & Kegan Paul.
Mannheim, Karl. 1936. *Ideology and Utopia*. New York: Harcourt, Brace & World.
Manning, Philip. 1992. *Erving Goffman and Modern Sociology*. Stanford: Stanford University Press.
Marcuse, Herbert. 1964. *One-Dimensional Man*. Boston: Beacon.
Marks, John. 1989. "The Search for Common Ground" (organizational publication). Washington, D.C.: Search for Common Ground.
Martineau, Harriet. [1837] 1985. *Society in America*. Selections reprinted in *Harriet Martineau on Women*, ed. by G. G. Yates. New Brunswick, N.J.: Rutgers University Press.
Marx, Karl. [1852] 1963. *The Eighteenth Brumaire of Louis Bonaparte*. New York: International.
————. [1859] 1970. "Preface." In *A Contribution to the Critique of Political Economy*. New York: International.
————. [1867] 1967. *Capital*. New York: International.
————, and Frederick Engels. [1846] 1947. *The German Ideology*. New York: International.
————, and Frederick Engels. [1848] 1955. *The Communist Manifesto*. Arlington Heights, Ill.: Harlan Davidson.
Marx, Leo. 1964. *The Machine in the Garden*. London: Oxford University Press.
Mauss, Marcel. [1925] 1990. *The Gift*. London: Routledge.
Maynard Smith, John. 1982. *Evolution and the Theory of Games*. Cambridge, UK: Cambridge University Press.
McCloskey, Deirdre/Donald. 1985. *The Rhetoric of Economics*. Madison: University of Wisconsin Press.
————. 1990. *If You're So Smart: The Narrative of Economic Expertise*. Chicago: University of Chicago Press.
————. 1994. *Knowledge and Persuasion in Economics*. Cambridge, UK: Cambridge University Press.
McFague, Sallie. 1982. *Metaphorical Theology*. Philadelphia: Fortress Press.
McHugh, Peter. 1968. *Defining Situations*. Indianapolis: Bobbs-Merrill.
McLuhan, Marshall. 1951. *The Mechanical Bride*. New York: Vanguard.
————. 1964. *Understanding Media*. New York: McGraw-Hill.
McPartland, Thomas A. 1959. *Manual for the Twenty Statements Problem*. Kansas City, Mo.: Kansas City Mental Health Foundation, Department of Research.
Mead, George Herbert. 1934. *Mind, Self and Society*. Chicago: University of Chicago Press.
Meadows, Donella, Dennis Meadows, Jørgen Randers, and William W. Behrens, III. 1972. *The Limits to Growth*. New York: Universe Books.
Meadows, Donella, Dennis Meadows, and Jørgen Randers. 1992. *Beyond the Limits*. Post Mills, Vt.: Chelsea Green.

Merchant, Carolyn. 1990. *The Death of Nature*. New York: Harper & Row.

Merton, Robert K. [1948] 1968. *Social Theory and Social Structure*. New York: Free Press.

———. 1973. *The Sociology of Science*. Chicago: University of Chicago.

Michelfelder, Diane P., and Richard E. Palmer, eds. 1989. *Dialogue and Deconstruction: The Gadamer-Derrida Encounter*. Albany: SUNY Press.

Michener, H. Andrew. 1992. "Game Theory and Strategic Interaction." In *Encyclopedia of Sociology*. Vol. 2, ed. by E. F. Borgatta and M. L. Borgatta. New York: Macmillan.

Microsoft Corporation. 1998. "The Digital Nervous System." URL: microsoft.com/dns/ overviews/DNSoverview2.htm (December 4, 1998.)

Mill, John Stuart. [1859] 1986. *On Liberty*. London: Penguin.

Miller, Eugene. 1979. "Metaphor and Political Knowledge." *American Political Science Review* 73: 155–70.

Miller, James B. 1994. *The Corporate Coach*. New York: Harper Business.

Miller, James G. 1978. *Living Systems*. New York: McGraw-Hill.

Miller, Jonathan. 1978. *The Body in Question*. New York: Random House.

Mills, C. Wright. 1956. *The Power Elite*. New York: Oxford University Press.

———. 1958. *The Causes of World War Three*. New York: Simon & Schuster.

———. 1959. *The Sociological Imagination*. New York: Oxford University Press.

Minsky, Marvin. 1985. *The Society of Mind*. New York: Simon & Schuster.

Miringoff, Marc, and Marque-Luisa Miringoff. 1999. *The Social Health of the Nation*. New York: Oxford University Press.

Mises, Ludwig von. [1949] 1966. *Human Action: A Treatise on Economics*. Chicago: Regnery.

Monroe, Kristen, ed. 1991. *The Economic Approach to Politics*. New York: HarperCollins.

Moore, Christopher W. 1986. *The Mediation Process*. San Francisco: Jossey-Bass.

Moore, Sonya. 1976. *The Stanislavski System*. New York: Penguin Books.

Morgan, Gareth. 1997. *Images of Organization*, 2d ed. Beverly Hills, Calif.: Sage.

Morgenstern, Oskar. 1968. "Game Theory: Theoretical Aspects." In *International Encyclopedia of the Social Sciences*. Vol. 6, ed. by D. L. Sills. New York: Macmillan.

Morrison, Toni. 1992. *Playing in the Dark: Whiteness and the Literary Imagination*. New York: Vintage.

Morton, Brian. 1990. "How Not to Write for *Dissent*." *Dissent* (Summer): 299.

Moynihan, Daniel Patrick. 1993. "Defining Deviancy Down." *The American Scholar* (Winter): 17–30.

Mueller-Vollmer, Kurt, ed. 1989. *The Hermeneutics Reader*. New York: Continuum.

Mura, Susan Swan. 1983. "Licensing Violations: Legitimate Violations of Grice's Conversational Principle." In *Conversational Coherence*, ed. by R. Craig and K. Tracy. Beverly Hills, Calif.: Sage.

Murray, Charles. 1984. *Losing Ground*. New York: Basic.

Myrdal, Gunnar. 1944. *An American Dilemma*. New York: Harper.

Neumann, John von, and Oskar Morgenstern. 1944. *Theory of Games and Economic Behavior*. Princeton: Princeton University Press.

Nietzsche, Friedrich. [1885] 1954. "Thus Spake Zarathustra." In *The Portable Nietzsche*, ed. by W. Kaufman. New York: Viking.

Nisbet, Robert. 1969. *Social Change and History*. New York: Oxford University Press.

———. 1973. *The Social Philosophers: Community and Conflict in Social Thought*. New York: Crowell.

———. 1976. *Sociology as an Art Form*. New York: Oxford University Press.

———. 1986. *Conservatism*. Minneapolis: University of Minnesota Press.

Norris, Christopher. 1987. *Derrida*. Cambridge: Harvard University Press.

Nussbaum, Martha. 1999. "The Professor of Parody." *New Republic* (February 22): 37–45.

Ogburn, William F. 1922. *Social Change*. New York: Huebsch.

Ollman, Bertell. 1978. *Class Struggle* (board game). New York: Class Struggle.

Olson, Mancur. 1965. *The Logic of Collective Action*. Cambridge: Harvard University Press.

Ortony, Andrew, ed. 1993. *Metaphor and Thought*. Cambridge, UK: Cambridge University Press.

Orwell, George. 1949. *1984*. London: Secker & Warburg.

Osborne, David, and Ted Gaebler. 1992. *Reinventing Government*. New York: Plume/Penguin Books.

Ostman, Charles. 1996. "The Internet as Organism." *21st Century Online* (online magazine). Microsoft Network (MSN). URL: www.msn.com (March 20, 1996).

Pareto, Vilfredo. [1916] 1935. *The Mind and Society*. San Diego: Harcourt.

Parsons, Talcott. 1951. *The Social System*. Glencoe, Ill.: Free Press.

———. 1961. "Some Considerations on the Theory of Social Change." *Rural Sociology* 26: 219–39.

———. 1966. *Societies: Evolutionary and Comparative Perspectives*. Englewood Cliffs, N.J.: Prentice-Hall.

Peel, J. D. Y. 1972. "Introduction." In *"Herbert Spencer on Social Evolution*. Chicago: University of Chicago Press.

Peirce, Charles S. [1932] 1957. *Essays in the Philosophy of Science*, ed. by V. Thomas. Indianapolis: Bobbs-Merrill.

Pepper, Stephen C. 1942. *World Hypotheses*. Berkeley: University of California Press.

Perrow, Charles. 1979. *Complex Organizations: A Critical Essay*, 2d ed. Glenview, Ill.: Scott Foresman.

Peterson, Trond. 1994. "On the Promise of Game Theory in Sociology." *Contemporary Sociology* 23: 498–502.

Phillips, Derek L. 1993. *Looking Backward: A Critical Appraisal of Communitarian Thought*. Princeton: Princeton University Press.

Pinker, Steven. 1994. *The Language Instinct*. New York: Morrow.

———. 1997. *How the Mind Works*. New York: Norton.

Pitkin, Hanna Fenichel, and Sara M. Schumer. 1982. "On Participation." *Democracy* 2: 43–54.

Plant, Judith. 1991. "Ecofeminism." In *The Green Reader*, ed. by A. Dobson. San Francisco: Mercury House.

Plato. [ca. 370 B.C.E.] 1979. *The Republic*, ed. and trans. by R. Larson. Arlington Heights, Ill.: Harlan Davidson.

Popper, Karl. 1950. *The Open Society and Its Enemies*. Princeton: Princeton University Press.

———. 1963. *Conjectures and Refutations*. New York: Harper.

Postman, Neil. 1989. "Learning by Story." *Atlantic* (December): 119–24.

Poundstone, William. 1992. *The Prisoner's Dilemma*. New York: Anchor.

Pribram, Karl. 1971. *Languages of the Brain*. Englewood Cliffs, N.J.: Prentice-Hall.

Pugh, Sharon L., Jean Wolph Hicks, Marcia Davis, and Tonya Venstra. 1992. *Bridging: A Teacher's Guide to Metaphorical Thinking*. Urbana, Ill.: National Council of Teachers of English.

Putnam, Robert. 1995. "Bowling Alone." *Journal of Democracy* 6: 65–78.

———. 2000. *Bowling Alone: The Collapse and Revival of American Community*. New York: Simon & Schuster.

Radcliffe-Brown, A. R. 1935. "On the Concept of Function in Social Science." *American Anthropologist* 37: 395–96.

Ramsey, Douglas. 1987. *The Corporate Warriors*. Boston: Houghton Mifflin.

Rand, Ayn. 1964. *The Virtue of Selfishness*. New York: New American Library.

Rapoport, Anatol. 1960. *Fights, Games and Debates*. Ann Arbor: University of Michigan Press.

Raser, John R. 1969. *Simulation and Society*. Boston: Allyn & Bacon.

Reggio, Godfrey (film director). 1983. *Koyaanisqatsi*. Santa Fe, N. Mex.: IRE.

Rheingold, Howard. 1991. *Virtual Reality*. New York: Simon & Schuster.

Richards, I. A. 1936. *The Philosophy of Rhetoric*. New York: Oxford University Press.

Ricoeur, Paul. 1970. *Freud and Philosophy*. New Haven: Yale University Press.

———. 1977. *The Rule of Metaphor*. Toronto: University of Toronto Press.

———. 1981. *Hermeneutics and the Human Sciences*, ed. by J. B. Thompson. Cambridge, UK: Cambridge University Press.

Rifkin, Jeremy. 1980. *Entropy*. New York: Viking.

———. 1987. *Time Wars*. New York: Simon & Schuster.

Rigney, Daniel. 1979. "Analogies: A Hindu Fable" (poem). *American Sociologist* 14: 170. Updated version available online at URL: www.geocities.com/Athens/Delphi/8822.

———. 1991. "Three Kinds of Anti-intellectualism: Hofstadter Revisited." *Sociological Inquiry* 61: 34–51.

———, and Donna Barnes. 1979. "Patterns of Interdisciplinary Citation in the Social Sciences." *Social Science Quarterly* 61: 114–27.

———, and Michael Kearl. 1994. "A Nation of Gray Individualists: Moral Relativism in the United States." *Journal of Social Philosophy* 25: 20–45.

Riker, William H. 1990. "Political Science and Rational Choice." In *Perspectives on Positive Political Economy*, ed. by J. E. Alt and K. A. Shepsle. Cambridge, UK: Cambridge University Press.

Roberts, Wess. 1985. *Leadership Secrets of Attila the Hun*. New York: Warner.

Roloff, Michael E. 1981. *Interpersonal Communication: The Social Exchange Approach*. Beverly Hills, Calif.: Sage.

Ronan, Colin A. 1974. *Galileo*. New York: Putnam.

Rorty, Richard, ed. 1967. *The Linguistic Turn*. Chicago: University of Chicago Press.

———. 1979. *Philosophy and the Mirror of Nature*. Princeton: Princeton University Press.

Rosenblatt, Paul C. 1994. *Metaphors of Family Systems Theory*. New York: Guilford Press.

Rousseau, Jean-Jacques. [1762] 1973. *The Social Contract*. London: Dent.

Rowan, Carl. 1996. *The Coming Race War in America*. Boston: Little, Brown.

Rubin, Lillian. 1990. *Erotic Wars*. New York: Farrar, Straus & Giroux.

Ruether, Rosemary Radford. 1987. *Contemporary Roman Catholicism: Crises and Challenges*. Kansas City, Mo.: Sheed & Ward.

———. 1989. *Disputed Questions*. Maryknoll, N.Y.: Orbis.

Runciman, W. G. 1983/1989/1997. *A Treatise on Social Theory* (3 vols.). Cambridge, UK: Cambridge University Press.

Sacks, Sheldon, ed. 1979. *On Metaphor*. Chicago: University of Chicago Press.

Sahlins, Marshall. 1976. *The Use and Abuse of Biology*. Ann Arbor: University of Michigan Press.

Said, Edward. 1978. *Orientalism*. New York: Pantheon.

St. Clair, Robert N. 1994. *Social Metaphors: Essays in Structural Epistemology*. Lanham, Md.:

University Press of America. [Current edition available from author, Department of English, University of Louisville, Ky.]

Sale, Kirkpatrick. 1991. "Bioregionalism." In *The Green Reader*, ed. by A. Dobson. San Francisco: Mercury House.

Samuelson, Robert. 2000. "Gliding to a Soft Landing?" *Newsweek* (June 26): 38.

Sandel, Michael. 1996. *Democracy's Discontent*. Cambridge: Harvard University Press.

Sanderson, Stephen K. 1990. *Social Evolutionism: A Critical History*. Cambridge, Mass.: Basil Blackwell.

Sapir, J. David, and J. Christopher Crocker, eds. 1977. *The Social Use of Metaphor*. Philadelphia: University of Pennsylvania Press.

Saussure, Ferdinand de. [1916] 1966. *Course in General Linguistics*. New York: McGraw-Hill.

Saxe, John Godfrey. 1900. "The Blind Men and the Elephant: A Hindoo Fable." In *The Poetical Works of John Godfrey Saxe*. New York: Houghton Mifflin.

Scanzoni, John. 1982. *Sexual Bargaining*, 2d ed. Chicago: University of Chicago Press.

Schank, Roger E. 1990. *Tell Me a Story*. New York: Scribner.

———, and Robert Abelson. 1977. *Scripts, Plans, Goals and Understanding*. Hillsdale, N.J.: Earlbaum.

Schell, Jonathan. 1982. *The Fate of the Earth*. New York: Avon.

Schelling, Thomas. 1960. *The Strategy of Conflict*. Cambridge: Harvard University Press.

Schön, Donald. 1967. *Invention and the Evolution of Ideas*. Formerly entitled *The Displacement of Concepts*. London: Tavistock.

Schumacher, E. F. 1973. *Small Is Beautiful*. New York: Harper & Row.

Schur, Edwin. 1980. *The Politics of Deviance*. Englewood Cliffs, N.J.: Prentice Hall.

Schutz, Alfred. 1967. *The Phenomenology of the Social World*. Evanston: Northwestern University Press.

Scott, John. 1995. "Rational Choice and Social Exchange." In *Sociological Theory: Contemporary Debates*, ed. by J. Scott. Hants, UK: Edward Elgar.

Searle, John. 1995. *The Construction of Social Reality*. New York: Free Press.

Seavey, C. A., P. A. Katz, and S. R. Zalk. 1975. "Baby X: The Effect of Gender Labels on Adult Responses to Infants." *Sex Roles* 1: 103–9.

Segal, Erich, ed. 1986. *The Dialogues of Plato*. Toronto: Bantam.

Seidman, Steven, ed. 1996. *Queer Theory/Sociology*. Cambridge, Mass.: Blackwell.

———. 1998. *Contested Knowledge*. Malden, Mass.: Blackwell.

———, and David G. Wagner, eds. 1992. *Postmodernism and Social Theory*. Cambridge, Mass.: Blackwell.

Sennett, Richard. 1977. *The Fall of Public Man*. New York: Knopf.

———, and Jonathan Cobb. 1993. *The Hidden Injuries of Class*. New York: Norton.

Shakespeare, William. [1600] 1971. "As You Like It." In *The Complete Works of William Shakespeare*. London: Spring Books.

———. [1606] 1971. "Macbeth." In *The Complete Works of William Shakespeare*. London: Spring Books.

Shannon, Claude, and Warren Weaver. 1949. *The Mathematical Theory of Communication*. Urbana: University of Illinois Press.

Shaw, Marvin E., and Philip Costanzo. 1982. *Theories of Social Psychology*, 2d ed. New York: McGraw-Hill.

Sherif, Muzafer. 1966. *In Common Predicament*. Boston: Houghton Mifflin.

Shubik, Martin. 1971. "The Dollar Auction Game." *Journal of Conflict Resolution* 15: 545–47.

Sills, David L., and Robert K. Merton, eds. 1991. *The Macmillan Book of Social Science Quotations*. New York: Macmillan.

Silverman, David. 1998. *Harvey Sacks: Social Science and Conversation Analysis*. New York: Oxford University Press.

Simmel, Georg. [1908] 1955. *Conflict*, ed. and trans. by K. H. Wolff. New York: Free Press.

Simon, Herbert. 1983. *Reason in Human Affairs*. Stanford: Stanford University Press.

———, and Allen Newell. 1956. "The Uses and Limitations of Models." In *The State of the Social Sciences*, ed. by L. D. White. Chicago: University of Chicago Press.

Singer, Peter. 1999. *The Darwinian Left: Politics, Evolution and Cooperation*. New Haven: Yale University Press.

Sjoberg, Gideon, ed. 1967. *Ethics, Politics and Social Research*. Cambridge, Mass.: Schenkman.

———, and Roger Nett. 1997. *A Methodology for Social Research*. Prospect Heights, Ill.: Waveland Press.

Skinner, B. F. 1974. *About Behaviorism*. New York: Knopf.

Slayden, David, and Rita Kirk Whillock, eds. 1999. *The Soundbite Culture: The Death of Discourse in a Wired World*. Thousand Oaks, Calif.: Sage.

Sloterdijk, Peter. 1987. *Critique of Cynical Reason*. Minneapolis: University of Minnesota Press.

Smith, Adam. [1759] 1982. *The Theory of Moral Sentiments*. Indianapolis: Liberty Fund.

———. [1776] 1937. *An Inquiry into the Nature and Causes of the Wealth of Nations*. New York: Modern Library.

Smith, Dorothy. 1987. *The Everyday World as Problematic: A Feminist Sociology*. Boston: Northeastern University Press.

———. 1990. *The Conceptual Practices of Power: A Feminist Sociology of Knowledge*. Boston: Northeastern University Press.

———. 1999. *Writing the Social*. Toronto: University of Toronto Press.

Snyder, James M. 1990. "Campaign Contributions as Investments." *Journal of Political Economy* 98: 1195–227.

Sokal, Alan. 1996. "Transgressing the Boundaries: Toward a Transformative Hermeneutics of Quantum Gravity." *Social Text* 14: Spring/Summer.

Sontag, Susan. 1989. *Illness as Metaphor and AIDS and Its Metaphors*. New York: Anchor Doubleday.

Spencer, Herbert. [1860] 1972. "The Social Organism." In *Herbert Spencer on Social Evolution*, ed. by J. D. Y. Peel. Chicago: University of Chicago Press.

———. [1864–67] 1966. "The Principles of Biology." In *The Works of Herbert Spencer*. Vol. 2. Osnabrück, Germany: Otto Zeller.

———. [1876] 1906. *The Principles of Sociology*. New York: Appleton.

Spengler, Oswald. 1926. *The Decline of the West*. New York: Knopf.

Spickard, James V. 1998. "Rethinking Religious Social Action: What Is 'Rational' about Rational Choice?" *Sociology of Religion* 59: 99–115.

Spivak, Gayatri Chakravorty. 1988. "Can the Subaltern Speak?" In *Marxism and the Interpretation of Culture*, ed. by C. Nelson and C. Grossberg. Urbana: University of Illinois Press.

Spretnak, Charlene. 1986. *The Spiritual Dimension of Green Politics*. Santa Fe, N.Mex.: Bear.

Stack, Carol. 1974. *All Our Kin: Strategies for Survival in the Black Community.* New York: Harper & Row.

Stanislavski, Konstantin. 1949. *Building a Character.* New York: Theatre Arts Books.

———. 1961. *Creating a Role.* New York: Theatre Arts Books.

———. 1963. *An Actor's Handbook,* ed. and trans. by E. R. Hapgood. New York: Theatre Arts Books.

Stefik, Mark. 1996. *Internet Dreams.* Cambridge: MIT Press.

Steiner, Claude. 1974. *Scripts People Live.* New York: Bantam.

Sternberg, Patricia, and Antonina Garcia. 1989. *Sociodrama.* New York: Praeger.

Stewart, John Q. 1948. "Demographic Gravitation: Evidence and Applications." *Sociometry* 11: 31–58.

Stout, Jeffrey. 1988. *Ethics after Babel.* Boston: Beacon.

Sumner, Wiliam Graham. 1883. *What Social Classes Owe to Each Other.* New York: Harper.

———. [1906] 1940. *Folkways.* Boston: Ginn.

Sudnow, David. 1979. *Talk's Body: A Meditation between Two Keyboards.* New York: Knopf.

Sun Tsu. [ca. 500 B.C.E.] 1963. *The Art of War.* Oxford, UK: Oxford University Press.

Swanson, Carl P. 1983. *Ever-Expanding Horizons: The Dual Informational Sources of Human Evolution.* Amherst: University of Massachusetts Press.

Swanson, Charles. 1977. "The Social Marketability of the Self." *Sociological Focus* 10: 263–74.

Tannen, Deborah. 1990. *You Just Don't Understand: Women and Men in Conversation.* New York: Morrow.

———. 1994. *Gender and Discourse.* Oxford, UK: Oxford University Press.

———. 1998. *The Argument Culture.* New York: Random House.

Taylor, Charles. 1989. *Sources of the Self: The Making of the Modern Identity.* Cambridge: Harvard University Press.

Taylor, Frederick. 1911. *The Principles of Scientific Management.* New York: Harper & Row.

Theodoreson, George A., ed. 1961. *Studies in Human Ecology.* Evanston, Ill.: Harper & Row.

Thomas, W. I., and Dorothy Swaine Thomas. 1928. *The Child in America.* New York: Knopf.

Thoreau, Henry David. [1849] 1983. *Civil Disobedience.* Harmondsworth, UK: Penguin.

Thurow, Lester. 1980. *The Zero-sum Society.* New York: Basic.

———. 1996. *The Future of Capitalism.* New York: Morrow.

Tilley, Christopher. 1999. *Metaphor and Material Culture.* Oxford, UK: Blackwell.

Toffler, Alvin. 1980. *The Third Wave.* New York: Bantam.

———, and Heidi Toffler. 1995. *Creating a New Civilization.* Atlanta: Turner.

Toulmin, Stephen. 1972. *Human Understanding.* Princeton: Princeton University Press.

Toynbee, Arnold. 1934–54. *A Study of History* (10 vols.). New York: Oxford University Press.

Tracy, David. 1981. *The Analogical Imagination.* New York: Crossroads.

———. 1987. *Plurality and Ambiguity.* New York: Harper & Row.

Trainer, Ted. 1991. "The Technological Fix." In *The Green Reader,* ed. by A. Dobson. San Francisco: Mercury House.

Trask, Maurice. 1971. *The Story of Cybernetics.* London: Institute of Contemporary Arts.

Treitschke, Heinrich von. [1898] 1965. *Politics.* San Diego: Harcourt.

Tsebelis, George. 1990. *Nested Games.* Berkeley: University of California Press.

Turbayne, Colin. 1962. *The Myth of Metaphor.* New Haven: Yale University Press.

Turkle, Sherry, 1984. *The Second Self: Computers and the Human Spirit*. New York: Simon & Schuster.

———. 1995. *Life on the Screen*. New York: Simon & Schuster.

Turnbull, Colin. 1972. *The Mountain People*. New York: Simon & Schuster.

Turner, Frederick Jackson. 1920. *The Frontier in American History*. New York: Holt.

Turner, Jonathan. 1991. *The Structure of Sociological Theory*, 5th ed. Belmont, Calif.: Wadsworth.

———. 1998. *The Structure of Sociological Theory*, 6th ed. Belmont, Calif.: Wadsworth.

———, and Leonard Beeghley. 1981. *The Emergence of Sociological Theory*. Homewood, Ill.: Dorsey.

Turner, Victor. 1974. *Dramas, Fields, and Metaphors*. Ithaca: Cornell University Press.

———. 1982. *From Ritual to Theatre*. New York: PAJ Publications.

———. 1986. *The Anthropology of Performance*. New York: PAJ Publications.

Tyrrell, G. N. M. 1951. *Homo Faber*. London: Methuen.

United Nations. 1948. "Universal Declaration of Human Rights." URL: www.un.org/rights/50/decla.htm (October 18, 1998).

Ussher, Jane M., ed. 1997. *Body Talk*. New York: Routledge.

Vaihinger, Hans. 1925. *The Philosophy of "As If."* New York: Harcourt Brace.

Waldrop, M. Mitchell. 1992. *Complexity: The Emerging Science at the Edge of Order and Chaos*. New York: Simon & Schuster.

Walker, Jim. 1981. "The End of Dialogue: Paulo Freire on Politics and Education." In *Literacy and Revolution*, ed. by R. Mackie. New York: Continuum.

Wallace, Walter L. 1969. *Sociological Theory*. Chicago: Aldine.

———. 1971. *The Logic of Science in Sociology*. Chicago: Aldine Atherton.

Wallerstein, Immanuel. 1974/1980. *The Modern World System* (2 vols.). New York: Academic.

Wallerstein, Judith, and Sandra Blakeslee. 1995. *The Good Marriage*. Boston: Houghton Mifflin.

Walster, Elaine. 1972. *Equity: Theory and Research*. Boston: Allyn & Bacon.

Watson, John. 1924. *Behaviorism*. Chicago: University of Chicago Press.

Weber, Max. [1904–17] 1949. *The Methodology of the Social Sciences*, ed. by E. Shils and H. Finch. Glencoe, Ill.: Free Press.

———. [1918] 1958. "Science as a Vocation." In *From Max Weber*, ed. by H. Gerth and C. W. Mills. New York: Oxford University Press.

———. [1921] 1958. "Politics as a Vocation." In *From Max Weber*, ed. by H. Gerth and C. W. Mills. New York: Oxford University Press.

———. [1922] 1958. *Economy and Society*. Selections reprinted in *From Max Weber*, ed. by H. Gerth and C. W. Mills. New York: Oxford University Press.

Weisberg, Robert W. 1993. *Creativity: Beyond the Myth of Genius*. New York: Freeman.

Wertsch, James V. 1991. *Voices of the Mind*. Cambridge: Harvard University Press.

West, Cornel. 1993. *Race Matters*. Boston: Beacon.

Whitehead, Fred, ed.. 1994. *Culture Wars: Opposing Viewpoints*. San Diego: Greenhaven.

Whorf, Benjamin. 1956. *Language, Thought and Reality*. Cambridge: MIT Press.

Wiener, Norbert. 1948. *Cybernetics*. Cambridge: MIT Press.

Willer, David. 1967. *Scientific Sociology: Theory and Method*. Englewood Cliffs, N.J.: Prentice-Hall.

———. 1992. "The Principle of Rational Choice and the Problem of a Satisfactory Theory."

In *Rational Choice Theory: Advocacy and Critique*, ed. by J. S. Coleman and T. J. Fararo. Newbury Park, Calif.: Sage.

———, ed. 1999. *Network Exchange Theory*. Westport, Conn.: Praeger.

Williams, Simon J., and Gillian Bendelow. 1998. *The Lived Body*. New York: Routledge.

Wilshire, Bruce. 1982. *Role Playing and Identity: The Limits of Theatre as Metaphor*. Bloomington: Indiana University Press.

Wilson, Edward O. 1975. *Sociobiology: The New Synthesis*. Cambridge: Harvard University Press.

———. 1978. *On Human Nature*. Cambridge: Harvard University Press.

———. 1998. *Consilience: The Unity of Knowledge*. Cambridge: Harvard University Press.

Wilson, R. Jackson, ed. 1989. *Darwinism and the American Intellectual: An Anthology*. Chicago: Dorsey.

Wilson, William Julius. 1999. *Bridges over the Racial Divide*. Berkeley: University of California Press.

Winch, Peter. 1958. *The Idea of a Social Science*. London: Routledge & Kegan Paul.

Wittgenstein. Ludwig. 1953. *Philosophical Investigations*. New York: Macmillan.

Wolfe, Alan. 1993. *The Human Difference*. Berkeley: University of California Press.

Wolfe, Tom. 1976. "The 'Me' Decade and the Third Great Awakening." *New York* (August 23): 26–40.

Wright, Robert. 2000. *Nonzero: The Logic of Human Destiny*. New York: Pantheon.

Wright, Will. 1989 *SIMCity* (urban planning computer simulation game). Walnut Creek, Calif.: Maxis.

Wrong, Dennis. 1961. "The Oversocialized Conception of Man in Modern Society." *American Sociological Review* 26: 183–93.

Yates, Gayle Graham, ed. 1985. *Harriet Martineau on Women*. New Brunswick, N.J.: Rutgers University Press.

Zeitlin, Irving. 1981. *Ideology and the Development of Sociological Theory*, 2d ed. Englewood Cliffs, N.J.: Prentice-Hall.

Zinn, Howard. 1980. *A People's History of the United States*. New York: Harper.

Zurcher, Louis. 1972. "The Poor and the Hip: Some Manifestations of Cultural Lead." *Social Science Quarterly* 53: 357–87.

———. 1977. *The Mutable Self*. Beverly Hills, Calif.: Sage.

Index

About the Author

~

Daniel Rigney is professor of sociology and director of the honors program at St. Mary's University in San Antonio, Texas, where he has previously served as assistant to the president. He has published research in the areas of social theory, the sociology of knowledge, the sociology of religion, and cultural criticism, including studies of anti-intellectualism and ethical relativism in the United States. His current interests include Matthew effects and applications of set theory to cultural analysis.